Religious Responses to Sex Work and Sex Trafficking

This book examines the history, theological beliefs and current contextual practices of faith-based NGOs who work in the area of human trafficking that involves the sex industry. There are hundreds of religious organizations around the globe who minister with human trafficking survivors and sex workers, but what is really happening on the ground and how do theological beliefs support a faith-based response?

Many of these groups represent their work as a cosmic battle against evil forces, yet important structural critiques are ignored in the urgency to rescue women and children. Using perspectives from both NGO staff and sex workers, an interdisciplinary panel of contributors examine specific organizations, highlight marginalized voices, and analyze undergirding methodologies. In doing so, the authors provide clear critiques and establish best practice guidelines for faith-based NGOs and future religious leaders, affirming an intersection of justice based upon critical reflection and careful action.

This book addresses with nuance an important topic that is often over-simplified. It will, therefore, be of great interest to scholars studying the interaction of religion to sex work and human trafficking, as well as academics of religious studies and theology more generally.

Lauren McGrow resides on the southern edge of Australia and her research focus includes sex work, gender, the body, and play. She is Research Fellow at Charles Sturt University, Australia and is the author of *Missionary Positions: A Postcolonial Feminist Perspective on Sex Work and Faith-Based Outreach from Australia* (2017).

Routledge Studies in Religion

Religious and Non-Religious Perspectives on Happiness and Wellbeing
Edited by Sharada Sugirtharajah

Metamorphoses of Religion and Spirituality in Central and Eastern Europe
Edited by Sławomir H. Zaręba, Maria Sroczyńska, Roberto Cipriani, Marcin Choczyński, and Wojciech Klimski

Balkan Contextual Theology
An Introduction
Edited by Stipe Odak and Zoran Grozdanov

Begging, Street Politics and Power
The Religious and Secular Regulation of Begging in India and Pakistan
Sheba Saeed

Religious Responses to Sex Work and Sex Trafficking
An Outrage Against Any Decent People
Edited by Lauren McGrow

Muslims of Post-Communist Eurasia
Edited by Galina M. Yemelianova and Egdūnas Račius

Christian Orthodox Migrants in Western Europe
Secularization and Modernity through the Lens of the Gift Paradigm
Maria Hämmerli

Domestic Demons and the Intimate Uncanny
Edited by Thomas G. Kirsch, Kirsten Mahlke and Rijk van Dijk

For more information about this series, please visit: https://www.routledge.com/religion/series/SE0669

Religious Responses to Sex Work and Sex Trafficking

An Outrage Against Any Decent People

Edited by
Lauren McGrow

Routledge
Taylor & Francis Group
LONDON AND NEW YORK

First published 2023
by Routledge
4 Park Square, Milton Park, Abingdon, Oxon OX14 4RN

and by Routledge
605 Third Avenue, New York, NY 10158

Routledge is an imprint of the Taylor & Francis Group, an informa business

British Library Cataloguing-in-Publication Data
A catalogue record for this book is available from the British Library

Library of Congress Cataloging-in-Publication Data
A catalog record has been requested for this book

ISBN: 978-0-367-34876-2 (hbk)
ISBN: 978-1-032-34082-1 (pbk)
ISBN: 978-0-429-32882-4 (ebk)

DOI: 10.4324/9780429328824

Typeset in Sabon
by Taylor & Francis Books

Contents

List of Figures vii
List of Contributors viii
Acknowledgements ix

Introduction: An Outrage Against Any Decent People 1
LAUREN MCGROW

1 Abolition Mommas: Evangelical Women as Exceptional Citizens in the Fight to End "Global Sex Trafficking" 8
CARLY DANIEL-HUGHES

2 Do You See This (Wo)man? Lessons Learned from Sex Workers 29
HANNAH ESTABROOK

3 Walking with Women in Sex Work: An Appraisal of the Role of the Nigerian Conference of Women Religious 44
NKIRUKA OKAFOR AND LAUREN MCGROW

4 Human Dignity in Sex Work and the Catholic Tradition 66
MARK A. LEVAND

5 'A Catholic and an Agnostic Walk into a Homeless Camp…' Collaborating Across Religious Differences 86
YVONNE C. ZIMMERMAN

6 Towards an Ethical Framework for Practice: Three "Touchstones" for Faith-based Organizations at the Margins 106
LAUREN MCGROW

7 Jesus Ate With Pras: Christianity and Commercial Sex Work in the Caribbean 130
ANNA KASAFI PERKINS AND DANE C. LEWIS

8 When Survival Precedes Faith: Decolonial Perspectives on the Ethical Dilemma Confronting Female Christian Sex Workers in Africa 155
BEATRICE DEDAA OKYERE-MANU, MARGARET SSEBUNYA AND SOPHIA CHIRONGOMA

Afterword: To Shape the Changes for Which We Long 174
YVONNE C. ZIMMERMAN

Index 189

Figures

1.1 and 1.2	Images from A21's "Can You See Me" Ad Campaign for U.S. Used with permission	9
6.1	Floating red umbrellas at the Sex Worker Pop-Up in NYC, March 2020. Photo by author	116

Contributors

Sophia Chirongoma is Research Fellow at the Research Institute for Theology and Religion (RITR) in the College of Human Sciences, University of South Africa (UNISA) and Senior Lecturer, Midlands State University, Zimbabwe.

Carly Daniel-Hughes is Professor, Concordia University, Montreal, Canada.

Hannah Estabrook is a professional clinical counsellor, has worked with survivors of the sex trade for over a decade and runs a non-profit called Sanctuary Night in Columbus, Ohio, USA, which offers drop-in services for those still "in the life."

Mark A. Levand is a sexuality educator and researcher at several USA colleges and universities including Widener University, Villanova University, and the University of North Carolina Wilmington, USA.

Dane C. Lewis is a human rights activist for the LGBT+ and HIV+ communities with a background in communications affiliated with CariFLAGS and Larry Chang Foundation, Jamaica.

Lauren McGrow is Research Fellow at Charles Sturt University, Australia and is the author of *Missionary Positions: A Postcolonial Feminist Perspective on Sex Work and Faith-Based Outreach from Australia* (2017).

Nkiruka Okafor is a scholar at Luther Seminary, St. Paul, Minnesota USA and Madonna Renewal Center, Freeport, Illinois, USA.

Beatrice Dedaa Okyere-Manu is Senior Lecturer at the University of KwaZulu-Natal, South Africa, and the International Research Training Group (IRTG): Transformative Religion.

Anna Kasafi Perkins is a Jamaican Roman Catholic researcher at the University of the West Indies and St Michael's Theological College, Kingston, Jamaica.

Margaret Ssebunya is Lecturer at the University of Kisubi, Uganda.

Yvonne C. Zimmerman is Associate Professor of Christian Ethics and Associate Academic Dean at the Methodist Theological School in Ohio.

Acknowledgements

This work has been tested by the circumstances of 2020–22 and yet, here it is, abundant, complete. I would like to congratulate all authors who studied, wrote, and submitted work while facing their own challenges. You've increased my skills and knowledge and your conceptual thinking has been an enrichment for this text. Yvonne Zimmerman and Letitia Campbell were beacons for the project; your scholarship is ground-breaking, and your support is uplifting. Beatrice Okyere-Manu, Sophia Chirongoma and Naomi Goldenberg were also loving and generous during the intensity of 2020. I'm grateful to have met and know the work of Hannah Estabrook, Anna Perkins, Dane Lewis, and Mark Levand – passionate activists and practitioners flung around the globe. I also thank Alex Kain from the Red Umbrella Fund for your incisive words and brilliant activism.

I would like to thank the Routledge Religion editors for believing in this text from the very beginning as we huddled at a table in the American Academy of Religion book hall in Denver, Colorado in November 2018 throwing ideas around with Rebecca Shillabeer. I also thank Joshua Wells, Katherine Ong and R. Yuga Harini, whose steady hands and optimism have improved this work greatly. Anonymous peer review of our book proposal was also immensely helpful, thank you.

Friends and family always contribute unquantifiable support to an academic volume, mine have given spirit and helped me wrestle with ideas amid practical difficulties. We've faced it together and I wouldn't choose anyone else. I particularly thank Lyn Wiseman, Lisa Holswich, Shane Clifton, Leanne Morrison, Hilary and Chris Haeusler, Gabriella Lytras, Bethany Wilkinson, George the Brave, Clayton Sheridan, Kim Sheridan, Jane Cusick, Nicky Stewart, Aminah Vaughan, Lucy Whitehead, and Charlie Burton for being there through the ups and downs of this experience.

Chris Brennan is a gem. Thank you for the index.

I'd like to thank Stacey Aslangul and Andie Patchett for insights and friendship. In the end, that's what it's all about.

Introduction

An Outrage Against Any Decent People

Lauren McGrow

Introduction

> "Human trafficking is a human tragedy. It's an outrage against any decent people."[1]

I came across this quote when organizing a panel for the American Academy of Religion conference in Denver, Colorado, USA in 2018 and used it to name the panel. It suited our purposes, to have a catchy title and attract people to the session, yet also hinted at deeper questions about conservative beliefs in relation to sex, work, and trafficking.

The quote is from American political commentator, Mark Shields, by all accounts a thoughtful and sincere man, a decent person.[2] To be outraged by trafficking is a rational stance for sure, but the statement lacks critical context about the realities of migration, agency, social systems, and the politics of respectability as it impacts the lives of people trading sex and other bodily commodities, including across borders. It also doesn't account for the competing definitions of the word trafficking,[3] and fails to acknowledge that there is little evidence of widespread sexual slavery.[4] Used interchangeably with consensual sex work, the ideology of sex trafficking has become a shortcut way of denying nuanced voices and the insights of sex workers across the globe. The glaring problem with this sentiment, *it's an outrage against any decent people*, is that sex workers and survivors are positioned as objects to be acted upon by decent citizens. This often stems from an insidious "moral gentrification of the world"[5] undertaken via the colonizing imperative. In essence, the good guys are maintaining traditional family values from a privileged place and victims and bad guys best beware.

But Who Is a Decent Person?

To be a decent person means to conform to prevailing moral standards, therefore sex workers and sex trafficking survivors are mostly on the wrong side of this word *decent*. Condemnation, injustice, and violence are commonly dished out for their perceived breaches of decency. This is truly the outrage and a key

DOI: 10.4324/9780429328824-1

reason for writing this text – a plea for higher standards of justice. Yet, a further meaning of the word *decent* is to act proportionate to the situation at hand. If so, then the narrative voices of sex workers disseminated in this volume reveal a streak of decency so illuminating as to call into question all faith-based beliefs about people in the sex trade.

Does Indecency Count for Anything?

To be indecent, then, is to be treated like a rock star in some quarters.[6] This is what happened to Marcella Althaus-Reid at the American Academy of Religion conference many years ago. Her theological project, *Indecent Theology*, was to render visible the sexual oppression at the heart of liberation theology. She helped develop an ironic, fierce discourse that challenged theologians to take account of gender, sex, and fucking. Our vision is that, in time, the indecent thinking of Althaus-Reid continues to bear fruit in this pastoral context and sex workers and sex trafficking survivors may be known as representatives of God, instead of outcasts, as educators and community builders, instead of victims, as included to transform social structures instead of stigmatized.

For religious people this means a change of perspective and a challenge to vanilla theology, as Althaus-Reid named it. Whether decent or indecent theology speaks to you, reflecting upon one's own sexual ethics is a starting point for faith-based work in this space, and doing so in rigorous conversation with sex workers and sex-trafficking survivors. This will be a sure-fire way to come into new pastoral paradigms of radical awakening; where the indecent person can be a rockstar and sexual respectability is not the foremost criteria of judgement.

Background Themes

Over the last 25 years, Christians have globally engaged human trafficking as a policy issue and an occasion for humanitarian action, bringing discourses of rescue and rehabilitation to bear on people at the sexual margins. Confrontational techniques like brothel raids have become an established part of the religious imagination, even as these practices have been called into question.[7] As Christian attention to sex trafficking has intensified, moreover, many faith-based organizations have benefitted from the financial support of Western governments, to increase their status and power as benevolent institutions, with limited critical assessment of their work. It is no exaggeration to say that sex trafficking is widely treated as a cause célèbre within Christian networks.[8] Prayer, donations, and practical assistance from the global church support this agenda.

Many religious organizations adopt a problem-solving approach, identifying the *problem* of trafficking with the sex industry and advocating, as a solution, projects that aim to facilitate exit from sex work. Thus evangelism, skill-building for future employment, returning women and young people to families of origin, prosecution of traffickers and political advocacy for morality are hallmarks of faith-based programs designed to address this problem. By closely associating trafficking with commercial sex, and sex work with slavery, many Christians have taken up this agenda as a fight against slavery, becoming the self-proclaimed new abolitionists. This phenomenon has been well documented by scholars like Kamala Kempadoo,[9] Elizabeth Bernstein,[10] Laura Agustin,[11] and Elena Shih.[12]

Critical insights are often absent from these religious approaches, among them: Attention to undergirding theological frameworks of sexual purity and control; an understanding of the ways in which a benevolent use of power functions to maintain the low status of marginalized women, and the silencing of alternative perspectives on sex; and a lack of recognition of the structural inequalities of race, class, and gender. These silences have practical, if unintended, consequences for vulnerable communities. The most prominent peer-based sex worker activist group in Thailand, Empower, estimates that "there are more women in the Thai sex industry being abused by anti-trafficking practices than there are women exploited by traffickers."[13] They have called for powerful groups to listen to sex workers, insisting that they can make meaningful decisions about their own lives and livelihoods, including decisions about migrancy and work.

It Is In This Milieu That We Write

Over the past 15 years, the authors in this book have examined these broad trends within feminist scholarship, sociology, and Christian theology, also situating the issue in longer histories of colonialism and racism. We bring to bear the tools of critical feminist, queer, and postcolonial theories to develop nuanced perspectives about religion, sex, and trafficking.

More recently, our research has also brought us into contact with groups working on these issues in a wide range of contexts and with a varied set of moral, political, and theological commitments. Our scholarship notes how religious organizations may work differently in this space with greater ethical awareness. One of the goals of this text is to highlight the work of faith-based organizations moving beyond the dominant anti-trafficking rhetoric to see what can be learned from their experiences.

A driving questions has been: How can religious practices with people at the sexual margins take structural critique seriously? Several chapters outline ways for religious leaders to renew their work by addressing areas of theological consideration and change. This text wrestles with issues founded on historical missionary enterprises. As scholars, activists, and practitioners we emphasize here the need for structural analysis as being key to understanding the circumstances of people in the sex industry.

A second critical question also informs this text: What is happening in the "contact zone"[14] where religious groups are interacting with survivors, sex workers, and communities affected by trafficking? Whose histories, priorities, and perspectives are affirmed? Several authors analyze practices taking place at the grassroots, to affirm and challenge their perspective for the purpose of growth. A good question that any *decent* person may wonder is: How are faith-based organizations developing nuanced practices (or not) and what does this look like on the ground? Several chapters highlight the work of organizations moving beyond the dominant framework to see what can be learned from and strengthened in their practice. Serious (self) reflection to see whether faith-based interventions are helpful to sex workers is necessary and a consistent theme of this text.

We bring to the conversation a diverse set of geographic and academic locations and our goal is to build a picture of healthy praxis with trafficking survivors and sex workers, addressing theological frameworks while focusing on contextual examples. Trafficking – especially sex trafficking – has been widely researched over the past 15 years from legal, sociological, gender studies, primary health, and policy perspectives. Yet there has been limited study of this issue to assess what is happening amongst faith-based organizations and how pastoral action is driven, at times, by harmful ideologies. We particularly note that those most affected are often the ones silenced in scholarly texts and in the governance models of religious organizations. Our aim here is to make room for other voices, who reason and reflect in a way not often heard by religious people in their endeavours to rescue. Diverse theological models of inclusion that embrace decolonial, feminist, and queer scholarship are documented across the text, showing that there is no one way to be present with marginalized people in a faith-based setting, but diversity and understanding is critical. Engaging with this text can only strengthen future ministers and social helpers.

In Chapter 1, Carly Daniel-Hughes casts a probing, critical eye on the international Pentecostal organization A21, particularly the motives of its founder, Christine Caine. Daniel-Hughes assesses the evangelical belief system of women's sexual victimization at the heart of the organization. Daniel-Hughes wants to bring unconscious motives to the surface to be understood in the context of feminist and anti-racist practice and she asks practitioners to interrogate the long-term effects of their charitable work. In Chapter 2, we have a voice from the grassroots, Hannah Estabrook who reflects upon her own work with sex workers both in the American legal system and in a faith-based organization. Estabrook notes a radical change in her approach, especially towards sex workers and to law-making, as she learnt from the women she worked with, and documents her growth as an open-hearted practitioner.

Chapter 3, by Nkiruka Okafor and Lauren McGrow, is concerned with what is happening at the grassroots in Nigeria as nuns interact with sex workers. Where are they similar and different as both classes of women are living beyond the traditional roles of wife and mother? Nigerian sex worker voices call into question any approach to faith-based restoration that does not consider the material circumstances of poverty, and they push back against religious judgement and condemnation, boldly claiming for themselves the salvation of God and protection. It is in this light that a new pastoral model emerges not based on rescue but rather listening and empowerment. Chapter 4 by Mark A. Levand continues the Catholic theme with a reflection upon human dignity and the social good of sex work through the lens of Catholic Social Teaching. In doing so, he develops, step by step, a robust theological framework for understanding sex commerce so that Catholic people may be able to support sex workers in their activism for full equality.

In Chapter 5, Yvonne C. Zimmerman investigates what is happening on the ground as a Catholic pastoral worker interacts with a non-religious social service provider in anti-trafficking work. This chapter recognizes that people with different beliefs can form a strong alliance that takes them beyond their current perspective, for the benefit of young people. Surely this is important work in a politically polarized society? Chapter 6 by Lauren McGrow builds upon this discussion by drawing out the ethical attributes required for practitioners in faith-based organizations to work well at the margins, and does so through an analysis of the benchmarks of best practice that arose from interviews with organizations in Australia.

Chapter 7 by Anna Kasafi Perkins and Dane C. Lewis presents a thorough examination of the conditions of sex work and church response in the Caribbean. These authors clearly show the inadequacy of current theological understanding about sexuality, gender, work conditions, and traditional morality, raising their voices to challenge Christian leaders in the region to rethink their perspectives. The final chapter by Beatrice Dedaa Okyere-Manu, Margaret Ssebunya, and Sophia Chirongoma is based on extensive research and interviews with sex workers in locations across Africa. The powerful voices of women question why they have been so excluded by the Christian church and reveal that in doing so, sex workers are subject to structural and personal violence that is truly an outrage. Can the church be the one to take a stand against this immoral exclusion of people in the sex industry? These authors show that they can using a postcolonial-African-feminist conceptual framework that places African women at the centre to proactively transform all of life.

Finally, in the Afterword, Yvonne C. Zimmerman explores emergent themes of scholarship in this field. This is the first text to bring together multiple scholars in theology and related disciplines who examine what it can mean to be present in a healthy way with people in the sex industry. Collectively, what needs to be addressed so that sex workers and sex trafficking survivors gain the most benefit from religious organizations? Zimmerman answers this question with a deep reflection on the crux of the issues as she sets the stage for the further institutional change that is now required.

Why It Matters

Empirical studies have not kept pace with publications driven by ideological imperatives[15] and this is especially true in the context of a religious response to trafficking and sex work. Yet there are hundreds of faith-based organizations daily intervening in the lives of sexually marginalized people across the globe. This book appraises the activities of anti-trafficking work in different parts of the world and helps to establish more expansive theological foundations, safe organizational protocols, and respectful pastoral responses.

If religious leaders are to engage ethically in ministry, solidarity, and the work of care with marginalized people in the pursuit of a just society, then conversations that challenge and reconstruct approaches to human trafficking and sex work are desperately needed. We hope that this text stimulates interaction and questions from students and religious practitioners. The "how" of practice is important but deeper work also needs to be accomplished on the "why" of faith-based practice with people in the sex industry.

Further, there is an "overwhelming need for improvement in the sexuality education provided to seminarians."[16] We take this call to action seriously and so *Religious Responses to Sex Work and Sex Trafficking: An Outrage Against Any Decent People:* examines one aspect of sexuality education providing a space for reflection and to consider future steps towards sexual justice. A key argument here is the need for a serious reconsideration of laws that keep sex workers oppressed and vulnerable to institutional and individual violence. Also required is a change of heart from religious leaders, those who have the power to influence parishioners, and society at large, to see sex workers as those who are worthy of greater respect, including for the work they do. What is clear from this text is that more often than not, people at the sexual margins are the decent ones, supporting families, acting compassionately, and speaking truth to power.

Notes

1 "Human Trafficking Quotes," Social Justice Resource Center, accessed January 26, 2022, https://socialjusticeresourcecenter.org/quotes/human-trafficking/.

2 David Brooks, "Mark Shields and the Best of American Liberalism," *The New York Times*, December 17, 2020, https://www.nytimes.com/2020/12/17/opinion/mark-shields-liberalism.html.

3 Kamala Kempadoo, "Introduction: From Moral Panic to Global Justice: Changing Perspectives on Trafficking," in *Trafficking and Prostitution Reconsidered: New Perspectives on Migration, Sex Work, and Human Rights*, eds. Kamala Kempadoo, Jyoti Sanghera, and Bandana Pattanaik (Boulder: Paradigm, 2005), vii.

4 Kempadoo, "Introduction," vii.

5 Nicola Mai, *Mobile Orientations: An Intimate Autoethnography of Migration, Sex Work, and Humanitarian Borders* (Chicago: University of Chicago Press, 2018), 4.

6 Marcella Althaus-Reid, ed, *Liberation Theology and Sexuality* (London: Ashgate, 2006), xii.

7 Aziza Ahmed and Meena Seshu, "'We Have the Right Not to Be "rescued"…': When Anti-Trafficking Programmes Undermine the Health and Well-Being of Sex Workers," *Anti-Trafficking Review* 1/1 (2012): 149–165.

8 Ruth Graham, "How Sex Trafficking Became a Christian Cause Célèbre," *Slate*, March 5, 2015, https://slate.com/human-interest/2015/03/christians-and-sex-trafficking-how-evangelicals-made-it-a-cause-celebre.html.

9 Kamala Kempadoo, Jyoti Sanghera, and Bandana Pattanaik eds., *Trafficking and Prostitution Reconsidered: New Perspectives on Migration, Sex Work, and Human Rights* (Boulder: Paradigm, 2005).

10 Elizabeth Bernstein, *Brokered Subjects: Sex, Trafficking and the Politics of Freedom* (Chicago: The University of Chicago Press, 2018).

11 Laura Maria Agustin, *Sex at the Margins: Migration, Labour Markets and the Rescue Industry* (London: Zed Books, 2007).
12 Elena Shih, "Not in My 'Backyard Abolitionism': Vigilante Rescue against American Sex Trafficking," *Sociological Perspectives* 59/1 (Spring 2016): 66–90.
13 Subhatra Bhumiprabhas, "Sex 'Trade', Not 'Traffic,'" *The Nation*, March 6, 2012, http://www.nationmultimedia.com/life/Sex-trade-not-traffic-30177322.html.
14 Mary Louise Pratt, "Arts of the Contact Zone," *Profession* (1991): 33–40.
15 Molly Dragiewicz, "Introduction," in *Global Human Trafficking: Critical Issues and Contexts*, ed. Molly Dragiewicz (New York: Routledge, 2014), 1.
16 Kate M. Ott and Amanda J. Winters, "Sex and the Seminary: Preparing Ministers for Sexual Health and Justice," *American Journal of Sexuality Education* 6 (2011), 55.

Bibliography

Agustin, Laura Maria, *Sex at the Margins: Migration, Labour Markets and the Rescue Industry*, London: Zed Books, 2007.

Ahmed Aziza and Meena Seshu, "'We Have the Right Not to Be "rescued"…': When Anti-Trafficking Programmes Undermine the Health and Well-Being of Sex Workers," *Anti-Trafficking Review* 1/1 (2012): 149–165.

Althaus-Reid, Marcella, ed. *Liberation Theology and Sexuality*, London: Ashgate, 2006.

Bernstein, Elizabeth, *Brokered Subjects: Sex, Trafficking and the Politics of Freedom*, Chicago: The University of Chicago Press, 2018.

Bhumiprabhas, Subhatra, "Sex 'Trade', Not 'Traffic.'" *The Nation*, March 6, 2012, http://www.nationmultimedia.com/life/Sex-trade-not-traffic-30177322.html.

Brooks, David, "Mark Shields and the Best of American Liberalism," *The New York Times*, December 17, 2020, https://www.nytimes.com/2020/12/17/opinion/mark-shields-liberalism.html.

Dragiewicz, Molly, ed. *Global Human Trafficking: Critical Issues and Contexts*, London: Routledge, 2015.

Graham, Ruth, "How Sex Trafficking Became a Christian Cause Célèbre," *Slate*, March 5, 2015, https://slate.com/human-interest/2015/03/christians-and-sex-trafficking-how-evangelicals-made-it-a-cause-celebre.html.

Kempadoo, Kamala, Jyoti Sanghera, and Bandana Pattanaik, eds. *Trafficking and Prostitution Reconsidered: New Perspectives on Migration, Sex Work, and Human Rights*, Boulder: Paradigm, 2005.

Mai, Nicola, *Mobile Orientations: An Intimate Autoethnography of Migration, Sex Work, and Humanitarian Borders*, Chicago: University of Chicago Press, 2018.

Ott, Kate M., and Amanda J. Winters. "Sex and the Seminary: Preparing Ministers for Sexual Health and Justice," *American Journal of Sexuality Education* 6 (2011): 55–74.

Pratt, Mary Louise, "Arts of the Contact Zone," *Profession* (1991): 33–40.

Shih, Elena, "Not in My 'Backyard Abolitionism': Vigilante Rescue against American Sex Trafficking," *Sociological Perspectives*59/1 (Spring 2016): 66–90.

Social Justice Resource Center, "Human Trafficking Quotes," accessed January 26, 2022, https://socialjusticeresourcecenter.org/quotes/human-trafficking/.

1 Abolition Mommas[1]

Evangelical Women as Exceptional Citizens in the Fight to End "Global Sex Trafficking"

Carly Daniel-Hughes

> "Who could say that I had not been born into a reasonably affluent and free society for such a time as this (Esther 4:14)? For a time when I could see the injustice and crying need so common throughout the world and stand up to combat it? ... The darkness surrounds us and it is growing. But *you* are the light to combat that darkness. As am I."[2]
>
> —Christine Caine, Undaunted: Daring to Do What God Calls You to Do

A self-described caffeine-charged, petite dynamo, the Australian Christine Caine is an evangelical star on a mission to end global human slavery. Her inspirational Christian books fold in the story of the explosive growth of her ministry, the NGO "The A21 Campaign," which stands for "Abolishing Injustice in the 21st Century,"[3] with a larger message of how God's saving grace transforms lives, including her own. For that transformation to occur, writes Caine, a Christian must dig deep by conquering adversity and self-doubt, replacing these with confidence in God. Themes of triumph over struggle define Caine's particular blend of self-help therapy, humanitarianism and Christian devotionalism directed to evangelical women. Titles like *Undaunted, Unstoppable, Unashamed* and *Unshakable* lean into narratives of how Caine, and those in her organization—and so too, *you*—can face down despair, rid yourself of shame, trust in God's love and advance His plan to heal the world. Caine's contribution to that larger vision is to free women and girls from "sex slavery."[4]

But it was not always so. Caine explains that she had to first see the victims of this human tragedy. Once she did, she could do nothing other than respond. She wants *you* to do the same. A21s "Can You See Me?" ad campaign (Figs. 1 and 2) rehearse Caine's own coming to awareness of sexually trafficked and exploited girls. In them tear-stained or dead-eyed, racialized young girls stare into the camera, driven by traffickers, likewise young racialized men, who, it appears, roped them into this humiliating condition.[5] In the second ad, we spy in the distance a white woman getting into her car looking onto the scene. (In the longer ad, this white woman, we discover, is the girls' high school teacher who witnesses this young woman slowly become prey to a boyfriend who sells her for sex). The girls' pitiable faces echo those that adorned the "Missing Persons" posters Caine reportedly saw in the Thessaloniki airport and awakened in her the passion to fight human trafficking over a decade ago.[6] The white woman, looking on, operates as a stand-in for the "*you*" targeted by the ad.

DOI: 10.4324/9780429328824-2

Figure 1.1 and 1.2 Images from A21's "Can You See Me" Ad Campaign for U.S.[7] Used with permission.

Christian evangelical anti-trafficking campaigns, like "The A21 Campaign" (from this point onward referred to as A21) sit in a larger field of humanitarian efforts to fight so-deemed human slavery. These campaigns have been criticized for housing racist and imperialist agendas, and for advancing carceral solutions to social problems that enhance, rather than reduce, the vulnerability of marginalized people globally. Despite two decades of pushback from various scholars as well as activists, the "anti-trafficking juggernaut rolls on," to cite scholar Kamala Kempadoo.[8] What accounts for the durability of anti-sex trafficking campaigns? More particularly for my purposes: what accounts for their attractiveness to affluent Protestant Christian women—the implicit *you* invoked by Caine?

In what follows, I sketch the main critiques of anti-trafficking campaigns, both secular and Christian, and attend to the rescue narratives that activists in this humanitarian effort circulate. My analysis then pivots to asking why these campaigns have attracted evangelicals, especially younger women. Caine's work is directed to evangelicals who see themselves as both "globally conscious citizens" and committed to empowering women in the Church and the world (though, importantly, still retaining heterosexual marriage and gender complementarianism as normative values). Caine's ministry offers a contemporary spin on the "helping imperative," which animated the efforts of affluent, and white, Protestant women in the late nineteenth and early twentieth centuries to agitate for their own rights. Anti-sex trafficking campaigns, I argue, can serve as unrecognized negotiations for evangelical women, such as Caine and her followers, of tensive gender politics inside of their own communities. The "helping imperative" gone global is a form of heroic action in and on the world. But in this, it is likewise a performance and assurance of religious power and authority, the very aspirations so often curtailed for evangelical women. In this, however, evangelical women may not be so exceptional at all—a point to which I turn at the end of this chapter.

Locating and Critiquing Anti-Trafficking Campaigns

> "What keeps Kalli and the rest of our A21 staff at locations around the world going day after day, year after year, even though they must repeatedly face the discouragement and emotional pain of seeing bruised and battered young women trapped in slavery? Passion."[9]
>
> —Christine Caine, *Unstoppable: Step into Your Purpose, Run Your Race, Embrace the Future*

In the last two decades, the call to end "human trafficking," or "sex trafficking" (often featured as its paradigmatic form), has galvanized Christian communities, including evangelical ones. This constituency was drawn to this humanitarian cause actively in the United States during the Bush administration. Establishing the Office of Faith-Based Initiatives, President George W. Bush gave conservative Christian organizations new access to federal funds for their charitable work.[10] This humanitarian issue, however, has since made its ways across Anglophone countries, becoming something of an evangelical mission in the United States as well as Australia, the United Kingdom and Canada.[11] It is now a cause that permeates evangelical culture in these countries. There are prayer weekends, bible studies, praise and worship songs, slave-free goods to purchase, all devoted to fighting trafficking. There are even memoirs and self-help titles by Christians, such as Christine Caine, who have taken up the effort and want others to do the same.[12] Her organization's "Walk for Freedom" is likewise aimed at raising awareness of the plight of human slaves and securing funding for the NGO's growing operations. According to an A21 promotional video, the 2019 walk took place in over 50 countries and 500 cities. Participants were outfitted in t-shirts and grasped placards with the hopeful slogan: "abolish slavery with every step."[13]

A21 is but one campaign in an expanding field of Christian faith-based organizations dedicated to eradicating slavery.[14] But its global footprint is growing. A21's success owes much to its slick media presentations and to the charisma of its female co-founder, Pentecostal evangelist, Christine Caine. Founded in Australia (where Caine got her start on the pastoral staff of the mega successful Hillsong Church),[15] A21 is presently headquartered in Costa Mesa, California. The organization operates in seventeen locations around the world, including South Africa, Thailand, Cambodia and parts of Europe. Though not the largest such Christian organization, A21's size is notable given it began only a decade ago in Thessaloniki with one safe house.[16] The size and reach of Christian organizations vary with those, like A21 or "International Justice Mission," having global operations, and others with a smaller and more local focus.[17] Across these organizations, however, the approach to the problem of trafficking is largely the same. In the words of A21 the aim is to "reach, rescue and restore."[18] This entails the production of education materials about "modern slavery" and its prevention, staffing of national hotlines where people can report incidents of trafficking, as well as sustaining aftercare programs and safe houses for women and girls leaving the sex trade. (A21 reportedly addresses other forms of exploitative labor impacting men, but as is common for these campaigns, Christian and secular, promotional materials foreground racialized women and girls.)[19] A21, like other Christian and secular anti-trafficking NGOs, also partners with law enforcement and foreign governments to secure criminal convictions of "sex traffickers."[20]

Many historians, cultural theorists, legal scholars and sex work activists have been critiquing the discursive frame of sex trafficking for over two decades.[21] What concerns critics is that these NGOs depend on carceral and juridical solutions to the perceived problem of "human slavery," approaches that ultimately increase police surveillance and governmental interventions that stigmatize and criminalize vulnerable communities and individuals, making their lives even more perilous.[22] In light of larger attention right now to inhumane border conditions and extensive police violence in the United States and elsewhere, we can perhaps better understand that carceral solutions naively assume the benevolence of police, courts and border officials toward racialized and other marginalized people. Moreover, while anti-trafficking activists assert that modern-day slavery is a variegated social problem entailing all kinds of labor, their literature—like A21's "Can You See Me" ads—foreground the sexual exploitation of young women and girls, particularly racialized ones and those from poorer countries and the global south.[23] Sex slavery is ubiquitous, but hidden, anti-trafficking activists argue, leading to under-reporting and inexact figures of the extent of this phenomenon. Those espousing this view often conflate all sex work with sexual slavery, resulting in widely discrepant statistics.[24] What constitutes "human slavery" is so definitionally vague that it is rife with empirical imprecision.[25]

In anti-sex trafficking work by Christian NGOs, and secular varieties of anti-trafficking activism, there are simplistic definitions of sexually trafficked victims at play. Laws to prohibit sex trafficking presume its victims lack volition, are innocently frauded or manipulated, and eager to return to their countries of origin (in the case of migrants).[26] Such a frame places pressure on people to identify with a particular trafficking script to gain protections. Few do, or perhaps even can.[27] The line separating a trafficked "victim" from a criminal turns out to be much more opaque than anti-trafficking campaigns admit. This is not to say that no one accesses A21 or other such safe houses or facilities; rather it points back to an inconvenient fact that any individual person's story is more complicated and tainted with "illegality" than the crisp moral narrative of innocence versus criminality that Christian and other anti-trafficking NGOs promote.

As a humanitarian cause, in other words, the fight to end slavery obscures complicated and fluid realities of exploitative labor conditions, migration, and sex work, and promotes a binary of agency or victimhood.[28] Campaigns imply that "sexually trafficked people" (i.e., regularly racialized young girls)[29] are in need of rescue from Western outsiders, because they cannot advocate for themselves, and of rehabilitation, because sex work is the quintessential human rights violation, always to be avoided, and never a considered, complicated or good choice.

The link between prostitution and "slavery" is even more potent for conservative Christians. The frame of "slavery" and its opposite, "freedom," echoes conservative Christian theological and cultural imaginaries. Rescue narratives—as we will see—follow the trajectory of a classic Protestant redemption story from damnation to salvation: horrific tales that end on a hopeful note. Girls and women are sold into slavery, then restored and made whole. This narrative arch is woven through with Protestant ideals about gender and sexuality, explains Yvonne Zimmerman in *Other Dreams of Freedom.*[30] What makes prostitution "bad" sex is that it is not freely given within the context of heterosexual marriage.[31] Sexual relations outside of marriage are then imagined as a form of bondage. Such attitudes have long history, rooted in the Protestant Reformation, but since the 1970s, espoused by conservative Christian women quite actively. This constituency has variously argued that true liberation derives from assuming traditional gender roles and promoting "family values," and not being enslaved to the vapidity of a secular and, ultimately, corrupting culture.[32]

As Elizabeth Bernstein has more recently pointed out, however, the evangelical women who have been most passionate about the cause of anti-sex trafficking are often not those who would rally around more conservative, even polarizing causes, like gay marriage and abortion. Instead, they are populated by evangelicals and other Christians who frame their humanitarian cause in terms "of women's rights and social justice."[33] This shift represents a convergence of secular feminists and left-leaning evangelical Christians around neoliberal configurations of gender and sexuality, Bernstein argues, "one that locates social problems in deviant individuals rather than mainstream institutions," and is committed to "egalitarian heterosexual marriage and professional-sphere equality."[34] Caine's particular brand of female-empowered writing and ministry fits well with Bernstein's larger analysis. What constitutes "freedom" for anti-trafficking activists, however, is defined not only by heterosexual marriage and family values, it also implies freedom of the market. For anti-trafficking activists, whether Christian or secular, rescue is understood in terms of carceral and militarized solutions, such as surveillance, prosecution, and repatriation. Rehabilitation takes the form of neo-liberal capitalist solutions. Women and girls are saved from sex work by making food or clothing for purchase by humanitarian-minded consumers.[35]

Unstoppable? Rescue Narratives and Christian Anti-Trafficking Campaigns

> "Yun was moved around to at least fifteen different brothels and strip clubs, forced to service up to thirty clients a day … her disgust and shame over the things she was forced to do ate away at any remaining sense of self-worth. Even so, she discovered a tiny spark, a longing … she longed for freedom."[36]
>
> —Christine Caine, *Unashamed: Drop the Baggage, Pick Up Your Freedom, Fulfill Your Destiny*

Despite criticisms, anti-sex trafficking campaigns continue to proliferate and garner the interest of conservative Christians, and many other groups, including mainline Christian denominations, secular NGOs, corporations, and Western governments.[37] What accounts for the success of human trafficking as a humanitarian cause lies in large part in the melodramatic narratives of rescue that anti-trafficking activists circulate—narratives designed to grab the attention of Western and Christian audiences. Sometimes male audiences are hooked with adrenaline-laden, muscular stories of risk and rescue in seedy, urban, and racialized underworlds. Men travel to a "dangerous" neighborhood, often in the poorest countries, and pose as johns in order to infiltrate a brothel and aid in a police raid.[38] A21's narratives, however, pivot in a different direction. They tend to generate horror to amplify a sense of moral urgency. Caine herself speaks of girls crammed into shipping containers; drowned at sea; locked in apartments and brothels; made to have abortions, or as she claimed in an interview: "they give birth and the babies are sold into pedophile rings"; these girls, "you must understand are raped twenty maybe thirty times every day."[39] In a promotional video, Malina Enlind, Director of the A21's Child Advocacy Center in Pattay, Thailand recounts an even more astounding incident: a three-year old girl, painted in makeup, scantily clad, drugged and made to dance for seven hours. "For years we tried to get this girl off the streets, but we couldn't because there was a loophole in the law that allowed her to be there," she reports in an A21 promotional video.[40]

Such anecdotes invite a lurid gaze, stopped short, a chance for Christian audiences to flirt with "a sex saturated culture...without becoming contaminated by it," explains Bernstein.[41] A21 recounts scenes of sexual deviancy and abuse, but it does not linger on them. Details are sparse; narratives are impressionistic. The point is not to outline carefully the situation being described; rather, it is to highlight how dramatically positive (and necessary) the interventions of A21's programs can be. That three-year Thai girl who was drugged and made to dance for money? Music swells in A21's promotional video as Malina Enlind recounts a happy outcome when the young girl finally came to their Child Advocacy Center: "she got new clothes and she turned into a child...she was working at the age of three and being drugged. Now she is one of the first in her class. She has an amazing family. She has four kittens...and she's doing gymnastics."[42] Girls are saved from conditions of utter despair and made whole (returned to a state of innocence thought to define "girlhood" as well). Threading narratives with prurient details, like this, Bernstein argues, protects the discourse of sex trafficking "from deep intellectual interrogation."[43] Who among us wants to investigate such repulsive scenes: children, drugged and used for sex; women and girls chained to beds and confined in brothels; migrants treated like herd animals? What would that say about *us*? We lose sight of the fact that we are not hearing from "victims" themselves. We are hearing from their rescuers about them.[44] Our interest turns to disgust. Stories of "sex gone bad" both excite and repel. This is their power. They cry out, in the words of two modern-day Christian abolitionists, Shayne Moore and Kimberly McOwen Yim: "Refuse to Do Nothing!"

Sensationalized, melodramatic narratives of discovery and rescue, apart from dulling critical inquiry, also consolidate nationalist, imperialist and racist visions of Western nations, whether Canada, the United States, or Australia and Western Europe as free and open societies as compared to others. Punctuating rescue narratives with sex, often of the violent and taboo kind, not only pings particular themes around gender politics and the sanctity of heterosexual marriage that define evangelical culture (they also negotiate tensions around these, as I elaborate below), these images likewise rely on ethnocentric logic that feeds Western exceptionalism. Bad sex occurs somewhere else in cultures where patriarchal power arrangements persist.[45] Such narratives prop up rich, neocolonialist societies, writes Barbara Heron, as "places of greater civilization, of order, cleanliness, and a truly good quality of life."[46] If bad sex persists inside of Western societies, on evangelical accounts, this is so often the result of misapplied or unrealized proper sexual values.

Anti-trafficking campaigns, in other words, recount stories about sex trafficking and global slavery that do an incredible amount of work for Western and Christian audiences: they sort through global injustice, obscure ongoing legacies of colonialism and racism, while enabling soft-power and militarized interventions by the former colonizing countries into poor regions around the world. Using the term "slavery" and its opposite, freedom, anti-trafficking discourse recycles theological scripts familiar to Christians, and, at the same time, calls up troubling racial and settler colonial histories in a gesture that obscures the on-going impact of these. "Slavery," on this account, belongs to a past that has been overcome; it does not reflect the valuation of freedom and human rights that are imagined as defining liberal states now.[47] (Indeed, one wonders if the evocation of "slavery" partly explains why the cause seems to have solicited greater enthusiasm from white evangelicals, and not those of color?)[48] Yet for conservative Christian women, there is more: the fight against sex trafficking serves as a proxy for painful gender politics inside conservative Christian communities. In this way, contemporary evangelical women share an unacknowledged commonality with nineteenth-century female abolitionists whose memory they evoke.

Abolition Mommas, Then and Now

> "I've become inspired by my abolitionist sisters of two hundred years ago ... during the nineteenth-century abolitionist movement, women could not vote, were not public speakers or teachers, held no political office and could not be clergy. And yet women played a central role in bringing an end to the trans-Atlantic slave trade."
>
> —Shayne Moore and Kimberly McOwen Yim, *Refuse to Do Nothing!: Finding Your Power to Abolish Modern-Day Slavery*[49]

Caine's ethical imperative, her assertion that she and her (putatively Western) audience are called to save women and girls elsewhere from "sexual slavery" calls up an older historical script, one that circulated in the nineteenth and early twentieth century, amongst female reformers. In that period, white, Protestant women's subjectivity was sutured to the performance of moral virtue, and the uplift of unfortunate others, indigenous and enslaved people, and the lower classes in particular.[50] This century saw the emergence of a separate-spheres ideology in which bourgeois women were tied to domesticity and motherhood, and men to public life and service. Cultivation and performance of a maternal morality enabled these women to find a wedge, however narrow, into social and political life. Protestant women's battle against prostitution began in the mid-nineteenth century initially with attempts by women moral reformers, like Britain's Josephine Butler, to guard poor, working class women against draconian laws and intrusive medical examinations outlined in the Contagious Diseases Acts (1864–1869).[51] Over the years, this effort ballooned into larger attempts to curtail prostitution altogether as a social vice and a danger to women's purity.[52]

In the United States, the cry to save girls from lives of prostitution became a charge of Frances Willard's Christian Women's Temperance Union (WCTU). Willard presented prostitution as a social vice, likened to alcoholism, which threatened family welfare as well as the moral probity of the nation. Willard's WCTU also undertook its own active campaign to expose the "trade" in girls. This "White Slave Panic" blossomed out of the sensationalized reporting of a Christian evangelist, William Stead, and his infamous, eventually discredited, "Maiden Tribute of Babylon" published in London's *Pall Mall Gazette* (1885).[53] This moral panic was largely fabricated, fueled by fears of lower-class white girls ensnared by racialized immigrant men into prostitution. The notion that poor girls were duped by false proposals of marriage or work into the sex trade was repeated by many women Christian reformers. Responding to the trade in girls set an agenda for much of Christian women's lobbying and humanitarian action.[54]

The nineteenth- and early-twentieth-century Christian women's crusade was animated at its start by concerns about the difficult and degrading labor and material conditions that lower-class girls and women endured. (It should be noted that Butler did much to roll back the CD Acts and to raise the age of consent, a concern picked up by the WCTU as well.) Yet for women social reformers, the charge to eradicate prostitution was likewise part of a larger strategy that allowed them to agitate for their own advancement, namely the right to vote, hold property, and garner pastoral authority.[55] Prostitution obtained the interest of Christian women because its existence could undermine the superior moral character of women as a group. Indeed, moral uprightness was the virtue on which white women reformers' very authority was waged. The goal was to restore all women and girls—degraded by poverty and low-class (racialized) men—to women's natural condition as pure and unsullied, in short, good. "Courage, my darlings," Josephine Butler reportedly said on a visit to a Liverpool brothel, "You are women, and a woman is a beautiful thing. You have been dragged deep in the mud, but you are still women."[56] When

Christian women fought to eradicate prostitution and to improve lower-class women and girls, then, they constituted their own subject positions as social and political actors as well as evangelists. This imperative to help the "downtrodden," however, smuggled in racist and nativist logics about who demanded rescue, and who was a threat and menace to social life. In this way, the "White Slave Panic" was linked to bourgeois women's status just as it also registered nativist fears about incoming immigrants and the shifting demographics that this entailed.

Organizations like Caine's A21 offers a modern spin on the helping imperative that female abolitionists in the nineteenth and early twentieth century deployed to insist on their own social and political power. The ability to save other women elsewhere, in this case, confirms Caine and her supporters' position as globally conscious citizens of benevolent nations, and their access to the rights this is thought to guarantee, including over "their own bodies and sexualities."[57] Caine writes for instance of one Nadia: "For years Nadia lived on dreams...She would travel. She would see a beautiful world, a world in which she had a helpful role to play," writes Caine of a woman in A21's safe house in Greece. "But girls in poor Georgian villages did not go to school beyond the second grade. They needed to learn only how to cook and clean, not read and write. What man, after all, would want to marry a woman more educated than he?" Her aspirations diminished by a patriarchal culture, Nadia finds herself victim to a trafficker who tricks her into coming to Greece as a nurse, but then forces her into a brothel. "Her new life was to be a sex slave," Caine reveals.[58]

We know how this story will unfold. Nadia does not stay in that brothel. The fierce love of a healing God and the determination of Christian women, like Caine, spare her, and other unfortunate women like her. "Now that I have found you," Caine reportedly told young women in an A21 safe house: "I will find other girls like you. I will do everything I can to stop this."[59] Caine's rhetoric indicates her position as what scholar Inderpal Grewal calls an "exceptional citizen" who improves herself by "helping others."[60] For affluent evangelical women, however, the call has the additional appeal of confirming not only their status as the citizen of a benevolent nation, but their particular Christian identity too. Because of their own salvation—figured in this as both a theological condition *and* socio-political one—(Western) Christian women are called to facilitate the redemption of others by sparing women and girls from patriarchal cultures that have degraded them. "When I lay down to sleep at night," Caine explains in *Undaunted*, "my life seems far removed from the lives of those who are trapped, pleading, broken—worlds apart, in fact. I am happily married, with healthy and happy children, living in a loving and safe home... My future is filled with dreams, plans, goals, vision. I am free. Yet in the work of A21...I meet so many who are languishing, forgotten, without justice, love, hope, or any promise in their lives."[61]

Caine's anecdotes about women like Nadia, Kalli, or Yun are entangled with racist and imperialist logics that, we have seen, inform anti-trafficking campaigns more generally.[62] Here, however, I want to suggest that Caine's confident assertions that she, and her audience, are "free" and can save other women and girls can also be read as a compensation for stubborn, and painful, gender politics operative within her own evangelical context. Caine, like other evangelical women celebrities, has proven masterful in recent decades at gathering audiences and developing mega ministries whose popularity can swell even into mainstream markets.[63] These women have wedged their way into leadership by taking up positions that are less apparently threatening to the pastoral authority of men. They are leaders of women's ministries; they are counselors and advisors; they are singers and performers; they are co-pastors and pastor's wives; but rarely are they simply "the pastor."[64] Conservative women leaders, argues historian Kate Bowler in *The Preacher's Wife: The Precarious Power of Evangelical Women Celebrities*, must perform "a delicate balance between professed submission to men and implicit independence from them."[65] Evangelical women have grabbed up the authority to preach and lead through calibrated performances of marriage and motherhood, deference to powerful men, apparent compliance with gender complementarianism, and by putting their own life struggles carefully on display.

Caine's celebrity testifies to these very dynamics, and to the frustrations that they have engendered. Her self-help books, threaded with personal confessions, are the ground upon which her efforts to evangelize are made. This is standard fare in evangelical sermonizing and writing, but it is a powerful form of speaker authentication for evangelical women especially. And it is one that Caine has mastered. A miscarriage, a history of sexual abuse, a late-in-life discovery that she was abandoned by her birthmother, a battle with cancer, as well as her marriage to Nick Caine and the birth of their two daughters—these are Caine's disclosures and her successes.[66] She peppers them throughout her books; she trots them out in her preaching. They are also her credentials, necessary in a world that routinely denies women the trapping of institutional authority. Carefully calibrated reveals offer testimony that Caine has endured and prevailed, that she is God's own instrument.[67] "I can see how Jesus is using all the painful parts of my life to bring healing, hope, and life to people. Through the work of A21, God has taken the shame I carried of abuse, adoption, and abandonment, and is redeeming it…" she writes in *Unashamed*.[68]

Caine, nonetheless, has expressed exhaustion with the performance the spotlight demands. "I never wanted to graduate to women's ministry," she told Bowler in an interview, "because it is always women's *miseries*, the repetition of the same sad story again and again: 'I was never loved. I was never whole. I was never'…Look, I want women to get *free*."[69] And Caine has done much to try and advance her vision of female empowerment for Christian women. She launched "Propel Women" in 2015, an initiative designed to support women to take up positions of authority in the church and in the world.[70] Incredibly, she did it from the stage of the Southern Baptist school, Liberty University.[71] Caine's charge to the evangelical community toward egalitarianism and uncompromising support for women's leadership is a departure from a calibrated performance of "submission" that regularly define evangelical women's rhetoric.[72] It is also notable for its bravery—especially when we remember that the Southern Baptist Convention has taken an uncompromising stand against women's religious leadership.[73] In her speech, Caine declared to the mass of graduating Liberty students:

> "Because of equal opportunity, affirmative action, like it or lump it, there is a world that is full of women and men, and we need the Church to stop running from that world, condemning that world, judging that world, and to begin to love that world, and go into that world, and bring the light, and the life, and the mercy, and the hope, and the grace of the Lord Jesus Christ into that world because it is dying, girls in that world are dying.
>
> And we've got militant left-wing feminists rising up because they are trying to fill a gap we've been hiding from because we're afraid to use two words in the same sentence: women and leader. And I'm like, really? What planet are we living on? ... I'm not going to leave my legacy where I'm going to rescue slaves and lose young women from the Church."[74]

Yet while Caine presents her lean-in evangelical feminism (though she does not use this term) with persuasive power, bubbling underneath is a palpable frustration with the way that the Church has and continues to marginalize women.

In fact, although conservative Christian women, like Caine, have acquired celebrity and fame, they have proven to have an uncertain hold on power inside their communities. "It's always been this way for women in evangelical leadership—hard to rise and easy to fall," explains Kate Bowler.[75] If a woman does manage to have a prolific career as an evangelical leader, there is little institutional backing to secure her efforts in the long run.[76] The challenges women in these communities face extend beyond the fight to obtain spiritual leadership. They also vary in the ways that they play out for evangelical women of color (who are often in communities with differing church structures and who must negotiate gender scripts that do not precisely follow that of their white counterparts). Recent allegations of sexual misconduct and harassment by high-profile pastors and inside of Christian seminaries have exposed extensive sexism and racism inside these communities that unsettled evangelicals, just as "ME TOO" has rattled the broader culture.[77] There is a clamoring by some evangelical women, like Caine, for change. Yet for those who push for it, the cost can be high. Indeed, Caine's friend, Southern Baptist phenom, Beth Moore, was chastised by male pastors and lost some of her own female supporters when she spoke out against Donald Trump's *Access Hollywood* tape.[78]

Will Caine's attempts to shake up the sexist culture in the Church persuade audiences of younger evangelicals, and the larger evangelical world? On the school's newspaper website there appears a debate about whether LU should have permitted Caine to speak, whether in fact, women even have the right to preach. (Proponents can be found on both sides of the issue, cutting right down gender lines.)[79] The work required to reckon with troubling legacies of sexism inside conservative Christian circles is mammoth, and its success is far from sure. Gender complementarianism, the doctrine that has defined contemporary evangelical gender politics, makes it exceedingly hard to simultaneously insist on gender parity. Sexes are separate, distinctive, with their own gifts, yes, but equally suited to ministry and evangelism? That is a tougher sell.[80]

One tactic is to speak *as if* gender egalitarianism is the gospel light too long hidden under the bushel of sexism, *as if* women's inferiority is but devil-talk. This is a strategy right out of Caine's playbook:

> "I want women to know God can use everything the enemy meant for evil in their life for good. He can take their stories of shame and redeem them—first for their own freedom and then to help others.
>
> I want women to know that they are not less than, weaker, second, or not enough. They are created in God's image—greatly valued, loved, chosen, wanted, and adored by the Creator of the universe."[81]

What to do, then, when this God-given fact proves elusive? Bowler's study, *The Preacher's Wife*, provides rich accounting of just such moments: a head pastor position goes to a man, and his mega ministry get bequeathed to a son, and not a talented and experienced daughter; men in seminaries, churches and para-church organizations sexually assault and harass minors or women, and get away with it;[82] single women find that they are ignored or sidelined because they are not mothers and wives; or female celebrities, and wives of male ones, find themselves under incredible scrutiny, and their hold on the spotlight tenuous and fleeting. What to do when the demands of motherhood are confining, so consuming that leadership and action seems impossible, or is radically limited? The fight to end "sex slavery" for affluent evangelical women, as I have argued, offers assurances that they possess the rights and privileges of "exceptional citizenship" in neo-liberal democracies; indeed, it has this pull for secular and Christian activists alike. Yet the desire to end the slavery of women and girls outside evangelical communities is a declaration, if unrecognized as such, that Christian women might escape the suffocation of pervasive sexism; that they have been selected by God to act, to do something grand, even world altering. "The world," Caine tells her readers, "will be forever changed because of *you*."[83]

Christian anti-trafficking campaigns shore up narratives of national and Christian exceptionalisms, as I have elaborated. For affluent, Christian women to whom they appeal (the "you" in A21's "Can You See Me?" ads) these campaigns propagate appealing moral narratives of rescue and redemption, giving flight to fantasies of heroism and assurances of their privilege and power as well. To save others, of course, is to demonstrate one's moral goodness. This is a requisite performance of Christian womanhood that defined it stretching back to the nineteenth century. To save others in another country, another culture, another community, is today, however, also a compensation for the impossibilities of resolving nagging gender politics in one's own life. This possibility makes anti-trafficking activism potent for some conservative Christian women. It likewise makes that activism problematic, and even dangerous, for the women and girls, outside of these communities, who it claims to help, because, in the end, are these Christian anti-trafficking campaigns *really* about those women and girls?

Some Concluding Thoughts, of the More Personal Kind

In closing, I acknowledge that the arguments that I have made are unlikely to persuade A21 to jettison their carceral approach to sex trafficking. (In 2016–2017, A21 appealed to the government of New South Wales to return to a former policy of criminalizing sex work despite the positive outcomes of decriminalization for sex workers there.)[84] The chapter aims instead to capture a textured history of a moment in Christian culture, and to foreground the power of Caine's celebrity and her organization within it. If we are going to look at religious responses to sex trafficking, we should account for powerful women like Caine in shaping these.

And yet…I do feel disheartened by the possibility that my arguments may do little to change the attitudes of conservative Christian women to sex work and sex workers either. There is a disparity between my assessment of evangelical women's humanitarian work against sex trafficking and the explicit rationale that these women would recognize, or even claim as their own. Conservative Christians, including Caine and her supporters, see their anti-trafficking work as motivated by the gospel and faith. Evangelicals are mandated to salvific action, both locally and globally. This is absolutely fundamental to evangelical culture and mission. It is born out of a recognition of human suffering and a particular understanding of the remedy to it. It is catalyzed by cultural values about sexual purity and gender roles too, and a religious context that sees women as uniquely suited to particular forms of charitable ministry, as we have seen. To fight sex trafficking, on this account, may seem morally incumbent on evangelical women.

My analysis identifies a discordance that can emerge in charitable work, between what one thinks one is doing and the subtler, less conscious motivations that propel one to particular kinds of humanitarian efforts, and with this, an inability to understand fully their effects. Human intentions are complex and knotty, in all cases, obviously, and not only for evangelicals. Intentions are especially problematic, however, when they include unexamined legacies of racism and colonialism in which white, affluent evangelicals are caught—but, and this is important to note, so are many well-meaning Christians.

I, too, was raised inside a Protestant community where charitable work defined our faith; it was certainly required of the women in that community to be seen as "good Christians." Charity was what enabled my mother, in particular, to ascertain her value as a person and a Christian. It would seem that we mainline Protestants share this with evangelical women. Christian charity entailed making a lot of donations, of money and food, or volunteer work at the church or in shelters. But it could smuggle in a blunt kind of moralizing. Help was what good people gave to the less fortunate. Little interrogation of what the help looked like, or how it felt for those upon whom it was enacted, was required of us. There was too little interrogation of why we were in the position to give it too, or it was a way of managing our guilt, our privilege. The whole scene generated by charity did not allow critique, not really, or allow those accessing or given that charity to offer it, at least not freely.

I have struggled with concluding this chapter because I want to say something affirmative about Caine and her organization. I struggle because I respect her boldness in tackling gender discrimination in evangelical churches (from the stage of Liberty University, no less). I struggle, too, because I understand the equation that she and her followers are making—in acting on behalf of others, they assert their own value and power in a culture that does not guarantee them. I watched the women in my own family, especially my hard-working mother, make the same calculus. I also watched her burn out at times being charitable to others (my mother was by nature self-effacing; she did not have Caine's self-aggrandizing talents). Charity did not regularly improve my mother's social standing or the horizons of her own life. Watching her, the narrative of Christian charity with which I was raised started to unravel. I eventually questioned the whole landscape of it so that now I cannot see the world as the Christian women who aim to save victims of trafficking might. I suspect that I inhabit a murkier moral space. Who are the saviors? Who are the victims? Are we so sure that we know? Not everyone is lead to such interrogations. Questions can be uncomfortable because they can entail loss, of what we think we know, of who we are. But such losses, in this case, might be one more affluent Christians, evangelical or otherwise, should consider?

The cause of anti-trafficking has now made its way onto the agendas of numerous mainline churches, just as it has that of secular Western governments. The notion of affluent women helping less affluent ones is a powerful call for those of us steeped in cultural feminism, extra potent when it is combined with the call of Christian charity. The appeal of anti-trafficking activism, thus, is hardly limited to a Christian subculture, even if it does flourish there at present. Maybe in the midst of public outcries over racial violence, and the awareness of vast economic disparities that Covid-19 has revealed, there is a greater will to expose racist and colonialist structures, to reimagine what safety might mean for everyone, and, with this, what help and so-called "Christian kindness" could entail. We could follow Caine and assert that (some) Christians are "propelled" into the world to heal and save it. Like Queen Esther, these Christians are born into privilege as part of God's plan to aid the less fortunate and those in need. Or alternatively might we remember that the gospel demands humility too? Can this realization push us towards humanitarian action that supports the humanity and moral agency of other people to determine their lives and secure their wellbeing?

Notes

1 This research was supported by a seed grant from the Office of the Vice President, Research and Graduate Studies at Concordia University. Thank you to my research assistants, Laurel Andrew, Alessia Infantino, and Olivia Schultz, as well as to editor

Lauren McGrow for insightful comments throughout the research and writing of this chapter. Any errors are entirely my own.

I borrow this title from Shayne Moore and Kimberly McOwen Yim, see *Refuse to Do Nothing: Finding Your Power to Abolish Modern-Day Slavery* (Downer's Grove, IL: Intervarsity Press, 2013). "Abolition Mommas" is the name of Yim's organization in San Clemente, CA.

2 Caine, *Undaunted: Daring to Do What God Calls You to Do* (Grand Rapids, MI: Zondervan Press, 2012), 158. Caine's comment here is a reflection on Esther 4:14. Esther was married to the Persian King Ahasuerus (Xerxes I). As Queen of the Persian Empire, she manages to save the Judean people from genocide. The story is commemorated in the Jewish festival of Purim. The passage that Caine is referencing reads: "Who knows but that you have come to your royal position for such a time as this?"

3 Caine, *Undaunted*, 178.

4 Other titles mentioned here, Caine, *Unstoppable: Step into Your Purpose, Run Your Race, Embrace the Future Do* (Grand Rapids, MI: Zondervan Press, 2014); *Unashamed: Drop the Baggage, Pick Up Your Freedom, Fulfill Your Destiny* (Grand Rapids, MI: Zondervan Press, 2016); *Unshakeable: 365 Devotions for Finding Strength in God's Word* (Grand Rapids, MI: Zondervan Press, 2017).

5 The larger ads outline the "scenario" entailed in this image. The descriptions can also be found on A21's website, see https://www.a21.org/content/can-you-see-me-usa/gouyi8.

6 See A21, "Missing Persons: A21 a 10 Year Film" Youtube, last modified June 18, 2018, accessed Jan. 4,2022. https://www.youtube.com/watch?v=4JQDYt0rVRY&feature=emb_rel_end

7 Printed with permission of "The A21 Campaign."

8 Kempadoo, "The Anti-Trafficking Juggernaut Rolls On," in Kempadoo, eds. with Jyoti Sanghera and Bandana Pattanaik, *Trafficking and Prostitution Reconsidered: New Perspectives on Migration, Sex Work, and Human Rights*, Second Edition (Boulder, CO: Paradigm Publisher, 2012), 249–260.

9 Caine, *Unstoppable*, 126.

10 Yvonne C. Zimmerman, *Other Dreams of Freedom: Religion, Sex and Human Trafficking* (New York, NY: Oxford University Press, 2013), 21–76.

11 It is also policy of the UN, see "Protocol to Prevent, Suppress and Punish Trafficking in Persons, Especially Women and Girls," adopted in 2000: https://www.ohchr.org/en/professionalinterest/pages/protocoltraffickinginpersons.aspx. Regarding the expansion of this discourse across Anglophone democracies, see Julia O'Connell Davidson, *Modern Slavery: The Margins of Freedom* (New York, NY: Palgrave Macmillan Press, 2015), 8–9.

12 Other examples include Moore and Yim, *Refuse to Do Nothing!*; Daniel Walker, *God in a Brothel: An Undercover Journey into Sex Trafficking and Rescue* (Downer's Grove, IL: Intervarsity Press, 2001); Mary Frances Bowley, *A League of Dangerous Women: True Stories from the Road to Redemption* (Colorado Springs, CO: Multinomah Books, 2006); Gary Haugen, *Just Courage: God's Great Expedition for the Restless Christian* (Downer's Grove, IL: Intervarsity Press, 2008); Zach Hunter, *Be the Change: Your Guide to Freeing Slaves and Changing the World* (Grand Rapids, MI: Zondervan Press, 2009); Eddi Byun, *Just Awakening: How You and Your Church Can Help End Human Slavery* (Downer's Grove, IL: Intervarsity Press, 2014).

13 A21, "Walk for Freedom 2021," A21 Website, accessed January 2, 2022, https://www.a21.org/content/walk-for-freedom-2021-dayof-walk/gsnbgg.

14 The number of organizations is expansive and includes "International Justice Mission" (IJM), "Not For Sale," "Exodus Cry," "Shared Hope" and "Defend Dignity," among others.

15 See the editorial by Elle Hardy, "From Hillsong to the Bible Belt," *The Monthly*, February 2019, https://www.themonthly.com.au/issue/2019/february/1548939600/elle-hardy/hillsong-bible-belt?cb=1598134874#mtr. About Hillsong's women's ministry in the previous decade, see also see Marion Maddox, "Rise Up Warrior Princess Daughters: Is Evangelical Women's Submission a Mere Fairy Tale?" *Journal of Feminist Studies in Religion* 29.1 (2013), 12–13.

16 See Caine, *Unstoppable*, 129–132. A21's webpage provides information about their offices and centers, see https://www.a21.org/content/where-we-work/gnde9k.

17 For instance, Wellspring Living, accessed January 4, 2022, https://wellspringliving.org/.

18 "Our Solution," A21 Website, accessed January 4, 2022, https://www.a21.org/content/our- solution/grdphc. https://www.a21.org/content/our-solution/gn9pjs. Similar wording appears on the website of the International Justice Mission, "Our Work," accessed Jan.4, 2022, https://www.ijm.org/our-work. According to sociologist Elizabeth Bernstein, IJM, the most established of these Christian NGOs has set the agenda of a "militarized humanitarianism" the defines the work of most anti-trafficking campaigns with global reach, whether Christian or secular, see *Brokered Subjects: Sex, Trafficking, and the Politics of Freedom* (Chicago, IL: The University of Chicago Press, 2018), 78–83.

19 Women and girls from Eastern Europe and the Global South are similarly foregrounded in Caine's own writing, e.g. *Unashamed*, 101–106.

20 "Traffickers," writes Jyoti Sanghera, are regularly "small-time operators," known and even procured by the so-called victim through familial or other social networks, see "Unpacking Trafficking Discourse," in *Trafficking and Prostitution Reconsidered*, 15–16.

21 E.g. Kempadoo et al., *Trafficking and Prostitution Reconsidered*; Bernstein, *Brokered Subjects*; O'Connell Davidson, *Modern Slavery*; Julietta Hua, *Trafficking in Women's Human Rights* (Minneapolis: MN: The University of Minnesota Press, 2011); Jo Doezma, *Sex Slaves and Discourse Masters: The Construction of Trafficking* (New York, NY: Zed Books, 2010); Laura Maria Agustin, *Sex at the Margins: Migration, Labor Markets and the Rescue Industry* (New York: NY, Zed Books, 2007).

22 Bernstein, *Brokered Subjects*, 78–83; Sanghera, *Trafficking and Prostitution Reconsidered,* 20; Julie Kaye, *Responding to Human Trafficking: Dispossession, Colonial Violence, and Resistance among Indigenous and Racialized Women* (Toronto, ON: University of Toronto Press), 11.

23 See Melissa Ditmore, "Trafficking in Lives: How Ideology Shapes Policy," in *Trafficking and Prostitution Reconsidered*, 107–126. Also see O'Connell Davidson, *Modern Slavery*, 82; Jo Doezma, "Ouch! Western Feminist's Attachment to the 'Third World Prostitute'," *Feminist Review* (2001): 16–38.

24 Carole S. Vance, "Innocence and Experience: Melodramatic Narratives of Sex Trafficking and Their Consequences for Law and Policy," *The History of the Present* 2 (2011): 200–218.

25 See O'Connell Davidson, *Modern Slavery.*

26 Hua, *Trafficking in Women's Human Rights*, 27–48.

27 Hua, *Trafficking Women's Human Rights*, 9; Sanghera, *Trafficking and Prostitution Reconsidered*, 9.

28 Gretchen Soderlund, "The Rhetoric of Revelation: Sex Trafficking and the Journalistic Exposé," *Humanity* 2 (2011), 193.

29 See note 22 above, and Bernstein, *Brokered Subjects*, 6.

30 Zimmerman, *Other Dreams of Freedom*, 103–129.

31 Zimmerman, *Other Dreams of Freedom,* 130–159.

32 Kate Bowler, *The Preacher's Wife: The Precarious Power of Evangelical Women Celebrities* (Princeton, NJ: Princeton University Press, 2019), 65–116. On attitudes

espoused by Hillsong Church's Women Ministries, under the leadership of Brian and Bobbie Houston, see Maddox, "Rise Up Warrior Princess Daughters."

33 Bernstein, *Brokered Subjects*, 77.

34 Bernstein, *Brokered Subjects*, 78 and 80.

35 Bernstein, *Brokered Subjects*, 92–95.

36 Caine, *Unashamed*, 120.

37 Bernstein, *Brokered Subjects*, 6.

38 Walker, *God in a Brothel*; Elena Shih, "Not in My 'Backyard Abolitionism': Vigilante Rescue against American Sex Trafficking." *Sociological Perspectives* 59 (2016): 66–90.

39 Comments such as these are found in interviews and promotional videos, for instance: A21, "Christine Caine, The A21 Campaign," Youtube, last modified June 20, 2013, accessed January 4, 2022, https://www.youtube.com/watch?v=YdsC0ait_OE. See also Jim Kavanaugh, "Abolishing Sex Slavery by Helping One Girl at a Time," CNN, June 16, 2011. https://thecnnfreedomproject.blogs.cnn.com/2011/06/16/abolishing-sex-slavery-by-helping-one-girl-at-a-time/.

40 A21, "Missing Persons: A21 a 10 Year Film," Youtube, last modified June 18, 2018, accessed January 4, 2022. https://www.youtube.com/watch?v=4JQDYt0rVRY @14.30.

41 Bernstein, *Brokered Subjects*, 86.

42 A21, "Missing Persons: A21 a 10 Year Film," Youtube, last modified June 18, 2018, accessed January 4, 2022, https://www.youtube.com/watch?v=4JQDYt0rVRY @15.00.

43 Bernstein, *Brokered Subjects*, 91.

44 Details about what goes on inside A21 facilities is sparse, as Elle Hardy also notes. See "From Hillsong to the Bible Belt."

45 Hua, *Trafficking Women's Human Rights*, 71–93.

46 Barbara Heron, *Desire for Development: Whiteness, Gender, and the Helping Imperative* (Waterloo, ON: Wilfrid Laurier Press, 2007), 34.

47 O'Connell Davidson, *Modern Slavery*, 1–27.

48 Bernstein's ethnographic research indicated that anti-trafficking activists tended to come from racial and class privileged positions. See *Brokered Subjects*, 57. Moreover, as Inderpal Grewal has noted, in media and news, it is invariably white "American, Christian Westerners" who are presented as the quintessential humanitarians. See *Saving the Security State: Exceptional Citizens in Twenty-First Century America* (Durham, NC: Duke University Press, 2017), 61 and 66.

49 Moore and Yim, *Refuse to Do Nothing*, 31.

50 Heron, *Desire for Development*, 31.

51 Gretchen Soderlund, *Sex Trafficking, Scandal, and the Transformation of Journalism 1885–1917* (Chicago, IL: University of Chicago Press, 2013), 29.

52 Judith R. Walkowitz, *Prostitution and Victorian Society: Women, Class, and the State* (Cambridge, UK: Cambridge University Press, 1980).

53 Soderlund, *Sex Trafficking, Scandal*, 72–73.

54 Katharine Bushnell was one of the most active members of the WCTU. See "Man's Prattle, Woman's World: The Biblical Mission of Katharine Bushnell," in Rosemary Skinner Keller, eds. *Spiritual and Social Responsibility: Vocational Vision of Women in the United Methodist Tradition* (Nashville, TN: Abingdon Press, 1993), 165–182; other examples include Jane Addams of the settlement movement. See Janet Beer and Katherine Joslin, "Diseases of the Body Politic: White Slavery in Jane Addams' 'A New Conscience and an Ancient Evil' and Selected Short Stories by Charlotte Perkins Gilman," *Journal of American Studies* 33 (1999): 1–18.

55 Soderlund, *Sex Trafficking, Scandal*, 72.

56 Jane Jordan, *Josephine Butler* (London, UK: John Murray Publishing, 2001), 81. Regarding William Stead, evangelist and author of the "Maiden Tribute," Soderlund concludes: "what Stead wanted was for working-class girls to be chaste, for them to exhibit the same alleged morality and calculative rationality as Victorian middle-class girls," *Sex Trafficking, Scandal*, 39.

57 Bernstein, *Brokered Subjects*, 85, quoting postcolonial feminist scholar Chandra Mohanty.
58 Caine, *Undaunted*, 16.
59 Caine, *Undaunted*, 24.
60 Grewal, *Saving the Security State*, 59–71.
61 Caine, *Undaunted*, 194.
62 See references above. Another telling example includes the rescue of Muslim girls from Uzbekistan in *Undaunted*, 188–189 and Favour, from Nigeria, in *Unstoppable*, 88.
63 See also Hardy, "From Hillsong to the Bible Belt."
64 Bowler, *The Preacher's Wife,* 170 and 172.
65 Bowler, *The Preacher's Wife*, 4.
66 All of these incidents are discussed to varying degrees in the popular books that I have cited here, *Undaunted, Unstoppable*, and *Unashamed.* The integrity of Caine's narrative in, *Unashamed*, however, was challenged by self-help author, Carey Scott, who claimed Caine plagiarized parts of her book, *Untangled.* See Leonard Blair, "Evangelical Christine Caine Sued by Colo. Author," September 26, 2018, https://www.christianpost.com/news/evangelist-christine-caine-sued-by-colorado-author-for-copying-book-227574/.
67 Caine writes: "I never imagined God would use an adopted, abused, marginalized, minority female…to open rescue homes for women sold as sex slaves around the world and to hire lawyers to win conviction of the organized criminals exploiting these women. To this day, I stand in awe that God uses me to travel across the globe…" See *Unstoppable*, 58.
68 Caine, *Unashamed*, 192.
69 Bowler, *The Preacher's Wife*, 182.
70 Propel Women, "About Us," accessed January 4, 2022, https://www.propelwomen.org/content/about/gjh6fc.
71 Drew Menard, "Christine Caine Launches Propel Women during Convocation," Liberty University Website, https://www.propelwomen.org/content/about/gjh6fc.
72 Even a departure from Caine's former Hillsong Church. See Maddox, "Rise Up Warrior Princess Daughters."
73 Bowler, *The Preacher's Wife,* 3 and 39–40.
74 Propel Women, "Propel Launch at Liberty University-Convocation with Christine Caine," Youtube, last modified April 9, 2015, accessed January 4, 2022. https://www.youtube.com/watch?v=yQ2lHnrn4zE@15.18.
75 Bowler quoted in Mark I. Pinsky, "At Trump's Right Hand: Paula White and the Prosperity Gospel," *Harvard Divinity Bulletin*, Spring/Summer 2020, 41.
76 Bowler, *The Preacher's Wife*, 250.
77 Eliza Griswold, "Silence is Not Spiritual: The Evangelical #METOO Movement," *The New Yorker*, June 15, 2018, https://www.newyorker.com/news/on-religion/silence-is-not-spiritual-the-evangelical-metoo-movement.
78 Bowler, *The Preacher's Wife,* 245.
79 Emily Hoosier, "New Initiative Propels Women," Liberty Champion, January 27, 2015 https://www.liberty.edu/champion/2015/01/new-initiative-propels-women/.
80 Within evangelical circles, the notion of biblical egalitarianism is being advanced by younger women. See, for instance, Sara Bessey, https://sarahbessey.com/christian-feminist/ and the late Rachel Held Evans, https://rachelheldevans.com/.
81 Caine, *Unashamed*, 196.
82 Caine's former church Hillsong in Australia has faced sexual assault charges waged against former pastor, Frank Houston, who was accused of sexually assaulting young boys. These actions were reportedly covered up by his son and current pastor. Report of the Royal Commission into Institutional Reponses to Child Abuse, "Report of Case Study No. 18," October, 2015, https://web.archive.org/web/20190204082855/https://www.childabuseroyalcommission.gov.au/sites/default/files/

file-list/Case Study 18 - Findings Report - Australian Christian Churches.pdf. Caine herself has not spoken out against Hillsong's handling of these allegations. See Ashley Easter, "Raising Caine over Christine Caine," December 4, 2018, https://www.ashleyeaster.com/blog/raising-cain-about-christine-caine. Accessed January 4, 2022.

83 Caine, *Unstoppable*, 175.

84 A21, "The A21 Campaign Submission to New South Wales Government-Legislative Council on Human Trafficking, Inquiry into Human Trafficking," February 2017, accessed January 4, 2022, https://www.parliament.nsw.gov.au/lcdocs/submissions/57033/0007%20A21.pdf.

Bibliography

A21, "Christine Caine, The A21 Campaign," *Youtube*, last modified June 20, 2013, accessed January 4, 2022, https://www.youtube.com/watch?v=YdsC0ait_OE.

A21, "Missing Persons: A21 a 10 Year Film," *Youtube*, last modified June 18, 2018, accessed January 4, 2022, https://www.youtube.com/watch?v=4JQDYt0rVRY&feature=emb_rel_end.

A21, "Our Solution," accessed January 4, 2022, https://www.a21.org/content/our-solution/grdphc.

A21, "The A21 Campaign Submission to New South Wales Government-Legislative Council on Human Trafficking, Inquiry into Human Trafficking ,"February 2017, accessed January 4, 2022, https://www.parliament.nsw.gov.au/lcdocs/submissions/57033/0007%20A21.pdf.

A21, "Walk for Freedom 2021," *A21 Website*, January 2, 2022, https://www.a21.org/content/walk-for-freedom-2021-dayof-walk/gsnbgg.

Agustin, Laura Maria, *Sex at the Margins: Migration, Labor Markets and the Rescue Industry*, New York, NY: Zed Books, 2007.

Beer, Janet and Katherine Joslin, "Diseases of the Body Politic: White Slavery in Jane Addams, 'A New Conscience and an Ancient Evil' and Selected Short Stories by Charlotte Perkins Gilman," *Journal of American Studies* 33 (1999): 1–18.

Bernstein, Elizabeth, *Brokered Subjects: Sex, Trafficking, and the Politics of Freedom*, Chicago, IL: University of Chicago Press, 2018.

Bessey, Sara, https://sarahbessey.com/christian-feminist/.

Blair, Leonard, "Evangelical Christine Caine Sued by Colo. Author," *Christian Post*, September 26, 2018, https://www.christianpost.com/news/evangelist-christine-caine-sued-by-colorado-author-for-copying-book-227574/.

Bowler, Kate, *The Preacher's Wife: The Precarious Power of Evangelical Women Celebrities*, Princeton, NJ: Princeton University Press, 2019.

Bowley, Mary Frances, *A League of Dangerous Women: True Stories from the Road to Redemption*, Colorado Springs, CO: Multinomah Books, 2006.

Byun, Eddi, *Just Awakening: How You and Your Church Can Help End Human Slavery*, Downer's Grove, IL: Intervarsity Press, 2014.

Caine, Christine, *Unshakeable: 365 Devotions for Finding Strength in God's Word*, Grand Rapids, MI: Zondervan Press, 2017.

Caine, Christine, *Unashamed: Drop the Baggage, Pick Up Your Freedom, Fulfill Your Destiny*, Grand Rapids, MI: Zondervan Press, 2016.

Caine, Christine, *Unstoppable: Step into Your Purpose, Run Your Race, Embrace the Future*, Grand Rapids, MI: Zondervan Press, 2014.

Caine, Christine, *Undaunted: Daring to Do What God Calls You to Do*, Grand Rapids, MI: Zondervan, 2012.
Ditmore, Melissa, "Trafficking in Lives: How Ideology Shapes Policy," in *Trafficking and Prostitution Reconsidered: New Perspectives on Migration, Sex Work, and Human Rights*. Second Edition, 107–126, Kempadoo, eds. with Jyoti Sanghera and Bandana Pattanaik, Boulder, CO: Paradigm Publisher, 2012.
Doezema, Jo, *Sex Slaves and Discourse Masters: The Construction of Trafficking*, New York, NY: Zed Books, 2010.
—"Ouch! Western Feminists' 'Wounded Attachment' to the 'Third World Prostitute'," *Feminist Review*67 (2001): 16–38.
Easter, Ashley. "Raising Caine over Christine Caine," December 4, 2018. Accessed January 4, 2022. https://www.ashleyeaster.com/blog/raising-cain-about-christine-caine.
Grewal, Inderpal, *Saving the Security State: Exceptional Citizens in Twenty-First Century America*, Durham, NC: Duke University Press, 2017.
Griswold, Eliza, "Silence is Not Spiritual: The Evangelical #METOO Movement," *The New Yorker*, June 15, 2018, https://www.newyorker.com/news/on-religion/silence-is-not-spiritual-the-evangelical-metoo-movement.
Hardy, Elle, "From Hillsong to the Bible Belt," *The Monthly*, February 2019, https://www.themonthly.com.au/issue/2019/february/1548939600/elle-hardy/hillsong-bible-belt?cb=1598134874#mtr.
Haugen, Gary, *Just Courage: God's Great Expedition for the Restless Christian*, Downer's Grove, IL: Intervarsity Press, 2008.
Hunter, Zach, *Be the Change: Your Guide to Freeing Slaves and Changing the World*, Grand Rapids, MI: Zondervan Press, 2009.
Held Evans, Rachel, https://rachelheldevans.com/.
Heron, Barbara, *Desire for Development: Whiteness, Gender, and the Helping Imperative*, Waterloo, ON: Wilfred Laurier University Press, 2007.
Hoosier, Emily, "New Initiative Propels Women," *Liberty Champion*, January 27, 2015 https://www.liberty.edu/champion/2015/01/new-initiative-propels-women/.
Hua, Julietta, *Trafficking in Women's Human Rights*, Minneapolis, MN: The University of Minnesota Press, 2011.
Jordan, Jane, *Josephine Butler*, London: John Murray Publishing, 2001.
International Justice Mission, "Our Work," accessed January 4, 2022, https://www.ijm.org/our-work.
Kavanaugh, Jim, "Abolishing Sex Slavery by Helping One Girl at a Time," *CNN*, June 16, 2011, https://thecnnfreedomproject.blogs.cnn.com/2011/06/16/abolishing-sex-slavery-by-helping-one-girl-at-a-time/.
Kaye, Julie, *Responding to Human Trafficking: Dispossession, Colonial Violence, and Resistance among Indigenous and Racialized Women*, Toronto, ON: University of Toronto Press, 2017.
Keller, Rosemary Skinner, "Man's Prattle, Woman's World: The Biblical Mission of Katharine Bushnell," in *Spiritual and Social Responsibility: Vocational Vision of Women in the United Methodist Tradition*, 165–182, Rosemary Skinner Keller, eds. Nashville, TN: Abingdon Press, 1993.
Kempadoo, Kamala, "The Anti-Trafficking Juggernaut Rolls On," in *Trafficking and Prostitution Reconsidered: New Perspectives on Migration, Sex Work, and Human Rights*, Second Edition, 249–260, Kempadoo, eds. with Jyoti Sanghera and Bandana Pattanaik, Boulder, CO: Paradigm Publisher, 2012.

Maddox, Marion, "Rise Up Warrior Princess Daughters: Is Evangelical Women's Submission a Mere Fairy Tale?" *Journal of Feminist Studies in Religion* 29 (2013): 9–26.
Menard, Drew. "Christine Caine Launches Propel Women during Convocation," *Liberty University Website*, https://www.propelwomen.org/content/about/gjh6fc.
Moore, Shayne and Kimberly McOwen Yim, *Refuse to Do Nothing: Finding Your Power to Abolish Modern-Day Slavery*, Downer's Grove, IL: Intervarsity Press, 2013.
O'Connell Davidson, Julia, *Modern Slavery: The Margins of Freedom*, New York, NY: Palgrave Macmillan, 2015.
Pinsky, Mark I., "At Trump's Right Hand: Paula White and the Prosperity Gospel," *Harvard Divinity Bulletin*. Spring/Summer 2020/Spring/Summer 2020 2020, accessed January 4, 2022, https://bulletin.hds.harvard.edu/at-trumps-right-hand/.
Propel Women, "About Us," accessed January 4, 2022, https://www.propelwomen.org/content/about/gjh6fc.
Propel Women, "Propel Launch at Liberty University-Convocation with Christine Caine," *Youtube*, last modified April 9, 2015, accessed January 4, 2022, https://www.youtube.com/watch?v=yQ2lHnrn4zE.
Report of the Royal Commission into Institutional Reponses to Child Abuse, "Report of Case Study No. 18," October, 2015, https://www.childabuseroyalcommission.gov.au/case-studies/case-study-18-australian-christian-churches.
Sanghera, Jyoti, "Unpacking Trafficking Discourse," in *Trafficking and Prostitution Reconsidered: New Perspectives on Migration, Sex Work, and Human Rights*, Second Edition, 3–24, Kempadoo, eds. with Jyoti Sanghera and Bandana Pattanaik. Boulder, CO: Paradigm Publisher, 2012.
Shih, Elena, "Not in My 'Backyard Abolitionism': Vigilante Rescue against American SexTrafficking," *Sociological Perspectives* 59 (2016): 66–90.
Soderlund, Gretchen, *Sex Trafficking, Scandal, and the Transformation of Journalism 1885–1917*, Chicago, IL: University of Chicago Press, 2013.
—"The Rhetoric of Revelation: Sex Trafficking and the Journalistic Exposé." *Humanity* 2 (2011): 193–211.
Walker, Daniel, *God in a Brothel: An Undercover Journey into Sex Trafficking and Rescue*, Downer's Grove, IL: Intervarsity Press, 2001.
Walkowitz, Judith R., *Prostitution and Victorian Society: Women, Class, and the State*, Cambridge: Cambridge University Press, 1980.
Wellspring Living, accessed January 4, 2022, https://wellspringliving.org/.
Vance, Carole S. "Innocence and Experience: Melodramatic Narratives of Sex Trafficking and Their Consequences for Law and Policy," *The History of the Present* 2 (2011): 200–218.
— "Thinking Trafficking, Thinking Sex," *GLQ* 17 (2010): 135–143.
Zimmerman, Yvonne C. *Other Dreams of Freedom: Religion, Sex and Human Trafficking*, New York, NY: Oxford University Press, 2013.
United Nations, "Protocol to Prevent, Suppress and Punish Trafficking in Persons, Especially Women and Girls," accessed January 4, 2022, https://www.ohchr.org/en/professionalinterest/pages/protocoltraffickinginpersons.aspx.

2 Do You See This (Wo)man? Lessons Learned from Sex Workers

Hannah Estabrook

36 One of the Pharisees asked Jesus[a] to eat with him, and he went into the
Pharisee's house and took his place at the table. **37** And a woman in the city, who
was a sinner, having learned that he was eating in the Pharisee's house, brought
an alabaster jar of ointment. **38** She stood behind him at his feet, weeping, and
began to bathe his feet with her tears and to dry them with her hair. Then she
continued kissing his feet and anointing them with the ointment. **39** Now when
the Pharisee who had invited him saw it, he said to himself, "If this man were a
prophet, he would have known who and what kind of woman this is who is
touching him—that she is a sinner." **40** Jesus spoke up and said to him, "Simon, I
have something to say to you." "Teacher," he replied, "speak." **41** "A certain
creditor had two debtors; one owed five hundred denarii,[b] and the other fifty.
42 When they could not pay, he canceled the debts for both of them. Now which
of them will love him more?" **43** Simon answered, "I suppose the one for whom
he canceled the greater debt." And Jesus[c] said to him, "You have judged
rightly." **44** Then turning toward the woman, he said to Simon, "Do you see this
woman? I entered your house; you gave me no water for my feet, but she has
bathed my feet with her tears and dried them with her hair. **45** You gave me no
kiss, but from the time I came in she has not stopped kissing my feet. **46** You did
not anoint my head with oil, but she has anointed my feet with ointment. **47**
Therefore, I tell you, her sins, which were many, have been forgiven; hence she
has shown great love. But the one to whom little is forgiven, loves little." **48**
Then he said to her, "Your sins are forgiven." **49** But those who were at the table
with him began to say among themselves, "Who is this who even forgives sins?"
50 And he said to the woman, "Your faith has saved you; go in peace."

Luke 7:36–50 New Revised Standard Version (NRSV)

It was December of 2014, and I had just started a new job working for the Franklin County Municipal Court in Columbus, Ohio, coordinating an innovative restorative justice program called *CATCH Court*, a specialized docket for "victims of prostitution and human trafficking."[1] In contrast to the standard (and randomized) docket of criminal and civil cases that a judge oversees, specialized dockets (also known as treatment courts) are filled with specific defendants referred to a specific judge who, along with a robust staff, can facilitate a more restorative process for specific marginalized groups instead of cycling them through the standard punitive process. The judge who founded and

DOI: 10.4324/9780429328824-3

presided over the CATCH Court program handed me a letter he had received from a woman named Heather (not her real name) in our local jail – she was on her way to prison, devastated at her sentence. I don't remember now why he showed me the letter, but I asked if I could go see her.

Local jails are not places of restoration. The deputy ushered me into a small visitation room with a steel table and an emergency button, and I waited. Heather walked in and, perhaps out of desperation, started talking. It wasn't long before she was weeping. I told her I had seen the letter and I knew she was on her way to prison. It was almost her birthday, she said. Heather had cycled through our court system with dozens of charges, including a hefty amount of prostitution-related charges. In all those times, she had never heard of CATCH Court, and now it was "too late." I remember thinking, *if justice is so restorative, why doesn't everyone get it?*

In this paper, I want to explore different models of justice while encouraging the reader to think critically about said models. Real-life stories will be shared to highlight the beauty and the limits of earthly justice. A nuanced understanding of entering the sex trade will be explored, with special attention given to the material conditions at play. I'll share some trends that I see in the field when it comes to working with "johns," or men who buy sex. Finally, I'll attempt to cast some vision for a way forward, grounded on the theological concept of *imago Dei* (the image of God) and on the hospitable way of Jesus. Mostly, I'm sharing things I've learned from sex workers along the way. I should also offer a word here about terminology: I use all the terms. What I mean is that peppered on these pages are words like *victim, survivor, prostitute, sex worker,* etc. I have my own personal preferences here, of course. And I recognize the flaws and limitations of words. If I say sex worker, you might imagine a strong and empowered individual and neglect the material conditions of their life that might make it seem *less* empowered. If I say sex trafficking victim or survivor, you might picture a person in some kind of cage needing to be rescued and released. Prostitute is an archaic slur but still used in legal documents, and by many women I know. Hooker is another slur that is also being "reclaimed" by some with lived experience. The reason I use all the terms is to represent the voices and stories and labels of the individuals that I've worked with. I invite you to notice your reactions to the various terms. And to always, always, use the preferred terms of those with the lived experience.

Justice Models

Most are familiar with the "traditional" retributive justice model, the approach focused on punishment aka "you do the crime, you pay the time." Meanwhile, *restorative justice* continues to build momentum, increasingly being applied in societal, educational, and criminal justice settings. Restorative justice:

> never diminishes the significance of a violation (crime); it summons all parties affected to collectively determine how to heal, repair, and restore

> relationships after the violation. It prioritizes disrupting cycles of harm and violence by creating pathways for healing and restoration. Restorative justice acknowledges that crime damages the perpetrator's relationship with the victim, the victim's community, the perpetrator's own community, and the perpetrator. It also acknowledges the offender's responsibility to help meet the needs of the victim(s) in restoring relationship and community.[2]

One example of this restorative justice momentum was the development of *specialized dockets*. Mental health dockets, for example, were developed for folks that had committed a crime due to an untreated and unaddressed mental health diagnosis. The same was true for folks with a substance use disorder – the evolution of the well-known drug court model. CATCH Court, a relatively new kind of specialized docket, started in 2009 for women who were picking up charges (mostly prostitution related) because, the court system assessed, they were likely victims of sex trafficking – an assessment that falls in line with the emerging movement of its time to view prostitution and sex trafficking as basically the same thing.

Do You See This Woman?

CATCH Court's founder was an evangelist for the "victim–defendant paradigm shift," or how he described the uniqueness of this population – the same women deemed "perpetrators" (defendants) were also victims of more serious crimes (namely, trafficking). In this case, restorative justice looks chiefly then like the community getting involved in *restoring* the individual to the community through all kinds of support, mentoring, various therapeutic healing modalities, and, of course, food. Women (defendants) would be able to voluntarily opt-in to CATCH Court instead of a stint in jail. They'd be placed on probation for a period of two years, and would come to court every week during that time to check-in directly with the judge. They'd meet with their probation officer and other court staff, as required. There were, of course, quite a few rules to follow. If this seems like a lot, that's for good reason. The requirements were high, but we'd argue that the benefits far outweighed the requirements. Participants would receive top-notch therapeutic services, housing, assistance with all kinds of basic needs, and a large community of other participants and champions who would "love you until you can love yourself."

The program worked (*it works if you work it*). We're not supposed to have favorites in this work, but Good Lord I couldn't help it. It was late 2015 and I kept getting calls about a woman named Brittany (not her real name). People kept talking about her like she was so *special*. She was incarcerated for a couple of felonies, or what we often called "big girl charges." She had some old prostitution-related charges on her rap sheet, but mostly she had advanced to some fancy game of stealing identities and committing fraud. Thanks to the experience I had with Heather, I had been working within the system to see felonies dropped to misdemeanors to access our program. Brittany proved to be our first "guinea pig." I met her in jail, like I did with almost every referral, and I *got it* – oh yeah, she's special, this one. We advocated for change; new processes and paperwork were created, and after a few months in jail, Brittany entered CATCH Court and went to live in a therapeutic community.

I'll never forget the day of her human trafficking assessment. She, per my request, set aside a few hours to come to my office and tell me her story – however much she felt comfortable sharing. What you might expect at this point is for me to share some gruesome details about the experience of being trafficked, but here's the part that broke our collective hearts the most: When Brittany was a teenager, she had been a good student and full-ride-scholarship-earning softball player. Yet, she longed for more attention from her neglectful father and she found it instead in an older married male neighbor – an elder at one of the local churches. Brittany, fifteen or sixteen at the time, started to spend time with him, and her longing was temporarily met. Willing to do whatever it took to maintain his attention, Brittany agreed to have sex with this man, and, she was quick to add, she mostly enjoyed it. She started calling him at home, even when his wife was there, a direct violation of his "rules." Eventually, *he filed charges* (phone harassment) against her. This, Brittany recognized, changed everything. She ended up on probation with a mound of community service hours to complete the summer before her senior year. Instead of her steady/healthy/positive group of friends, she started spending more time with the proverbial "wrong crowd." She wound up pregnant and gave up her full-ride scholarship. Crushed, she began using street drugs and the rest you can probably imagine. I share all of that to highlight this: In Brittany's story, there was a clear primary perpetrator – the older man who seduced her. But there was also a secondary perpetrator, and that was the criminal justice system. The same "system" that had brought Brittany and I together in this moment had previously *not seen* her. They saw a harassing delinquent instead of a neglected young woman. They saw a manipulative teenager instead of a violated kid. Brittany's most recent charges could have easily led to her third prison number, but the system owed it to this woman to try something else. Not making up for past wrongs by any stretch of the imagination, the system needed to look closer. What Brittany and I realized together that day was that she had been criminalized for her survival mechanisms and deepest desires since she was a kid. What she wanted when she was 16 and 44 was the same – to be fully seen and fully loved. So when Judge Paul Herbert walked over from the municipal court (misdemeanors) to the common pleas (felony) court basement to introduce himself to Brittany, who was locked up before her court date, she would later compare it to the Good Shepherd who leaves the 99 in search of the one who was lost. Seen. Known. Found. Loved. *Restored.*

In my years at CATCH, I witnessed women being reunited with their families and children. I saw women reach and surpass educational and professional goals. I've attended weddings, baby showers, and graduations for these women. I've also sat behind my computer and analyzed the data, watching the recidivism rates decrease for women who chose the path of restorative justice. I have had a front row seat to the transformation of lives. I've borne witness to the healing power of a judge who looks upon a person with kindness, curiosity, and compassion.

In addition, within a six-year period (2012–2017), only 4 percent of *prostitution-related charges* in this specific court were referred to the CATCH program. Some women, like the woman mentioned at the top of this paper, could go through the system and never hear about such a life-changing resource. Racially speaking, prostitution-related arrests matched the demographics of the larger city, but the referrals to the program didn't. CATCH Court, like most specialized dockets, is predominantly white, an inequity actively being discussed and addressed by the National Association for Drug Court Professionals, state supreme courts, and others. So where was this program (and other restorative justice programs) when the black community was being ravaged by crack cocaine in the 1980s and 1990s, and the demographic of women in prostitution in our city was primarily black? CATCH Court began as a result of a judge who noticed and was curious about bruises he saw on a (white) female defendant charged with prostitution. I guess it's true that black and blue marks are easier to see on white skin. How many black and brown women showed up to court with bruises and we never stopped to notice? Or care? Do you see *this* woman?

This program, and others like it, emerged in a time when sex trafficking became a very pervasive and sexy topic, and all sex work began to be assumed to be trafficking. As one sex worker highlights:

> Under these constructs, we have only two options: to be victims, which means we need to be rescued from our work—even if that rescue happens in handcuffs—or to be empowered sex workers, which means saying we've never experienced violence or constrained choice, that we love our jobs all day every day, and to be free we only need access to the free market.[3]

This all makes our terminology fraught with academic debate. When we ask about the difference between sex trafficking and prostitution, it actually seems to me that we're attempting to create a line of demarcation about where we should view women as victims (and therefore care about them) and criminals (and therefore care *less* about them). Federally, the accepted definition of human trafficking is a crime that involves the exploitation of a person by means of force, fraud, or coercion for labor, services, or commercial sex.[4] Instead of using the binary of "prostitute" or "trafficked victim," some have suggested thinking of it more as a continuum of trafficking to freedom.[5] I would suggest that a continuum certainly gets us closer but that perhaps the image of a braid or a spiral gets us even closer still. These things are always intermingled and complex – the thread of personal agency of someone in the sex trade, mixed with the threads of material conditions wherein she finds herself. If a woman from an impoverished urban area was bounced around from family member to family member, as a result of her parents' instability and substance use disorders, then drops out of high school after beginning to use cocaine, and ends up, by her early twenties, (choosing to) walk the streets and jump in and out of cars, would we call her a free agent? If a trans woman was kicked out of her home for being trans and can't get a job for the same reason, and ends up (choosing to) exchange sex for shelter and other basic needs, would we call her free? There is no question that there are scenarios in which young women and girls are kidnapped from the local suburban mall and groomed slowly or forced quickly into commercial sex. But the far more common scenario is that the poor, the uneducated, the gender nonconforming, or the woman of color, who has already suffered from many kinds of injustice, ends up walking "the block" in urban neighborhoods. The intermingled complexity here is that people are agents who generally make the best choices about their lives that they can, *and* that many marginalized people simply don't have as many choices as the more privileged. So much debate has existed around the role of choice in the sex trade – sex worker rights' activists wanting to emphasize agency and choice, and radical feminist communities wanting to emphasize the lack of choices and coercion into the sex trade. I'd advocate for a nuanced view that honors and respects individual choices while also working to change the material conditions that don't give people very many options. Or, as one former sex worker stated, "Fight the industry. Support the worker."[6]

The media doesn't help us here. Examples in the mainstream media, such as *Pretty Woman* or *The Girlfriend Experience,* depict prostitution as glamorous, fun, and easily escapable, which further masks the dangers of life in prostitution. Common presentations of prostitution in popular culture gloss over, or altogether erase, the frequent experiences of rapes, beatings, arrests, addiction, verbal abuse, kidnappings, and robberies that occur in prostitution.[7]

And who would choose *that*? Because there is a thread of choice (most often), it's important and helpful to understand the stages of prostitution, and to take a deeper look at what "entices" a person into prostitution.[8] This stage-based model suggests that the first stage, the enticement stage, involves any number of push factors and pull factors. Push factors/problems are anything about one's life that might "push" them into prostitution. This could be poverty, abuse and neglect, early exposure to drug use, etc. Pull factors are seemingly the "solution" that the lifestyle has to offer: Access to quick money and drugs, a sense of family and affection. And may we also remember that there are systemic factors at play in the ease of "enticement:"

> It is important to consider that while being tricked, boyfriended, abused, addicted, or forced were common mechanisms for entry into prostitution, using these factors alone to completely explain why women entered prostitution implies *individual factors* were the primary reasons for prostitution. Based on data gathered … there is significant evidence that people entered prostitution in large part because of structural oppression that devalued certain groups and societal barriers that made living-wage jobs, education, safe affordable housing, and healthcare nearly impossible for

members of these devalued groups, thus leaving prostitution as one of the only options for survival.[9]

Or, as a pair of researchers asked so eloquently: *If prostitution is a choice, why are those with the fewest options the ones in it?*[10]

I think it's crucially important to highlight this initial stage because it helps us understand the conditions of the person entering the sex trade – it helps us know what to *fight* when we "fight human trafficking" – things like poverty, childhood abuse and neglect, homelessness, etc. But it also acknowledges the very real benefits of the sex trade and contextualizes this choice in a way that frankly makes logical sense. Intermixed in the violence and horror stories of those in the sex trade are the moments of pleasure, and even joy. I remember a woman who got caught up in a police sting who was so knowledgeable about the "elements" that could get her arrested, she was able to bypass getting a ticket because she knew what *not* to do. So after the police couldn't charge her, they eventually brought her into a room where a bunch of social work types were present, which is where I met her. She talked for almost an hour about the places she'd been all over the country, and how much fun she was having. She was joking and laughing at her own jokes. She showed us pictures of her home in California. She was very proud of her dogs, and being a dog mama. She was hilarious and joyful and she broke all the molds. She wasn't shy to tell us about sex work, either. My advice when training staff and volunteers is that you don't just want to be comfortable talking about sex. You want to be comfortable talking about *fucking*.

Who and What Sort of Person This Woman Is

Most sex workers do not identify as victims or survivors of trafficking. This language can be alienating for many of the women I work with because it reduces them to damaged goods or a victim in need of our care and rescue, and they're so much more than that. Most women I've worked with blame themselves for the situations they're in, repeating a narrative that has existed since childhood. Most of you understand that perhaps the most insidious mark of child sexual abuse is the stain of shame and self-blame that it leaves on its victims.[11] It has been my experience that a high percentage of the women I've worked with still in or exiting the sex trade were also victims of child sexual abuse (CSA). I want to be clear here that CSA is not a precursor for entering the sex industry, as there are women in sex work who weren't abused as children, and many survivors of CSA who do not enter the sex trade. Because of my professional position (as a therapist, court personnel, social service provider), it is also likely that the majority of my experience is with those with higher needs and/or perhaps more experiences of trauma. Radical feminists, opposed to any form of the sex industry, claim that child sexual abuse is "bootcamp" for prostitution.[12] While that is increasingly viewed as a limited and controversial perspective, it does also highlight that for those sex workers who are also survivors of CSA, individuals may have been effectively "rehearsing" and reliving the storyline that they are bad and it's their own fault that bad things are happening.

Some of the research about women in prostitution refers to them as "the missing missing." When they go missing, no one really knows. A study of solved serial murder cases in the United States between 1970 and 2009 indicated that 32 percent of the serial murder victims were prostituted women.[13] For example, all 48 victims of the Green River Killer, Gary Leon Ridgway, were prostituted women. Ridgway explained: "I picked prostitutes as my victims because ... I knew they would not be reported missing. I picked prostitutes because I thought I could kill as many of them as I wanted without getting caught."[14] Do you see this woman?

A Whole New Monster

When we define a victim, we inevitably need a perpetrator. For decades, that has meant prosecuting (mostly black) men for the crime of human trafficking. For a long time, there was a double standard when it came to the men who purchased sex. Where do they fall in this process? Are they also victims of the traffickers? In a word: *No*. It seems to me, when it comes to men who buy sex, we've created a whole new monster. The women (typically) who sold sex used to be whores, and we've changed the narrative to make them victims (and worthy of being protected/rescued/helped). The men (typically) who buy sex used to be "boys being boys." Now we've demonized them – they're monsters worthy of ... punishment.

In a classic move of not learning from our mistakes, we've consented to a retributive model of justice for these monsters. New legislation is being introduced to increase penalties (punishment) for men who buy sex (aka "johns"). John schools (educational programs to assist men with understanding the negative impact of their purchase and, importantly, the dismissal of cases) are deemed insufficient. We should fine them. Incarcerate them. Call their wives to the scene. There's no question that this is a more equitable solution (since women who sell sex have been overincarcerated for decades), but I'm not sure this is the kind of equity we're looking for. It certainly isn't justice that restores.

As someone who has been "fighting human trafficking" for over a decade, specializing in the care of its victims, I frankly resonate with the revenge fantasies of *wanting someone to pay*. I've heard countless stories of horrific trauma. I've sought out counseling to address my own secondary trauma. Today, much of my time is spent with women still "in the life" who are on the streets and regularly present with fresh bruises and scars, reminders that violence is a predictable part of their world. Johns. Dope boys/dealers. Pimps. Traffickers. "Boyfriends." I've heard the stories. I've known rage coursing through my body and noticed my hands instinctively in fists, my jaw clenched. All that energy has to go somewhere, and *damn*, it feels satisfying to imagine some of these people (mostly men) suffering for what they've done.

A couple of things have been taking place around and in me that have shifted things for me here, and *praise God,* released some of that angry tension. Anti-trafficking activists in my local community started championing "end demand" strategies, also known as the Nordic model.

> The Nordic Model approach to prostitution (sometimes also known as the Sex Buyer Law, or the Swedish, Abolitionist, or Equality Model) decriminalises all those who are prostituted, provides support services to help them exit, and makes buying people for sex a criminal offence, in order to reduce the demand that drives sex trafficking.[15]

Locally, petitions began circulating and invitations to speak at legislative hearings showed up in my inbox. I froze. I recognized the part of me that wanted to see these men pay, but I wasn't sure I wanted to advocate for legislation just because I have strong feelings.

The other reality that emerged, of course, was the COVID-19 global pandemic. During this time, our drop-in center that served the women on the street had to close its doors to folks wanting to come inside. However, we were determined to be consistent and provide the resources we could. Our operation shifted to primarily outdoor work. Our volunteers started standing at the corner, passing out food and handwarmers, and still providing transportation when a woman said she was ready for treatment. Previous to this, we made it clear that our doors were open to *women.* But you can't keep people from hanging around a street corner. So we started interacting more and more with the men who hung around the women we knew and loved. In more than a few cases, we knew we were interacting with men who had abused and exploited the women that we served. But instead of sequestering them away from care, we got proximate. We looked them in the eye and started hearing about their realities. I don't and would never excuse abusive or exploitative behavior. But what I've also relearned (again and again) is that "othering" anyone does significant damage *to me.* Dehumanization is the first step to violence, and I don't want to become that which I hate. So I've been reminded of the utter humanity of these men. Maybe they're not monsters. As Brene Brown says, "People are hard to hate close up. Move in. Speak truth to bullshit. Be civil ..."[16] What might these men reveal to me about the image of God?

I had a client recently – a woman formerly in the sex trade. With several years out of "the life," she was invited to participate in a "john sting." This meant that she would sit with law enforcement officers and social workers who would survey individual men who were caught trying to purchase sex. She came to me with this opportunity, and like a good therapist, I encouraged her to think about possible triggers. I asked her about negative experiences with johns from her own life, and she had them. What if one of *them* was caught in this sting? What if she found herself sitting right across from him? What if she had flashbacks to that kind of evil? What if she got angry?

Well, she did get angry. But not at any of the dozens of johns arrested that day. And not even at law enforcement. She got angry at the social workers who, in her opinion, were not treating these men as well as they deserved. She described quite the opposite of what I expected to hear. On some level, I expected to hear about the anger she felt toward these men, but she was filled with compassion. She said that as they spoke of their lives and troubles, she got it. She would look at them and effectively say, "me too." She saw herself in them. She saw their humanity: the longing for connection and for things to be better. The longing to *be* better.

I recall another night when I was standing on the street corner with a survivor of the sex trade – a woman who had been standing on this very street corner for different reasons just a year prior. A man walked by, an old date. Instead of ignoring him or scoffing at him, she said hello, and began asking him questions. He was struggling, he said. He had relapsed and was thinking (he said) about getting into treatment. She offered to help him on the spot, calling a contact to see if there was a detox bed available that night. She offered to drive him, but he decided he wasn't ready. He carried two grocery bags of food, possibly heavier than his waif-like body. Running into this woman in recovery seemed to spark something in him – some reminder of who he was before addiction. He got out a phone to show us pictures of what he used to look like – more like a bodybuilder than this skinny man in front of me. I promise you I never would have talked to this man who walked by us. It was a survivor of over 20 years on these streets that showed me his humanity. She didn't see a monster. She saw something else – something human and maybe even something divine.

I don't know that this would be the terminology of my sex worker friends, but it would seem to me that they were able to see something of *the image of God* in these men. When it comes to the discourse around prostitution narratives, Christians have a substantive consideration to bring to the debate: The ways in which all people are like God, the *imago Dei* (Latin).[17] The biblical concept of the image of God in all humanity means that every person is uniquely imprinted by God, an extraordinary creation with fundamental value created with love by God's design. This might be the greatest theological foundation for resistance to the sex trade. But just as it is the foundation to remind us people are not to be commodified and consumed, it is also the foundation for how to view those who do the commodifying and the consuming.

Getting Biblical

I want to turn to a favorite passage from Luke. You might not agree with the interpretation that the woman who wept at the feet of Jesus was a prostitute. That's fine. Scholars have debated it; most seem to suggest that she was involved in some kind of sex work, but some just conclude that it doesn't matter – what matters is that we acknowledge her as a sinner. Interestingly, among those who name her as a prostitute debate whether she was the more common type of prostitute who would have been miserable, exploited, and enslaved ... or if she would have been a free courtesan or "companion" with a certain kind of status, which may have "mitigated the shamelessness attributed to her because of her occupation."[18] It seems the question of whether or not the woman in sex work is free and empowered, a hotly debated matter today, was relevant in the Hellenistic period (and every period before and after). It seems to me that irregardless of the precise mix of choice and oppression, the relative amount of trauma, or whether her clientele was wealthy or not, this is a woman who knew her need for liberation.

Which leads to a second debate around this passage: Is this a woman who is responding to the reality that she was forgiven and set free, or was this woman attempting to earn the Lord's grace? Is she a sinful woman or a forgiven woman? Spoiler alert: She's forgiven.[19] I'll admit here that reading commentaries (mostly written by men) on this passage can feel akin to listening to modern debates about what a girl was wearing at the time she was raped. How are we to interpret a woman with a short skirt? Or in this context, how do we interpret a woman who lets down her hair?[20] In short, we can either view this move as erotic or as humble reverence. What it can't be seen as (upon first glance) is *hospitable*. There's really no debate that this is a story about hospitality, and that this woman has proven to be more hospitable to Jesus than the intended host (Simon), but, importantly, we can't get there without Jesus' interpretation. The repeated kisses alone and the lengthy anointing make this an awkward hospitality scene, to say the least.[21] Bertschmann sums it up this way:

> Jesus thus imaginatively reframes the scene by interpreting the woman's ambiguous gestures as the deeds of a generous host. It is only in retrospect that we can see these actions as gestures of lavish hospitality ... In Luke, the woman's gestures might be a seriously embarrassing fondling of Jesus' feet with strong erotic overtones or an activity of deep, loving reverence and surrender. In either case, Jesus affirms her activities as both loving and appropriate – as appropriate in fact as the efforts made by a good host to honour his guest.[22]

Now to the question Jesus asks and which has been repeated a few times in this paper: *Do you see this woman?* As with many of Jesus' questions (e.g. "do you want to be made well?"), this has always sat with me as a ridiculous one. Her very presence and scandalous behavior makes her impossible not to see, not to mention hear (crying), and smell (perfume). Not only does Simon see her, but he is likely having a full body experience of her presence in the room. He sees her solely as a sinner, and one who should not be touching Jesus the way she is. Her actions, not turned away by Jesus, cause Simon to doubt that Jesus is indeed a prophet. Because he cannot *see* her (that she is beloved, humble, grateful, forgiven), he cannot see Jesus accurately either. He completely misjudges them both. Simon has failed in this story to understand the significance of his own cancelled debt.[23] Crabbe states,

> If there is a consistent difference in Luke between "sinners" and "Pharisees" (or "outsiders" and "insiders") in this respect, it is not that insiders are any

> less dependent upon the gracious forgiveness of a significant "debt." Rather, Luke's text suggests that by making judgements about others, insiders have insulated themselves against the significance of their own cancelled debt, creating a barrier from others, and thus making participation in the *koinonia* of such kingdom-experiences seem too costly. Here lies their tragedy.[24]

It feels important to remind myself and you that the woman in this passage never speaks. She never makes a verbal admission of guilt that we know of, nor does she declare her intention to change her life. This fact though resonates with my experience coming alongside sex workers. They are frequently the topic of our debates, but rarely the voice of it. And after trying to escape sex work handfuls of times already, one grows weary of expressing this kind of intention. I wonder if it was this understanding that led Jesus to say, "go in peace," and not "go and sin no more." Maybe the struggle wasn't over. Maybe He didn't eat with prostitutes so they'd change their behavior, but maybe so they'd know they don't have to be alone.

Simon, I Have Something to Say to You

I've loved and clung to this passage for years. Jesus' question for Simon, as His loving gaze remains on *this woman*, has been cause for internal cartwheels for a long time. I've preached it, meditated on it, and tattooed it. When Jesus asks His question, I'm compelled to worship Him. When He accepts her, I know my own acceptance and I *love much*. But in recent days, this passage has beckoned me once again. It summons me to greater complexity. I recognize that part of what I have always brought to this passage is that when Jesus asks His question *Do you see this woman?*, there is part of me that folds my arms across my chest and shouts, "Yeah, Simon?! Do you see her, you piece of shit?" I want Simon to see how wrong he is, and I even want him to pay. But what if what Jesus was doing was also with the heart to restore Simon? Perhaps Jesus was inviting us to consider a transformative justice that restores us, the lot of us. Because for justice to truly be restorative, it must be for everyone.

If I judge Simon harshly here or shame him for his failure, I have also become him. It's easy for me to see myself in the woman who is a known sinner. She points me to and helps me see Jesus. But I must also see myself in Simon, recognizing that I, too, get it wrong sometimes. When I see the woman through the gaze of Jesus, I see forgiveness. When I see Simon through the gaze of Jesus, I see the same.

Moving On

I ended up leaving my job at the court, but not before I had the remarkable experience of sitting in a courtroom as Heather (from above), five years sober, independent, employed, and thriving showed up for her expungement hearing. She sat with the same judge she had written to years prior. She shared her story, and the judge expunged her entire record. I no longer know if a courtroom gives us the best picture of what God is like, but I'm also aware of lots of Scripture passages that read like a courtroom scene (e.g. Micah 6, Isaiah 3, John 5) and I can tell you that watching a person have their entire record *expunged* is one of the most life-affirming, kingdom-bringing, shalom-looking things I have ever witnessed.

While I left the court, I surely did not leave the sex workers/sex trafficking victims/prostitutes/hookers. I helped launch a drop-in center for women still caught in "the life." There are many, many stories I could tell about this work that we have continued, but one sticks out because of how much it has impacted me personally. Years ago, a woman named Liz (not her real name) came into our drop in center after a recent release from jail. She had been incarcerated for several months, so I had not seen her, and frankly, barely recognized her. She sat down to eat and said a prayer over her food. So I asked her about her prayers. She prayed out loud that the women on the streets would feel "hugs and kisses" from God because of how loved they are. I asked her about that later, and she said that sometimes the wind felt like a hug from God, and a shooting star a kiss. She also prayed – as weary as her own can be – that God's feet would go beneath her feet as she walked. Is she asking God to enable her to walk the block somehow, like some kind of divine co-dependent? Or is she just saying: *Even here, even as I walk, I need Your presence.* She was contrite in her confession of sin as she prayed, and I was reminded again that the tangle she's in is much more disease and systemic oppression than choice.

Your feet beneath my feet. This has become a new centering prayer in my life with God. May we know a God that walks *with* us when we're not getting it right. May we learn to be like feet beneath weary feet. May we "eat at all the tables, because Jesus eats with everyone."[25]

The primary focus of my work remains with the beautiful and complicated women that are involved in the sex trade. For years, I thought this work gave me permission to *other* the men who paid for sex, and even to hate them. I still feel compelled by the Jesus who keeps his gaze upon the woman and asks the question *Do you see this woman?* But as I've had my gaze on *this woman* for a decade now, what I also see is that her gaze on the man towering over her is kinder than my gaze. And I can almost hear the question in her head: *Do you see this man? Do you* really *see him?* And because she asks this question, I know I'm beginning to see myself – and Jesus – more accurately too. I'm not ready to provide services to men who buy sex, but I have more imagination for it now. Together, may we imagine a world where sellers *and* buyers of sex find the restoration they deserve. Because we are all God's children.

Notes

1 "CATCH Court: Changing Actions to Change Habits." Franklin County Municipal Court. Accessed November 13, 2021. https://municipalcourt.franklincountyohio.gov/Departments-Services/Specialized-Dockets/CATCH-Court

2 Dominique DuBois Gilliard, *Rethinking Incarceration* (Downers Grove, IL: InterVarsity Press, 2018), 175.

3 Lorelei Lee, "Cash/Consent: The War on Sex Work," *n+1 Magazine,* Fall 2019, Issue 35. https://www.nplusonemag.com/issue-35/essays/cashconsent/?utm_source=digg

4 "Human Trafficking." The United States Department of Justice, last modified November 12, 2021. https://www.justice.gov/humantrafficking

5 Ronald Weitzer. "Sociology of sex work," *Annual Review of Sociology,* 35 (2009): 213–234. doi.org/10.1146/annurev-soc-070308–120025

6 Esperanza Fonseca, "The problem with the phrase 'sex work is work'," *Proletarian Feminist,* September 8, 2020. https://proletarianfeminist.medium.com/?p=bdac613eb2f0

7 Katherine A. Cascio, "Leaving 'The Life:' Exploring Services for Women Exiting Prostitution" (PhD dissertation, University of Kentucky, 2017), 58.

8 Gail Folaron and Celia Williamson. "Understanding the Experiences of Street Level Prostitutes," *Qualitative Social Work,* 2(3), (2003): 271–287.

9 Cascio, "Leaving the Life," 124.

10 Melissa Farley and Vanessa Kelly, "Prostitution: A critical review of the medical and social services literature," *Women & Criminal Justice,* 11(4), (2000): 29–64.

11 Judith Lewis Herman, "Posttraumatic Stress Disorder as a Shame Disorder," in *Shame in the Therapy Hour,* ed. Ronda Dearing and June Price Tangney (Washington, DC: American Psychological Association, 2011), 261–275.

12 Andrea Dworkin, "Pornography, prostitution, and a beautiful and tragic recent history." In *Not for Sale: Feminists resisting prostitution and pornography*, ed. Rebecca Whisnant and Christine Stark (North Melbourne, VIC, AU: Spinifex Press Pty Ltd., 2004), 137–148.

13 Kenna Quinet, "Prostitutes as victims of serial homicide: Trends and case characteristics, 1970–2009," *Homicide Studies*, 15, (2011): 74–100. doi.org/10.1177/1088767910397276

14 State of Washington v. Gary Leon Ridgway, No. 01-1-10270-9 SEA (Superior Court of King County 2003).

15 "What is the Nordic Model?," Nordic Model Now!. Accessed December 11, 2021. https://nordicmodelnow.org/what-is-the-nordic-model/

16 Brene Brown, *Braving the Wilderness* (London: Vermilion, 2017).

17 Tammy Schultz, "Prostitution Discourse: The Sexuality as a Commodity Debate and a Christian Response," *Journal of Psychology and Christianity*, 37(3) (2018): 256–268.

18 Evelyn R. Thibeaux, "'Known to be a Sinner:' The Narrative Rhetoric of Luke 7:36–50," *Biblical Theology Bulletin,* 23, (1993): 151–160.

19 Yuri Phanom, "Is She a Sinful Woman or a Forgiven Woman? An Exegesis of Luke 7:36–50," *Asian Journal of Pentecostal Studies*, 19(1), (2016): 59–71.

20 Charles Cosgrove, "A Woman's Unbound Hair in the Greco-Roman World, with Special Reference to the Story of the Sinful Woman in Luke 7:36–50," *Journal of Biblical Literature*, 124(4), (2005): 675–692.

21 Dorothea Bertschmann, "Hosting Jesus: Revisiting Luke's 'Sinful Woman' (Luke 7:36–50) as a Tale of Two Hosts," *Journal for the Study of the New Testament,* 40 (1), (2017): 30–50.

22 Bertschmann, "Hosting Jesus," 43–44.

23 Kylie Crabbe, "A Sinner and a Pharisee: Challenge at Simon's Table in Luke 7:36–50," *Pacifica,* 24, (2011): 247–266.

24 Crabbe, "A Sinner and a Pharisee," 263–264.

25 Nichole Nordeman, *Dear Me* (Brentwood: Sparrow Records, 2017).

Bibliography

Bertschmann, Dorothea H. "Hosting Jesus: Revisiting Luke's 'Sinful Woman' (Luke 7.36–50) as a Tale of Two Hosts." *Journal for the Study of the New Testament* 40(1) (September 2017): 30–50. https://doi.org/10.1177/0142064X17723476.

Brown, Brene. *Braving the Wilderness*. London: Vermilion, 2017.

Cascio, Katherine A., "Leaving 'The Life:' Exploring Services for Women Exiting Prostitution." *Theses and Dissertations–Educational, School, and Counseling Psychology*. 58 (2017). https://uknowledge.uky.edu/edp_etds/58.

Cosgrove, Charles H. "A Woman's Unbound Hair in the Greco-Roman World, with Special Reference to the Story of the 'Sinful Woman' in Luke 7:36–50." *Journal of Biblical Literature* 124 (2005): 675.

Crabbe, Kylie. "A Sinner and a Pharisee: Challenge at Simon's Table in Luke 7:36–50." *Pacifica* 24 (3) (2011): 247–266.

Dworkin, Andrea. "Pornography, prostitution, and a beautiful and tragic recent history." In *Not for Sale: Feminists resisting prostitution and pornography*, edited by Rebecca Whisnant and Christine Stark, 137–148. North Melbourne, VIC: Spinifex Press Pty Ltd., 2004.

Esperanza, Fonseca, "The problem with the phrase 'sex work is work'," *Proletarian Feminist*, September 8, 2020. https://proletarianfeminist.medium.com/?p=bdac613eb2f0.

Farley, Melissa and Vanessa Kelly. "Prostitution: A Critical Review of the Medical and Social Sciences Literature." *Women & Criminal Justice* 11 (4) (2000): 29–64. https://doi.org/10.1300/J012v11n04_04.

Franklin County Municipal Court. "CATCH Court: Changing Actions to Change Habits." AccessedNovember 13, 2021. https://municipalcourt.franklincountyohio.gov/Departments-Services/Specialized-Dockets/CATCH-Court.

Gilliard, Dominique Dubois. *Rethinking Incarceration*. Downers Grove: InterVarsity Press, 2018.

Herman, Judith Lewis. "Posttraumatic Stress Disorder as a Shame Disorder." In *Shame in the therapy hour*, edited by Ronda Dearing and June Price Tangney, 261–275. Washington, DC: American Psychological Association, 2011.

Lee, Lorelei. "Cash/Consent: The War on Sex Work," *n+1 Magazine*, Fall 2019, Issue 35. https://www.nplusonemag.com/issue-35/essays/cashconsent/?utm_source=digg.

Nordeman, Nichole. *Dear Me*. Brentwood: Sparrow Records, 2017. https://genius.com/Nichole-nordeman-dear-me-lyrics.

Nordic Model Now. "What is the Nordic Model?" Accessed December 11, 2021. https://nordicmodelnow.org/what-is-the-nordic-model/.

Phanom, Yuri. "Is She a Sinful Woman or a Forgiven Woman? An Exegesis of Luke 7:36–50," *Asian Journal of Pentecostal Studies* 19(1), (2016): 59–71.

Quinet, Kenna. "Prostitutes as Victims of Serial Homicide: Trends and Case Characteristics, 1970–2009." *Homicide Studies* 15(1) (2011): 74–100. doi.org/10.1177/1088767910397276

Schultz, Tammy. "Prostitution Discourse: The Sexuality as a Commodity Debate and a Christian Response." *Journal of Psychology and Christianity* 37(3). (2018): 256–268.

Thibeaux, Evelyn R. "'Known to Be a Sinner': The Narrative Rhetoric of Luke 7:36–50." *Biblical Theology Bulletin* 23(4) (November 1993): 151–160. https://doi.org/10.1177/014610799302300403.

U.S. Department of Justice. "Human Trafficking." Last modified November 12, 2021. https://www.justice.gov/humantrafficking.

Weitzer, Ronald. "Sociology of Sex Work." *Annual Review of Sociology* 35 (2009): 213http://www.jstor.org/stable/27800076.

Williamson, Celia, and Gail Folaron. "Understanding the Experiences of Street Level Prostitutes." *Qualitative Social Work* 2(3) (September 2003): 271–287. https://doi.org/10.1177/14733250030023004.

3 Walking with Women in Sex Work

An Appraisal of the Role of the Nigerian Conference of Women Religious

Nkiruka Okafor and Lauren McGrow

Introduction

Women Religious (Catholic Women in Vowed Life otherwise called nuns) in Nigeria have played critical roles in the rehabilitation of women in sex work both domestically and internationally. Women from Nigeria have travelled mostly to Italy and other European countries for sex roles. The accepted narrative is that these women are trafficked meaning they are taken against their will for sex work. The "trafficked model" serves as a model of relationship between pastoral care workers and women in sex work, as this preferred model elevates the pastoral agent as the one with moral authority that is "helping" the sex worker. Women sex workers can be objectified as the ones needing to have their problems solved using this model. Sex workers can feel judged by this model that pictures them as powerless and in desperate need of help. This chapter notes that pastoral care workers could listen more deeply to other narratives from sex workers, including that there are women who affirm that being in sex work is an expression of their autonomy and individual bodily choice. By listening to women's narratives and finding points of identification and mutual connection, Women Religious may be able to build solidarity networks between Nigerian pastoral care workers and Nigerian sex workers to expand the rights of women.

The Nigerian Conference of Women Religious (NCWR), which is the umbrella body of Major Superiors of Women Religious Institutes/Orders in Nigeria, has been at the forefront of working with trafficked women through its project the Committee for the Support of the Dignity of Woman (COSUDOW). Care for the women has been undertaken by the nuns at different levels, including at a national level and in collaboration with bodies, such as the Catholic Church, in Europe. At various institutes in Nigeria, Women Religious orders have engaged in the mission of creating awareness through education on the reality and circumstances of women trafficked for sex slavery, as well as assisting some women in sex work to chart a new course in life. Individual nuns have also taken up some projects to support women and developed trusting relationships with women in sex work. They support and work with women through education, rehabilitation, advocacy, and empowerment at their center

DOI: 10.4324/9780429328824-4

located in Benin in Nigeria. The work that Women Religious do with women in sex work goes unnoticed by the broader church, corporate bodies, and the public.

This chapter appraises the NCWR project COSUDOW for women in sex work, offering a description, theological framework, and a strategy for enhancing future work towards solidarity. As a nun of the Religious Institute of Sisters of the Immaculate Heart of Mary, Mother of Christ, Nigeria, I am an insider to orders of religious women. This order is the first Igbo indigenous Women Religious order founded in Nigeria in 1937. I have studied this NCWR project for women in sex work for my doctoral thesis, which led me to interview a small number of sex workers in Nigeria. The study inspired a personal transformation that I have written and published as an essay elsewhere.[1]

When I started this research, I was relating to the women from a distinct vantage point. I carried my privileges around since I was accustomed to the notion that women who choose vowed life are at the opposite pole with women who choose to use their bodies to make money through sexual acts. My conversion and transformation came from the breaking down of these prejudices. Through a painful journey of self-acceptance, I had to break down the gap between me and the women. My transformation is realizing that I am no different from the Other. Every categorization of women as saints or sinners, based on the use of their bodies, is violence to every woman. I interacted with ordinary women from all spheres of life where I was expecting to see victims. I was surprised to learn that not all women in sex work are there because of economic reasons but because of a multitude of circumstances. The work that nuns in Nigeria do with women in the sex industry, or trafficked women, is mostly seen from the view of the "higher women" helping the "lower women." This essay, and my research more broadly, seeks to break down such perspectives.

This will be done in six sections. Section one is the introduction. The second section presents the framework of the study by reviewing the paradoxical play around the female body in the church. This leads to the Madonna–Whore Dichotomy as articulated by Shannon Bell,[2] Gail Phetersen,[3] Carisa Showden[4] and many others. This section reviews some pastoral responses to sex work in the church in Nigeria. Section three situates and locates the reality of sex work in Nigeria. Data from my interviews demonstrates that representing women as being on two opposite poles on issues of sexuality does not consider the self-understanding of women nor does it consider the embodied oppression that Women Religious may face inside the church. The fourth section appraises the role of NCWR in combating the trafficking of women for sex work overseas. The final section is a summative constructive proposal linking *imago Dei* and the LIVE (Listening, Introspection, Validation and Emancipation/Empowerment) pastoral model of care for women involved in sex work, whether they are trafficked or there by choice. Doing this may help Women Religious to expand their understanding of women in sex work and provide an impetus for affirmation, connection, and, in a word, solidarity among equals rather than top-down rescue models.

The Female Body in the Church

Organized religion has an ingrained obsession with the female body setting the stage for the Madonna/Whore model of classifying women into good and bad roles.[5] Female bodies and sexuality have played significant roles in all religious settings and throughout recorded history.[6] This work is from a Christian perspective. Christianity, from inception, has shown its own variations of obsession with the female body. The birth of Christ from a virgin, whereby the virginity of Mary is more celebrated than her womanhood, is but one example of this relentless focus on female sexuality. Any sexual relationship pertaining to Mary, the mother of Jesus, must be excised (especially in the Catholic Church) to make her a symbol of purity whereby conjugal love is equally deemed an unholy aspect of her humanity. She is the epitome and model Madonna for others to follow. In such models, women are classified as belonging to the higher pedestal of virginity – the Madonna – or if they cannot meet this expectation, women are quickly relegated to the lowest pedestal of prostitution – the Whore. The Madonna/Whore model of categorizing women is fatally flawed because it does not allow for ethical complexity in women's lives, healthy self and sexual development or diverse sexual experiences. It also limits women's community, setting up these roles in opposition to each other rather than helping women build connections through mutual understanding and support. Church fathers and early theologians competed on who would denigrate the female body most to show that virginity transcends the curse of the female body.

Historically, theologians and pastors have read the Bible through the lens of patriarchy, which is rife in the church. Ruth Perry notes that such readings "devalues the *imago Dei* (image of God) in women – who were created to share dominion with men (Gen. 1:28) and are gifted by the Holy Spirit to build the Kingdom alongside their brothers (Gal. 3:28)."[7] St. Augustine of Hippo goes further to completely deny the image of God in a woman. He writes: "Woman was merely man's helpmate, a function which pertains to her alone. She is not the image of God but as far as man is concerned, he is by himself the image of God."[8] Augustine is the father and founder of the doctrine of original sin that shaped Christianity. Some of the writings of these church fathers are still held as doctrines by the church today, with accompanying denigration of the female body, for instance through non-ordination of women to the priesthood. Thomas Aquinas whose *Summa Teologiae* is the blueprint for formation of Catholic seminarians is (in)famous for his belief that a woman is a misbegotten male. He writes: "As regards the individual nature, woman is defective and misbegotten, for the active force in the male seed tends to the production of a perfect likeness in the masculine sex; while the production of woman comes from a defect in the active force or from some material indisposition, or even from some external influence."[9] Writings such as these can be confusing and contradictory to Women Religious who read the scriptures and see that "male and female God made them in his image and likeness."[10]

During the Reformation, Martin Luther took the words of Augustine and Aquinas to another level by speaking for God and to women, enclosing their humanity through binary roles. He states that "the word and works of God is clear, that women were made either to be wives or prostitutes."[11] Luther writes this piece to justify his raids of female monasteries, carrying away the nuns to be married forcefully like Katherine Ann Van Bora.[12] While some women were struggling to find ways towards spiritual and physical freedom from being defined in terms of their bodies and seeking solace in monasteries, male religious leaders were convinced of their prerogative to tell women how to live their sexuality before God.

The importance of women and the evaluation of their worth, in and out of the church, has relied on what they do with their own bodies. The writings quoted above, and subsequent theological beliefs, are still used to push every violence against the female body in church and society.[13] This type of theology complicates the way that religious women view their bodies. A woman is told that she is not good and equally hears that her body is good for the service of others excepting her sexuality. The church reinforces the model of Madonna/Whore covertly and overtly. The list is endless: downplaying Mary Magdalene as an apostle; downgrading her celebration in the Roman calendar to a memorial until very recently; tagging every female saint as a "virgin"; as well as the fact that there are only four doctors of the church in church history: making St. Jovita a male to hide that she was a deacon(ness); downplaying the role of women as theologians; promoting Mary as predominately a virgin, neglecting that she is a wife; and the refusal to give women significant and powerful roles in the church. This plays out as oppression in the lives of Women Religious who struggle to gain power that is not reliant on the debasement of their own bodies and sexuality in the church. Potentially, this is a point of connection between nuns and sex workers who also are judged badly in society because of how they use their bodies. This connection develops understanding and mutual empathy and may help to build a genuine community of support that centers women's agency in diverse places and circumstances.

Autonomy and Choice

Feminist theorists are helping to reshape conversations about gender and the female body and understanding of the place and role of women in the world and the church. Carisa R. Showden, a feminist political theorist, in her work *Choices Women Make: Agency in Domestic Violence, Assisted Reproduction, and Sex Work*, presents an understanding of agency in the lives of women that challenges the notion that women who engage in sex work have no choices in that way of life. Regarding agency as a product of autonomy and freedom, she posits that there must be deliberation on choices and having choices to deliberate on.[14] This is complex for women faced with difficult and, sometimes, impractical scenarios of poverty, family pressure and disability, for instance, especially with regards to choices around their bodies. For example, one of the women interviewed in my study recalled how she entered the sex industry:

> "I am a Ghetto girl, born in ghetto at Enugu. My mama is into runs [selling sex]. I do not know what a father is because my mama does not know how she even became pregnant or by who. Me, I started runs at 12. This is the only world I know. What else am I expected to do? I simply taking my own customers and left my mama's area and came to Awka ghetto."[15]

Women are easily categorized between two impossible extremes: either they are heroes with self-determining autonomy or are victims at the mercy of structural determinism. Showden argues that for women those two extremes do not fully represent how women make choices.[16] Women make choices in the continuum in between these poles. No single narrative captures women's experiences and the choices they make in their bodies, but it does depend on circumstances.

Drawing from feminist political and legal theory, as well as phenomenological and poststructuralist theory, she argues that the responses that women make are shaped by norms, values, needs of others, and forms of power that influence women's self-understanding.[17] The implication is that there should be respect for the choices a woman can make, even choices of subordination as we work together to expand choices for a more open life.[18] Women Religious, who are engaged in activism towards ordination and increased status within the church, know this only too well. Arguing that agency is both socially determined and socially enacted, sex workers are acting on the choices presented to them in the society, and, yet claim a form of agency in their choice. The task is discovering how each woman understands her own role in the use of her body and working to expand her rights for increasing agency.[19] Nuns have shared a similar journey in terms of asserting their own agency and self-determination while experiencing a perceived lack of choice, through the oppression of the patriarchal institution to which they have committed themselves.

Interviews with sex workers in India revealed that the top reasons women engage in sex work are "poverty, marital abuse, sexual abuse and the death of a parent or husband."[20] Yet, deciding to engage in sex work is itself a choice. Some women are forced into sex slavery through trafficking and their choices in these circumstances are unclear. This is the narrative that most pastoral workers prefer, yet it does not tell the entire story. For example, in a qualitative study of female commercial sex work in Tijuana, Mexico, financial need is the major factor driving women to trade sex at every age.[21] Many young women in sex work are single mothers who are supporting their children. There are identifiable positive aspects of the job, which includes flexibility in work shifts, and a good income. This case is true for women in sex work in Nigeria also, according to my own research.[22]

In regions of economic desperation, male family members and acquaintances at times sell women and girls into prostitution.[23] These are real victims of sex work who have very restricted agency and could be classified as subjected to human trafficking. Women trafficked as sex workers can suffer untold human degradation and find it difficult to reintegrate into society because of the stigma of being labeled a prostitute.[24] Violation of autonomy and agency can make it difficult to establish a trusted self in a new environment. In their study of Moldovan women returning after sex trafficking experiences, Brunovskis and Surtees note the complexity in reuniting women with spouses and children, especially around stigma and financial troubles.[25] Some of the women experience great shame and do not disclose they have been trafficked to families for fear of victimization, lack of understanding and being associated with prostitution. Some of their fears include unrealized migration expectations, and stressed behaviors upon return.[26] Unrealized migration expectation is the inability of the person who migrated to another country or city to achieve substantial material gain. Returning to their place of origin in a poorer condition means that migration has failed to give them the desired societal upward mobility. Stressed behaviors arise from shame associated with failure to achieve economic gains. Fear, distress, continued financial pressure and stigma can prevent women from reintegrating back into the community they left to seek a better life through sex work, as demonstrated in the Moldova study.[27]

In contrast to these trafficking narratives, Oso Casas finds that many Latin American women who do sex work in Spain are not trafficked or forced.[28] They make the choice because of the love they have for their family and wanting to support them, or to keep them socially mobile in society, or because of breakdowns in relationship.[29] Some get out of the industry on their own if they make enough money and are transient in the life. This orientation shifts the focus to the diverse experiences of women in different parts of the world and how they have different motivations and can function and even thrive in sex work.

Baumeister and Vohs studied sex work as a female resource in heterosexual interactions and found that the sexual economy could be analyzed using social exchange theory, which is summarized as the examination of individual and market factors that contribute to supply and demand factors around sex.[30] Generally, people refuse to openly acknowledge the exchange process in negotiating sexual activities outside of the sex industry.[31] This gives women leverage to use sex as an exchange for other values, such as long-term commitment and respect and includes economic gains. Their study concludes that women have some agency in choosing sex work because female sexuality is more valuable than men's sexuality and therefore women are in a better position to negotiate their material needs.[32]

Claiming a form of agency in sex work enables women to weigh up their circumstance and face the risks involved, particularly in a criminalized environment. Women in sex work are exposed to many risks, including STDs like HIV, harassment by law enforcement agents, rape, and in some, extreme cases, brutal death. Some women must abandon known territories for unknown ones to carry out their trade. Being involved in what is viewed as stigmatized work, they risk being exposed. Sex work can involve shame and guilt that can be internalized. In most societies, including ones where sex work is legal, sex workers are viewed with skepticism, disdain, or outright contempt. The sense of doing something that is not acceptable can be a heavy burden for women to carry. Paying attention to how sex workers place the material gains side by side with the cost helps to identify if it is worth all the risk. For a woman to remain in sex work by choice, she must have calculated the benefits and rewards against the cost and found the gains to outweigh cost.

Many sex workers in the interviews I conducted affirmed that the material gain outweighed the risks but also left women with a certain fatigue or weariness. Fatigue among the participants can be expressed as a desire to get married. Marriage is regarded as a means of social mobility and a sign of settling down as an adult. One woman narrates:

> "I am 36. Marriage is what I am begging God seriously to do for me, to be honest, this work is not a good work because God made night for us to sleep and have rest, is just that if you don't go out for search of money, you will not survive."[33]

Pastoral Model of Care for Sex Workers

Theologians and pastoral care workers mostly hold one model of the true experience of sex work when they make proposals about the pastoral care of women in prostitution. The often-held position stems from the feminist abolitionists' view that sex work is violence against women. There is no recognition of agency for women in sex work. The women are victims, whether they recognize it or not.[34] More recently, voices that call for solidarity with sex workers are growing in pastoral care and theology, including in this volume.[35] Two influential pastoral perspectives are reviewed from a Christian perspective. They include the liberation perspective by Margaret E. Guider and a loving response by Lia Claire Scholl.[36,37]

Prostitution and Liberation Theology

Margaret Guider, in her work *Daughters of Rahab: Prostitution and the Church of Liberation in Brazil* presents an example of what contextual liberation might look like for women in the sex industry. Her work is situated in Brazil. She writes from her experience as a missionary there. Guider claims that women in prostitution have some agency and that this confounds church and society.[38] The persistence of prostitution is a problem both for pastoral theology and in broader social structures. Persons who sell sex are rarely understood on their own terms. However, she notes that "despite the scrutiny and condemnation of church authorities, the religious imagination of prostitutes, as with other women, is beyond the control of any institution."[39] There exists ambivalence between beliefs and behaviors around women and prostitution in the history of Christianity, just as there has been ambivalence towards Women Religious, as noted earlier. As Guider so eloquently states, "Christianity prescribes chastity, obedience, and often times poverty as hallmarks of female virtue to be preserved and preferred even when a woman is threatened with the diminishment or loss of her life."[40] This is non-negotiable for the church. The ambivalence is that women who sell sex are marginalized yet praiseworthy, liminal yet independent, condemned yet desired and tolerated. Church fathers and theologians like Augustine and Thomas Aquinas called prostitution "a necessary evil."[41]

In what corresponds with Showden's political model for viewing women in the sex industry, Guider offers three patterns of interaction between the church and the phenomenon of prostitution in history: toleration, prohibition, and abolition. Toleration is marked by a sense of accommodation of a phenomenon judged to be a human situation; prohibition is marked by efforts to repress the phenomenon which normally yields no fruit; abolition is marked by moves by both ecclesial and civil authorities to liberate female sex workers from conditions of poverty, as poverty is easily explicated as the major factor that leads to prostitution. Sometimes, these patterns exist side by side while a particular pattern may dominate at a given time. None of the patterns favored by the church takes the agency of the women seriously. Guider shows that the church attempted to solve the problem of prostitution without involving the women in sex work in Brazil, instead focusing on job training and other ways of urging women to leave the industry.[42]

Critically reading the role of Rahab the harlot as documented in the Hebrew bible book of Joshua, Guider sees in the story a starting point for theological reflection on the church of liberation and the problem of prostitution. She suggests that Rahab should be incorporated into the Christian tradition as an exemplar of faith and justice. Rahab's neglect as an icon of faith and justice might relate to her profession as a harlot. Yet, her prostitute identity does not seem to be an issue before God who includes her as she is.[43] In her evaluation of women in sex work in Brazil, innumerable daughters of Rahab are involved in issues of faith and justice but are neglected and their stories not told because of their connection with the stigma of the sex industry and the church's reluctance to accept them on their own terms.[44]

The history of sex commerce in Brazil, like every other history, defies summation. An historical response in Brazil was the development of a specialized ministry to women who are marginalized, known as *Pastoral da Mulher Marginalizada* (P.M.M.) which was operational from approximately 1965 to 1990.[45] The process of establishing the ministry was interactive, focused on critical examination of the social ills of Brazil (including culture, gender, sexism and poverty) and eventually included sex workers who began to challenge the Catholic Bishop's Conference of Brazil in the late 1970s and early 1980s, to not use a top-down model of ministry.[46] The project evolved through the actual work of human beings who were connected and challenging the church while expressing their concrete needs. The women became known as agents of their own issues and their activism included letters to the Vatican requesting that the Catholic Church stop the marginalization of prostitutes in Brazil.[47] The women were taking back their agency in making their voices heard.

Guider sees this as a "process of evangelization and liberation that ultimately demanded the conversion of the Church itself, or if not its conversion, at least the admission of its complicity in the marginalization and oppression of all women."[48] The institutional silence in the church on the existence of prostitution is broken. Though the problem is not completely resolved, what is accomplished for the church is a shift away from a problem-solving model and a radical change in fundamental theological orientation towards liberation via the inclusion of very marginalized and typically condemned women. The church in Brazil has tried to prove an exception through ministry to marginalized women. Guider questions whether the church was successful, as much theology is still in the hands of men and sex workers have not had an entirely warm reception in their contribution to Christianity in Brazil. This is because they asked the church to be honest and acknowledge how Catholicism in Brazil fueled the sexism and racism that women experienced.[49]

Loving Response

A response that takes solidarity with sex workers seriously is the work of Lia Claire Scholl, a pastor who has ministered with sex workers for over 12 years, working with HIPS (Helping Individual Prostitutes Survive) in Washington and in her own project, called Star Light Ministries.[50] In her book *I Heart Sex Workers: A Christian Response to People in the Sex Trade* she articulates her ideas on what may constitute a loving Christian response to persons in sex work. On her motivation and experience, she writes:

> "Because I'm a minister—and candid about it—I've faced the stigma that comes with being an ally, especially a Christian ally, to people engaged in sex work. Sex workers often encounter do-gooders who want to rescue them from their situation. Because other Christians offer judgment, moralism, and evangelism, they expect those same attitudes from me. They expect me to be a 'Captain-Save-a-Ho,' a person who tries to rescue and change sex workers. When I don't try to 'save' the people I meet, just be their friend, over and over, they express surprise."[51]

She regrets her earlier years in the work when she tried to convert sex workers and states that perhaps Christians are the people who need conversion, echoing Guider's insight into what people in sex work offer the church.[52] She presents her theology and method of response to sex workers by using an overarching biblical story to retell the story of the sex workers whom she encounters. She writes of Tamar, who played the prostitute in the Bible to get her rights. She affirms the stories of women who enter sex work for various reasons, especially to reclaim their rights.[53]

An outstanding question she raises is: "What if we begin to see the people who engage in sex work as individuals who are seeking their own paths in an unjust world?"[54] The question becomes crucial when we realize that sex workers often face unjust choices. Scholl decries the media, cultural and Christian portrayal of sex workers, which invites derision and discomfort around the humanity of women. Using the models of agency as constructed by Showden, the women that Scholl encounters are in charge of their decisions and can be respected, supported, and loved. Scholl maintains that no singular experience captures the story of every woman in sex work. She notes that "sex work may be enslavement to one woman, but it may be liberation to another. The most liberating thing, for any woman, is to have her experience affirmed and believed, because women can be trusted."[55]

With the story of Esther, who was compelled to join the harem and later used her sexual prowess as a woman to win favor for her people, Israel, Scholl raises questions about what constitutes trafficking and choices when young women are faced with few choices in life.[56] Societal values and sexual preferences must change to accommodate ordinary expressions of self that are not sinful in themselves. Sex becomes a way women achieve power, at times find safety and get out of poverty.[57] This injustice, inevitably, must change if the root cause of sex work is to be addressed. Inequality is the foundation of sex work. Her three categories of entering sex work are choice, circumstances, and coercion.[58] However, she admits that the categories become blurred, as there are many reasons one enters sex work and because it is difficult to determine how circumstances differs from coercion and choice. In the story of Rahab, Scholl sees a lady who transitioned from a "madam" to a "mother."[59] Frequent transitions occur for women in sex work. This is extended to those transitioning from sex work to other ways of living. Becoming an ally with sex workers helps them to build agency and so Christians can be a friend to sex workers, rather than a rescuer.[60]

Scholl does not propagate a one-size-fits-all approach as she seeks to increase agency, listen, and learn from women, challenge injustice, be a safe minister and build equal relationship. This work aligns with my own position that the experiences of the women may be trusted. The women perceive their agency in different ways. Sources of influence in accepting or denying agency are to be examined in proposing a pastoral model of care. The person of the minister, the sex worker, the culture that produces and sustains sex workers, and the way that biblical stories are read are also factors to consider.

The NCWR and Sex Workers in Nigeria

Historical Context: Nigeria

Nigeria is the most populous country in West Africa. It is a conglomerate of over 300 tribes and ethnic groups with different languages, which was living independently as different nations and empires before the intrusion of Britain with colonization and the subsequent amalgamation of the different nations and empires into one nation.[61] Colonization, the trading of goods, and slavery are the major disruptive factors that opened Sub-Saharan Africa (to which Nigeria belongs) to other worlds.[62] Nigeria, as the nation we know today, is a product of the amalgamation of northern and southern protectorates in 1914 by the

British governor Lord Frederick Lugard and other colonial authorities.[63] The nation has rapidly evolved from traditional society to a modern country and is richly endowed with abundant natural resources like crude oil, tin, coal, limestone, zinc, and other commodities. Yet, the wealth from these resources is concentrated in the hands of a few politicians and their allies. Nigeria is a rich nation of poor people.[64] Thus, the populace, especially the youth, undertake any form of trade that offers hope for a means of livelihood. With urbanization, there is massive migration to the cities in search of jobs and better opportunities for living.

The commercial sex trade is regarded as one of the consequences of colonization, modernization, or globalization, and perhaps an aftermath of slave trade.[65] Europeans introduced commercial sex work into Nigeria and some parts of Africa through the use of colonial political powers, market capitalism, and increased social mobility in the 1800–1900s.[66] Sex workers are caught in the conundrum of being defined as deviant from many perspectives yet, as research has demonstrated, sex work is a profitable business for women and girls from Nigeria who are coping with grim economic situations.[67] Their place in traditional society is contested, with many still viewing sex workers as a threat to moral order, and sex workers suffer police crackdowns, neglect of rights, and high risk of violence and disease in modern African society.[68] They are not welcomed by the church. Yet, sex work thrives, and there exist a substantial number of women who boldly say that they chose to be in sex work and are advocating for acceptance, human rights, and changes to the law.[69,70]

Nigeria is one of the suppliers of female sex workers who go to Europe and Arab nations. Sex work, especially, woman trafficked under the guise of a better job abroad, has become a transnational and cross-continental dynamic that Nigerian women are navigating. While this phenomenon is often understood in terms of the disempowerment and oppression of women, and resulting social and moral disapproval, some of the women I interviewed for my research said that they paid to be taken out of Nigeria for sex work. One of the women reported, "it is the same thing you are doing here that you will do there, but you will be paid in dollars and Euro. So, why do it here for nothing?"[71,72] Another said that it was pressure from her mother that led her to international sex trade. She is from Edo state in midwestern Nigeria, which supplies a high number of young Nigerian women to work in Italy.[73]

Women who opt for sex work and those trafficked under the guise of better life abroad state clearly that sex work is the easiest way out of the economic conundrum that Nigeria has been in from the early 1990s. Sex work is seen as a way out of poverty and some women who have returned from abroad build decent homes for their families and buy houses in the big cities like Port Harcourt, Abuja, Lagos, and Enugu.[74] Though people know that these women were selling sex abroad, some parents hold them up as symbol of success to other female children. Many times, young girls also approach the rich madams to take them abroad to make money. Elderly women who have returned from abroad set up offices in Benin, the capital of Edo State, for recruiting young girls. They can serve as conduits to ship willing sex workers and unsuspecting girls to Europe. Because of proximity to female sex workers and traffickers, the project of the NCWR is in Benin City, Edo State, Nigeria.

Women Religious Working with Sex Workers in Nigeria: An Appraisal of COSUDOW, Nigeria

COSUDOW is the registered non-governmental organization (NGO) that the NCWR uses to draw attention to the "dehumanizing nature of the sexual exploitation of trafficked girls and women in Africa" and "put up a fight to liberate women from the shackles of their slave masters and they also investigate the cases of threat to lives of families of victims who have decided to abandon exploitative prostitution for a more decent living."[75,76] The organization is working from a single narrative, that of women being trafficked against their will and that sex work is slavery. Literature discussed above and data from interviews shows otherwise. The NCWR is the umbrella body for all women in vowed life in the Roman Catholic tradition in Nigeria. There are 57 religious orders, seven monasteries and four associate institutes that actively contribute to and support COSUDOW.

The efforts to combat sex trafficking of Nigerian women by Women Religious started from Italy.[77] Some Nigerian women who were held against their wish as sex slaves approached Nigerian sisters (nuns) in Italy for help. The women were initially housed in a convent in Italy. In 1998, the NCWR formed a committee to draw up a plan for further rescue with strategies of implementation. Sr. Blandina Ryan, MMM, and Sr. Florence Nwonuma, SSH with Bar. Eric Okojie and Bar. Victor. Ehizojie began the committee. The objectives of COSUDOW include:

- To reintegrate and rehabilitate young women who have voluntarily or involuntarily returned from Europe involved in sexual exploitation.
- To educate and enlighten families and the young people of the hazards or danger involved in travelling to Europe or elsewhere for greener pastures.
- To ensure that victims and their family members are securely protected after they have opted out of exploitative prostitution.
- To provide counseling services and spiritual direction to enable the girls regain their self-dignity and worth.
- To work in collaboration with Government agencies and non-Governmental agencies involved in the fight against human trafficking.
- To find ways of giving victims of trafficking marketable skills and help them set up ventures that will enable them have a source of livelihood.[78]

Funding for the initial take-off projects were provided by the Episcopal Conference of the Catholic Bishops of Italy, MissioAchen, Germany and SRTV, the Netherlands. The Conference of Major Superiors in Italy, *Unione Superior Maggiorid'Italia (USMI)-Italy*, provided funding for scholarships. Local church bodies and the NCWR contribute funds to keep the center running.[79]

The leadership of the major Superiors of Religious Institutes that formed the NCWR identifies a Women Religious order that could supply personnel to run the center for three years with renewal for another three years. The order so identified takes charge and assumes the position of Executive Director of the Center for the period so that leadership is shared between different women and religious orders.

From inception COSUDOW claims to have rehabilitated a total of 378 victims of trafficking (VOTs) whom they have helped to leave sex work, be reintegrated, and earn money from other means and livelihoods.[80] The center embarks on awareness campaigns in rural areas, in churches and schools with the aim of educating young girls on the reality of human trafficking for sex slavery. Parents are made aware of the dangers of giving out their female daughters to strangers for a trip to Europe.[81]

COSUDOW is the platform that women in vowed life are using to reach out to women in sex work. This is the first and only articulate Catholic platform in Nigeria that is dedicated to the issue of trafficked women. Yet trafficking does not explain the entire reasons women engage in sex work. A theology of the human person made in the image and likeness of God can help Women Religious in Nigeria to walk and work authentically with women in sex work whether it is defined as a choice or forced labor.

Imago Dei

Imago Dei affirms that every human being is created good. The fullness of the beauty of humanity is that we are created with flesh and blood. Embodiment makes us the humans that we are. Following the biblical narrative, this goodness was mixed with sinfulness at the fall of first humans. Incarnation is God taking human flesh (Jn 1:4) to restore the dignity that humanity had at creation. This theological concept invites openness and humility in encountering women involved in sex work.[82]

An example of dignity restored is found in the encounter that Jesus has with women identified as not using their bodies in a culturally approved manner. The story of Jesus' encounter with the woman caught in the very act of committing adultery (Jn 8: 1-11) will help us to understand the transformation that occurs in listening to women who are being condemned for making stigmatized choices.

Persons from differing theological perspectives might emphasize morality or sin in this issue.[83] Such a perspective might call for a condemnation of the sin of sex work while caring for the sinner (the human person). My response would be to call for listening and understanding rather than starting from a perspective of sin. Identifying sin so closely with the issue of sexuality has had little positive result for Christianity. Emphasis on sin in biblical interpretation has not reduced the presence of sexuality through the ages, rather, sinful sexuality is used to condemn women.[84] How about we emphasize the sin of the men around sexuality? In the narrative, Jesus does not condemn but understands, challenges the structures of the day, and shows deepest compassion for life.

Imago Dei makes us aware that every human person reveals God. This revelation is not limited to those whom society approves. Female sex workers reveal God in their bodies since the choice they make with their bodies does not remove their intrinsic worth as human beings created in the image and likeness of God. The Christian sex workers I interviewed clearly expressed that it is their trust in God that is keeping them in business and they pray for safety each day. I hope my theological perspective will aid in finding fullness of life with dignity and respect.

Reminding every human being of the dignity and worth of other human beings is necessitated by the various experiences of people treating others as less than human even in the church. Scholars of African origin are using concepts found in African traditional society to emphasize the dignity of every human person and highlight the interdependence of every person, which is something we are also trying to accomplish by noting the points of connection between Women Religious and sex workers in Nigeria.

The concept of *Ubuntu, umuntu,* and *Umunthu* capture the essence of being human in the African context.[85] *Ubuntu* is of Zulu, South African origin. *Umunthu, mtu, mundu, ntu* or *muntu* are from Bantu-speaking West Africa. These concepts are used to express the core idea of interdependence and relational understanding of the human person in African philosophy as expressed by the popular dictum of John Mbiti, "I am because we are; and since we are, therefore I am."[86]

In the Igbo language (Nigeria, West Africa), the word used to denote a human being is *mmadu,* which literally means the "beauty of life or the goodness of life or the crowning point of life" according to Andrew Isiguzo, George Ukagba, and Nkeonye Otakpor.[87] Further in their explication of the concept of the human person, interdependence on others in African life is emphasized. They write:

> "*Mmadu* is conceived, born, lives, and dies with in a dialogical milieu. Mmadu is not just born alone into a community. This fact is no qualification as or for a human being. Physical birth is not a predicate. To be authentically human is also not a function of a nametag. Physical birth and a name are necessary but not sufficient to qualify someone as a human being. We are humans principally because of the humanity of others. As a consequence human existence is understood as a double act of independence and interdependence. *Mmadu* needs the support of others to make life worthwhile. *Mmadu* needs the confident trust and reliance of others in order to attain that sublime state of goodness and beauty that are the essence of existence."[88]

My hope and desire are that women in sex work may find in the church the place to experience confidence and trust they need to flourish as humans. Women in sex work find themselves at the receiving end of being treated as less than human in the church and society. Affirmation of their dignity and worth could be a starting point of support.

Conclusion: Solidarity Through the LIVE Approach

The LIVE approach (Listening, Introspection, Validation, and Emancipation/Empowerment) is a culturally sensitive pastoral care model for women in sex work. The purpose is to understand the individual agency of Nigerian sex workers as a starting point for providing pastoral care. This would help Women Religious in Nigeria to work authentically with sex workers. Rather than thinking of every female trading sex as a victim, listening to individual narratives may help to know what drives the person and where the person needs assistance, providing flexible, targeted support. Another aspect to providing support that is self-aware is to understand the pressures and judgement that the roles of Madonna/Whore hoist onto women.

Nuns have privileges within church and society, garnering more respect than women in sex work. Vowed religious women and sex working women are located at two opposite ends of the spectrum in terms of how society and the church perceive our bodies and being in the world. Nuns receive accolades and praises for standing against what "those women" do with their bodies. Sex workers are shamed. Therefore, Women Religious must remain aware of these privileges as they seek to provide pastoral care, acknowledging the power differential, though they belong to the same race and ethnic group.

This perspective provides an opportunity for solidarity between nuns and sex workers, who may be able to join forces to expand options for all women in Nigeria while breaking down binary judgements aimed at the Madonna/Whore. For example, one of the research participants, a sex worker providing for her family, interprets her agency in a manner akin to salvation. Her name is Caro, and her story is one of saving others in the family. She says:

> "I am a nice girl. I come from a large family. We are nine kids. Sometimes, no food, nothing. I volunteered myself to start this work because I know I am beautiful, and men will carry me. We now have a house."[89]

Caro thinks of herself as a sort of "saviour," a messianic figure for the family when they had nothing. She is proud that she has accomplished something for the family. So, for her, it is her "niceness" and ability to "volunteer" for the salvific mission that matters. Therefore, she sees herself as one with agency. She is using her giftedness to save her family members. Could this be a point of recognition and affirmation with Women Religious who also interpret their roles in society as salvific?

In my research, all the women interviewed say that they are Christians and involved in a church. Most of them believe they have a lot of connection with God, which gives them a sense of having some agency in their relationship with God, self, and society. God is very much involved in day-to-day living, including sex working: "I don't go to church often, but I always pray before going out. I always ask God to guide and protect me as I go to that work because I did not intentionally engage myself into the work. It is as a result of bad conditions and not having a helper that led me into the work."[90] Another puts it this way:

> "I prayed God to forgive me since this is not going to be permanent because I know it is a sin before the sight of God. I know that my spirit is not always at rest each time I'm going out for this work and for that, I always pray to God to guide and protect me from the hands of ritualists or those that can harm me, that it will be better for me to remain without getting work than to go and fall into the hands of evil ones because I know I've a call or purpose of which God brought me into this world which I have not fulfilled."[91]

One woman added a dimension of asking grace while not keeping God's word, which she quotes. She says:

> "Well, God said that 'our body is the temple of the Holy Spirit,' but things of this world have really deceived us. So, we keep on asking for God's abundant grace in all that we do so that we will be safe from every trial and temptations of this life. I do go to church every Sunday."[92]

There seems to be this constant negotiation with God on how to act. From another interviewee, "I always pray to God to guide and protect me because I know God has a purpose for me on earth."[93]

The participants in this study are confident of their unmediated access to divine protection and love. Their sense of agency in their relationship with God is strong. This contrasts with their narrative about the various churches they attend. Relationships with the church are described with disappointment, where human beings, purporting to be acting in the name of God, usurp their agency through double standards of the sexual control of women and sometimes publicly shame and expel female sex workers.

Could this be a strong point of correlation between these sex workers and Women Religious in Nigeria? Both cohorts express deep faith in God with unmediated access to divine grace, while also struggling with oppression from within church structures and leadership. Nuns are all too familiar with judgement from church fathers and the historical expulsion of women for usurping authority or behaving in a manner that is out of male religious control. Recognizing similar experiences builds solidarity and may contribute energy for change for the benefit of all women, in church and society.

The LIVE model calls for openness, non-judgmental, and non-anxious presence to hear the diverse stories and perspectives of the women. *Listening* will help to build trust. Listening connects. Listening deeply to others, sex workers themselves, the context and culture, theology, and above all, listening to God, grounds the pastoral care worker while providing competent care for women in sex work. In listening, the message conveyed is "I hear you," "I see you," and "You matter." The story of every woman in sex work is different and each person is on a different spot on the continuum in negotiation of agency. Listening entails openness and a desire to learn. Listening to others with openness entails empathy. Deep listening is a skill practiced in humility. Empathic connection to feelings and needs of the person makes the humanity of the person come alive. Choosing what needs to meet at the time makes us realize our limitations as humans. This is where humility and discernment are indispensable in the art of practicing the compassionate love of God with others. Listening to female sex workers necessitates listening to other factors surrounding the choice of sex work, indicated through the narratives of the women.

The call to *introspection* helps the care provider to not take a one-up or better-than-thou attitude towards the women. It also challenges others who come into the relationship with sex workers to look inwards, rather than condemn from pre-conceived notions of who the women are. It is easier to condemn others than to see where we all participate or are implicated in the structure that keeps some persons, especially women, in a perpetually subservient position. The same people who patronize sex workers at night wake up in the morning to demand their condemnation. As Women Religious seeking liberation, we are invited to reflect on how we participate in evil structures that perpetually keep some persons subjugated. We all need repentance.

Validating the personhood of the women in sex work may go a long way in proving to them that they are still human. Some of the women believe they are nobodies. Raising a sense of hope in their being may help the women to breathe deeply and realize they are understood. This may also help them in their sense of trust and honesty instead of a manipulative attitude.

From a gender perspective, validation in the LIVE model assists pastoral agents to admit the painful situation of women in different cultures, including in religious life. Women, including nuns, have limited choices to make as human beings in the world. Agency and autonomy for women are stifled in many ways, as is evident in Catholic theology as described in this chapter. Women are held to higher standards than men when it comes to matters of sexuality. As in the days of old, men who buy sex are overlooked or even encouraged to be "manly," while women who sell sex are judged and oppressed. In the LIVE model, sex workers are validated as human persons struggling to live meaningfully in the world.

Emancipation occurs through *empowerment*. Empowerment is a buzzword in working with people on the margins. Beyond cosmetic and surface gestures of buying sewing machines for young women in the name of empowerment, this study calls on the church to break the cycles of evil that the women live. The process will be different for different women in different regions. Through listening, the point where the person needs empowerment can be discerned. Empowerment could mean pointing people to resources they may not be aware exist. It could mean opening the power within for the potentials to burst forth.

Empowerment means validation of one's sense of agency and autonomy in the world while taking responsibility for one's share in the interconnectedness of humanity. Through listening, introspection, validation and joining with others for emancipation through change in self and social structures, the church in Nigeria could be at the forefront of providing high-quality pastoral care to women in the sex industry.

The LIVE approach to pastoral care is simple and does not need elaborate training for implementation. Every human being is endowed with the capacity to listen to one another, while holding one's own judgments in check. A non-judgmental attitude helps to build rapport, trust, and confidence. Each sex worker's story differs from the other. Validating others comes from shared knowledge that every human person is made in the image and likeness of God. Empowerment and emancipation come from the desire to play a role in bringing justice on earth. Listening to people's narratives transforms lives. The life of the listener and the person telling the narrative can be transformed. Members of the church and Women Religious can be transformed when the depth of human suffering is shared, and compassion is given and received. Amid this suffering, we can point to resources and strengths that are found in the women's narratives and so live our mission as the Body of Christ.

At the parish (congregational), diocesan (synod), and any other level of church organization, a pastoral plan could be developed using the LIVE approach. The heart of such a plan would be listening, introspection, validating, and empowering the women to live the life they are called to in the life of the church. The church needs introspection at all levels. Pope Francis, following the example of Pope John Paul II, apologized for the sins of the church.[94] As a corporate entity, though also a divine reality, the church is sinful too. As these narratives indicate, some of the women simply need a listening church to validate their experiences as agents in the world. The women in sex work should be part of the formation and implementation of such plans for their own pastoral care. It is time to let the voices of women into the mainstream of the life of the church, as Women Religious have long argued.

Notes

1 Nkiruka Okafor, "Rethinking Agency for Women Prostitutes: A Transformative Personal Encounter," *Bulletin of Ecumenical Theology* 32 (2020), 52–63.

2 Shannon Bell, *Reading, Writing and Rewriting the Prostitute Body* (Indianapolis, IN: Indiana University Press, 1994).

3 Gail Pheterson, *The Prostitution Prism* (Amsterdam: Amsterdam University Press, 1996).

4 Carisa R. Showden, *Choices Women Make: Agency in Domestic Violence, Assisted Reproduction, and Sex Work* (Minneapolis, MN: University of Minnesota Press, 2011).

5 Roland Stringfellow, "Denouncing the Real Villains of Sex Work: Towards a Compassionate Theology for Sex Workers," *Religión e incidencia pública. Revista de investigación de GEMRIP* 2 (2014), 171–196.

6 For example, in traditional African Society, any charm/sacrifice prepared with a female person or body part is considered dangerous. The major deity honored in many ancient religions is mother earth and fertility deities.

7 Ruth Perry, "Quoting the Founding Fathers of Complementarian Theology," *The Beautiful Kingdom Warriors,* March 30, 2014, https://thebeautifulkingdomwarriors.com/2014/03/30/quoting-the-founding-fathers-of-complementarian-theology/.
8 Perry, "Quoting the Founding Fathers."
9 Perry, "Quoting the Founding Fathers."
10 Perry, "Quoting the Founding Fathers."
11 Perry, "Quoting the Founding Fathers."
12 Perry, "Quoting the Founding Fathers."
13 Carly Daniel-Hughes, "Prostitution," in *The Oxford Handbook of New Testament, Gender and Sexuality*, ed. Benjamin H. Dunning (New York: Oxford University Press, 2019), 645–660.
14 Showden, *Choices Women Make*, 161.
15 Interview with Nigerian FSW, July 6, 2014.
16 Showden, *Choices Women Make*, Chapter 4.
17 Showden, *Choices Women Make*, 160–161.
18 Showden, *Choices Women Make*, 2–3.
19 Showden, *Choices Women Make*, 165–166.
20 Sharvari Karandikar, Lindsay B. Gezinski and Jacquelyn C.A. Meshelemiah, "A qualitative examination of women involved in prostitution in Mumbai, India: The role of family and acquaintances," *International Social Work* 56/4 (2011), 506.
21 Jesus Bucardo, Shirley J. Semple, Miguel Fraga-Vallejo, Wendy Davila and Thomas L. Patterson, "A Qualitative Exploration of Female Sex Work in Tijuana, Mexico," *Archives of Sexual Behavior* 33/4 (2004), 346.
22 Nkiruka Okafor Ihm, "Transforming Narratives Through "LIVE": A Pastoral Model of Care for Women in Sex Work" (PhD Dissertation, Luther Seminary, 2016), Chapter 4.
23 Karandikar, Gezinski, and Meshelemiah, "A Qualitative Examination," 499.
24 Anette Brunovskis and Rebecca Surtees, "Coming home: Challenges in family reintegration for trafficked women," *Qualitative Social Work* 12/4 (2012), 455.
25 Brunovskis and Surtees, "Coming home," 457.
26 Brunovskis and Surtees, "Coming home," 460–462.
27 Brunovskis and Surtees, "Coming home."
28 Laura Oso Casas, "Money, Sex, Love and the Family: Economic and Affective Strategies of Latin American Sex Workers in Spain," *Journal of Ethnic and Migration Studies* 36/1 (2010), 47-65.
29 Oso Casas, "Money, Sex, Love," 49–50.
30 Roy F. Baumeister and Kathleen D. Vohs, "Sexual Economics: Sex as Female Resource for Social Exchange in Heterosexual Interactions," *Personality and Social Psychology Review* 8/4 (2004), 339–363.
31 Baumeister and Vohs, "Sexual Economics," 341.
32 Baumeister and Vohs, "Sexual Economics," 341–344.
33 Interview with Nigerian FSW, July 12, 2014.
34 Svati P. Shah, "Sex Work and the Women's Movements," *CREA Count Me In! Addressing Violence Against Marginalized Women in South Asia Report* (New Delhi: CREA, 2011), 7.
35 For a specifically Catholic perspective in this volume see, Mark Levand, "Human Dignity in Sex Work and the Catholic Tradition," in *An Outrage Against Any Decent People: Religious Responses to Sex Work and Sex Trafficking*, ed. Lauren McGrow (London: Routledge, 2023).
36 Margaret Eletta Guider, *Daughters of Rahab: Prostitution and the Church of Liberation in Brazil* (Minneapolis: Augsburg Fortress Press, 1995).
37 Lia Claire Scholl, *I Heart Sex Workers: A Christian Response to People in the Sex Trade* (St Louis: Chalice Press, 2012).
38 Guider, *Daughters of Rahab*, 96–97.

39 Guider, *Daughters of Rahab*, 12.
40 Guider, *Daughters of Rahab*, 12.
41 Rita Nakashima Brock and Susan Brooks Thistlethwaite, *Casting Stones: Prostitution and Liberation in Asia and the United States* (Minneapolis: Fortress Press, 1996), kindle location 1709 of 4914.
42 Guider, *Daughters of Rahab*, 99.
43 Guider, *Daughters of Rahab*, 35.
44 Guider, *Daughters of Rahab*, 35.
45 Guider, *Daughters of Rahab*, chapter three.
46 Guider, *Daughters of Rahab*, 94–97.
47 Guider, *Daughters of Rahab*, 96–103.
48 Guider, *Daughters of Rahab*, 103–104.
49 Guider, *Daughters of Rahab*, 127.
50 Scholl, *I Heart Sex Workers*, 2–4.
51 Scholl, *I Heart Sex Workers*, 3.
52 Scholl, *I Heart Sex Workers*, 2–5.
53 Scholl, *I Heart Sex Workers*, 9–15.
54 Scholl, *I Heart Sex Workers*, 15.
55 Scholl, *I Heart Sex Workers*, 20.
56 Scholl, *I Heart Sex Workers*, 55–56.
57 Scholl, *I Heart Sex Workers*, 65.
58 Scholl, *I Heart Sex Workers*, 88.
59 "Madam" is used to designate older women who have worked as sex hawkers but are now mentoring other upcoming sex workers. They can initiate people in the sex industry. Scholl uses Rahab as an example of older sex workers transitioning to other roles in the society.
60 Scholl, *I Heart Sex Workers*, 3.
61 "A Brief History of our Country," Embassy of the Federal Republic of Nigeria, Mexico, accessed November 13, 2021, https://www.nigerianembmexico.org/history-of-nigeria.
62 "A Brief History of our Country."
63 Akindare Okunola, "11 Facts You Should Know About Nigeria as It Celebrates 60 Years of Independence," Global Citizen, October 1, 2020, https://www.globalcitizen.org/en/content/facts-to-know-about-nigeria-independence/.
64 "11 Facts You Should Know."
65 Benedict B. B. Naanen, "'Itinerant Gold Mines': Prostitution in the Cross River Basin of Nigeria, 1930-1950," *African Studies Review* 34/2 (1991), 57–79.
66 Toyin Falola and Matthew M. Heaton, *A History of Nigeria* (New York: Cambridge University Press, 2008).
67 Pat Caldwell, "Prostitution and the Risk of STDs and AIDS in Nigeria and Thailand," *Health Transition Review Supplement to Volume* 5 (1995), 170.
68 Habeeb Abdulrauf Salihu and Olufemi Adeniyi Fawole, "Police Crackdowns, Human Rights Abuses, and Sex Work Industry in Nigeria: Evidence from an Empirical Investigation," *International Criminal Justice Review* 31/1 (2020), 41.
69 Otutubikey Izugbara estimates there are 60 000 sex workers in Nigeria. He cautions that these current statistics may be unreliable. We echo such caution as reliable statistics are complicated by the fact that sex work is illegal and clandestine. See C. Otutubikey Izugbara, "'Ashawo suppose shine her eyes': Female sex workers and sex work risks in Nigeria," *Health, Risk and Society* 7/2 (2005), 141–159.
70 "De-Criminalise Sex Work in Nigeria, Sex Workers Urge Govt.," *Vanguard*, July 27, 2017, https://www.vanguardngr.com/2017/07/de-criminalise-sex-work-nigeria-sex-workers-urge-fg/.
71 Foluké Abigail Badejo, Sharyn Rundle-Thiele and Krzysztof Kubacki, "Taking a wider view: A formative multi-stream social marketing approach to understanding

human trafficking as a social issue in Nigeria," *Journal of Social Marketing* 9/4 (2019), 473.
72 Interview with Nigerian FSW, August 01, 2014.
73 Badejo, Rundle-Thiele and Kubacki, "Taking a wider view," 474.
74 C. Otutubikey Izugbara, "'Ashawo suppose shine her eyes,'" 143.
75 "Committee for the Support of the Dignity of Woman (COSUDOW)," Nigeria Conference of Women Religious, accessed October 01, 2020, https://www.ncwr.org.ng/committee-for-the-support-of-the-dignity-of-woman.html.
76 "Committee for the Support."
77 "Committee for the Support."
78 "Committee for the Support."
79 "Committee for the Support."
80 "Committee for the Support."
81 "Committee for the Support."
82 Edwina Gateley, *I Hear a Seed Growing* (Maryknoll, NY: Orbis Books, 1990), Kindle location 675 of 3580.
83 Stringfellow, "Denouncing the Real Villains of Sex Work," 173.
84 Stringfellow, "Denouncing the Real Villains of Sex Work," 175–176.
85 For further discussion of the terms, see Elieshi Ayo Mungure, *Conflict Transformation in the Family: A Quest for a Contemporary Pastoral Care and Counseling Approach in Tanzania* (Neuendettelsau: Erlanger Verlag für Mission und Ökumene, 2013). See also Hilliard Kwashie Dela Dogbe, "The Living Well: An Ecclesial Response to Alcoholism in Ghana," (PhD dissertation, Luther Seminary, 2012), 153–166.
86 John S. Mbiti, *African Religions and Philosophy* (Oxford: Heinemann, 1982), 108.
87 Andrew Isiguzo, George Ukagba and Nkeonye Otakpor, "The Igbo Concept of a Person," *Africa: Rivista trimestrale di studi e documentazione dell'Istituto italiano per l'Africa e l'Oriente*. 59/2 (2004), 231–243.
88 Isiguzo, Ukagba and Otakpor, "The Igbo Concept of a Person," 238–239.
89 Interview with Nigerian FSW, August 20, 2014.
90 interview with Nigerian FSW, July 17, 2014.
91 interview with Nigerian FSW, July 17, 2014.
92 Interview with Nigerian FSW, July 12, 2014.
93 interview with Nigerian FSW, July 1, 2014.
94 Inés San Martín, "Pope Francis strives to back up apologies with action," *Crux*, August 15, 2016, https://cruxnow.com/vatican/2016/08/pope-francis-strives-back-apologies-action/.

Bibliography

Falola, Toyin, and Matthew M. Heaton. *A History of Nigeria*. New York: Cambridge University Press, 2008.

Gateley, Edwina. *I Hear a Seed Growing*. Maryknoll, NY: Orbis Books, 1990.

Guider, Margaret Eletta. *Daughters of Rahab: Prostitution and the Church of Liberation in Brazil*. Minneapolis: Augsburg Fortress Press, 1995.

Isiguzo, Andrew, George Ukagba, and Nkeonye Otakpor, "The Igbo Concept of a Person." *Africa: Rivista trimestrale di studi e documentazione dell'Istituto italiano per l'Africa e l'Oriente*. 59/2 (2004): 231–243.

Izugbara, C. Otutubikey. "'Ashawo suppose shine her eyes': Female sex workers and sex work risks in Nigeria." *Health, Risk and Society* 7/2 (2005): 141–159.

Karandikar, Sharvani, Lindsay Gezinski, and Jacquelyn Meshelemiah. "A Qualitative Examination of Women Involved in Prostitution in Mumbai, India: The Role of Family and Acquaintances." *International Social Work* 56/4 (2013): 496–515.

Mbiti, John S. *African Religions and Philosophy*. Oxford: Heinemann, 1982.

Mungure, Elieshi Ayo. *Conflict Transformation in the Family: A Quest for a Contemporary Pastoral Care and Counseling Approach in Tanzania*. Neuendettelsau: Erlanger Verlag für Mission und Ökumene, 2013.

Naanen, Benedict B. B. "'Itinerant Gold Mines': Prostitution in the Cross River Basin of Nigeria, 1930–1950." *African Studies Review* 34/2 (1991): 57–79.

Nakashima Brock, Rita and Susan Brooks Thistlethwaite. *Casting Stones: Prostitution and Liberation in Asia and the United States*. Minneapolis: Fortress Press, 1996.

Okafor, Nkiruka. "Transforming Narratives Through 'LIVE': A Pastoral Model of Care for Women in Sex Work." PhD Dissertation, Luther Seminary, 2016.

Okafor, Nkiruka. "Rethinking Agency for Women Prostitutes: A Transformative Personal Encounter," *Bulletin of Ecumenical Theology* 32 (2020), 52–63.

Okunola, Akindare. "11 Facts You Should Know About Nigeria as It Celebrates 60 Years of Independence." *Global Citizen*. October 1, 2020, https://www.globalcitizen.org/en/content/facts-to-know-about-nigeria-independence/.

Oso Casas, Laura. "Money, Sex, Love and the Family: Economic and Affective Strategies of Latin American Sex Workers in Spain." *Journal of Ethnic and Migration Studies* 36/1 (2010): 47–65.

Perry, Ruth. "Quoting the Founding Fathers of Complementarian Theology." *The Beautiful Kingdom Warriors*. March 30, 2014, https://thebeautifulkingdomwarriors.com/2014/03/30/quoting-the-founding-fathers-of-complementarian-theology/.

Pheterson, Gail. *The Prostitution Prism*. Amsterdam: Amsterdam University Press, 1996.

Salihu, Habeeb Abdulrauf and Olufemi Adeniyi Fawole. "Police Crackdowns, Human Rights Abuses, and Sex Work Industry in Nigeria: Evidence from an Empirical Investigation." *International Criminal Justice Review*31/1 (2020): 40–58.

San Martín, Inés. "Pope Francis strives to back up apologies with action." *Crux*. August 15, 2016. https://cruxnow.com/vatican/2016/08/pope-francis-strives-back-apologies-action/.

Scholl, Lia Claire. *I Heart Sex Workers: A Christian Response to People in the Sex Trade*. St Louis, MI: Chalice Press, 2012.

Shah, Svati P. "Sex Work and the Women's Movements." In *CREA Count Me In! Addressing Violence Against Marginalized Women in South Asia Report*. New Delhi: CREA, 2011.

Showden, Carisa R. *Choices Women Make: Agency in Domestic Violence, Assisted Reproduction, and Sex Work*. Minneapolis, MN: University of Minnesota Press, 2011.

Stringfellow, Roland. "Denouncing the Real Villains of Sex Work: Towards a Compassionate Theology for Sex Workers." *Religión e incidencia pública. Revista de investigación de GEMRIP*2 (2014): 171–196.

4 Human Dignity in Sex Work and the Catholic Tradition

Mark A. Levand

Introduction

Sex work holds a complex and often stigmatized position within the Catholic world. On the one hand, there is a message of valuing women and seeking to dismantle coerced sex trafficking leading to a pastoral response of support and charity. On the other hand, there is a long history of looking down on sex work as a profession and conflating consensual sex work with coerced sex trafficking. This latter view can lead to a lack of autonomy and a pejorative view of those who engage in sex work. Adding to this multi-layered view is the lack of clarity in the way church documents use the term prostitution.

One does not have to look far into the history of the Catholic Church to find language that disparages those working in the sex industry. We see this disparaging language in recent Catholic documents such as prostitution being an insult to human dignity,[1] prostitution as a form of slavery,[2] insinuating that sex workers are dead psychologically and spiritually,[3] and describing prostitution as a social scourge.[4] Even earlier, we see translators ascribing words like *harlot* or *prostitute* to Augustine and Aquinas, bringing with it an implication of lesser dignity.[5] This language can encourage others to treat those in the sex industry—both the sellers and consumers of sex—poorly, from a stance of moral superiority. In order to articulate a Catholic theological and pastoral understanding of support for sex workers, we must first clarify the terms we use today and their conflation in church writings. We can then briefly establish the dignity of the sex worker and the work itself from teachings on labor and recent studies that examine the outcome of sex work. We can then consider the concepts in Catholic social thought that offer clarity for why those in the sex industry should be treated with dignity and respect. Lastly, we will begin a dialogue about some moral complexities by considering some lesser-examined aspects of sex work.

Confusion and Clarity of Terms

In Catholic documents on sex work (often termed "prostitution"), there is a conflation or lack of clarity in how the topic is officially categorized. The

DOI: 10.4324/9780429328824-5

Catechism of the Catholic Church, for example, identifies the gender and age diversity of those in sex work,[6] but one of the most well-known documents on the pastoral responses to sex work largely discusses it as a form of slavery and violence against women.[7] While it is appropriate for the church to condemn slavery and violence against women, it can accidentally support and perpetuate the idea that only women (implying cisgender women) engage in sex work and that all sex work is slavery and violence. There is also a lack of clarity on the distinction between sex work and trafficking.

The human trafficking prevention group "Stop The Traffik" differentiates sex work from sex trafficking (or exploitation) largely by consent—*sex work* is the willing sale of sexual services and does not affect a person's human rights while *sex trafficking* is when a person is coerced into the sale of sex and is a violation of human rights.[8] The distinction between the willingness to sell sex versus coercion is seemingly obvious though often overlooked in public discourse. This lack of distinction is also present at times in Catholic documents on sex work.

In Church writings, the Catholic Church seems to be both aware of and unclear about the sex work v. trafficking distinction. For example, the Pontifical Council for the Pastoral Care of the Migrants and Itinerant People notes that "not all of those who have been trafficked are in prostitution and not all prostitutes have been trafficked."[9] There are some documents in which there is consistency in the description of "forced prostitution." In papal representative Archbishop Bernardito Auza's address to the United Nations, *Fight Against Human Trafficking*, every time prostitution is mentioned, it is condemned as something people are forced into or by which people are exploited.[10] In some church documents, it is explicitly only mentioned as a type of forced labor,[11] indicating that there is a form of un-coerced "prostitution."

In other instances, however, we see a conflation in language when describing "prostitution" as one of many topics underneath the umbrella of forced labor or as a type of slavery separate from human trafficking. For example, in *Pastoral Orientations on Human Trafficking*, prostitution is described as a type of forced labor.[12] We see this type of categorization again in Pope Francis' words about "the sexual exploitation of boys and girls, slave labour, including prostitution," marking it as a type of sexual exploitation with the implication of coercion under the umbrella term of slave labor.[13] Pope Francis does, however, use "sexual abuse" in a later statement to describe this "modern slavery," avoiding the use of the term prostitution, indicating an understanding of this difference.[14] In the *Compendium of the Social Doctrine of the Church*—the official presentation and summary of Catholic social teaching—prostitution is condemned as a type of slavery separate from the trafficking of human beings.[15] The *Catechism of the Catholic Church* describes prostitution as:

> a social scourge. It usually involves women, but also men, children, and adolescents (The latter two cases involve the added sin of scandal.). While it is always gravely sinful to engage in prostitution, the imputability of the offense can be attenuated by destitution, blackmail, or social pressure.[16]

In this description, it is clear that "prostitution" is seen as sinful and being coerced into sex work is the only circumstance that absolves people of accountability. While the assumption that "all prostitution is forced labor" may be made in good faith, the result of such an assumption blurs the distinction between trafficking and consensual sex work, limiting theological discourse about the latter.

In some instances, it is apparent that exploitation is being denounced, based on the assumption that no one would willingly enter the sex industry. In Pope John Paul II's letter to Archbishop Jean-Louis Tauran, he describes: "In particular, the sexual exploitation of women and children is a particularly repugnant aspect of this trade [the trade of human trafficking], and must be recognized as an intrinsic violation of human dignity and rights."[17] The subsequent sentence condemns the business or industry aspect of the sex trade because of the violation of freedom.[18]

It is clear that the Catholic Church condemns forced sexual labor of anyone, and specifically that of children. This condemnation is consistent with the ethos of many who advocate for the legalization and decriminalization of sex work. What is unclear, however, is that the Catholic Church's tradition of tolerating sex work in society remains unnamed in many of these recent church documents, and still perpetuates a view that sex workers do not have autonomy and moral agency.[19,20] When these Catholic documents overlook the moral agency of sex workers, there a greater potential of making social rhetoric unclear and subsequently may impact pastoral responses.

This lack of clarity between non-consensual trafficking and consensual sex work has the potential to cause confusion about the moral accountability regarding "degradation of the human person." When Catholics and other Christians discuss sex workers as "degrading themselves," this rhetoric could lead others to treat sex workers with less respect because of the belief that they are "selling their bodies," implying a diminished human dignity. To be clear—the Church upholds that whatever may be an "insult to human dignity" does not in any way detract from one's dignity, even if it is believed to be something someone is "doing to themselves."[21] This conflation between sex trafficking (coerced) and sex work (consensual) leads to a simplistic understanding with harmful implications: that all sex workers are victims and those who consume sex work are morally corrupt traffickers. This unnuanced view of sex work can lead to discriminatory thinking and policies causing undue harm to those in the sexual economy.[22]

Kate Lister lays out the importance of using the term "sex workers" to refer to people who sell sexual services rather than the pejorative or value-laden terms "prostitute" "whore," or "harlot."[23] Lister concludes that "we cannot and will not achieve social equality for anyone if the language we use to describe marginalised groups actually reinforces the stigma they face." In supporting sex workers today, one of the first pastoral steps Catholics can take is by understanding and respecting the language that is used in the industry. This pastoral practice upholds human dignity out of respect for the power of naming—a practice that is applied in other aspects of Catholic pastoral response.[24] Using language preferred by those in the profession can help restore human dignity by upholding rhetoric that frames sex workers as workers with human dignity.

The Dignity of Sex Work

Exploitation is obviously condemned vehemently both by the church and by those in the sex industry. When the conciliar document *Gaudium et Spes* discusses "disgraceful working conditions where [people] are treated as mere tools for profit rather than free and responsible persons" it notes the importance of people being treated (1) fairly, without exploitation, not as tools for profit and (2) as free and responsible persons. If we infantilize those who do sex work saying they would "never rightly choose sex work as a profession" then we have already violated this second principle. But if we treat sex workers as free and responsible persons, what can we learn about supporting sex workers as a church? Recent discussions on sex work as work and the dignity of workers can get us closer to a compassionate pastoral response.

Scholar of Christian ethics Kate Ward examined what sex worker advocates can teach the school of Catholic social thought by interrogating the claim that "sex work is work."[25] In her analysis, Ward notes that saying "sex work is work" distinguishes between trafficking and choice—naming it as *work* gives an accurate picture of sex work as a job in a capitalist society. Or as Clementine von Radics said, "as uncoerced as any labor under capitalism can be."[26] In Chapter 2 of their book, *Revolting Prostitutes: The Fight for Sex Workers' Rights*, Molly Smith and Juno Mac consider a number of rebuttals to the resistance people have to calling sex work "work," ultimately culminating in the premise that sex workers should not have to justify why their work deserves to be safe, not criminalized, and why they deserve to be considered workers.[27] Theologian Dan Finn observes that "all work is dignified and all work contributes to the worker's self-formation as an active, deciding person."[28] This understanding of work is derived from the church teaching that *all* work is dignified not because of *what* the work is, but because of *who* (a human person) is doing the work.[29]

Sex work can be stigmatized and shunned based on the morals and values of a society—legal scholar Amin Yacoub uses the term "objective dignity" to describe the dignity tied to these societal rules.[30] The basis by which this happens is what Melissa Gira Grant calls the "prostitute imaginary"—the fears and fantasies that people have of sex workers that enforce, encourage, and in turn operationalize the stigma.[31] Yacoub notes that objective dignity can vary by culture—some are more or less restrictive or stigmatizing of sex work, influencing how a given society assesses sex worker dignity.[32] While the dignity of the profession (and consequently the workers) might be critiqued by a societal moralism, the Catholic perspective on human dignity is that it is inviolable—unable to be removed by anything a person says or does, and respect and love are extended, even for those who act differently in social matters.[33,34]

If we see that the worker is dignified, and that the work is worthy of mention because it is *human* work, it is also helpful to observe that sex work can have positive outcomes for those involved. Several studies have examined the reasons people pay for sex. Male clients might seek out sex work for reasons including a desire for intimacy and affection, to seek sexual variety, and convenience.[35] In one study, female clients described motivations for buying sex including therapeutic reasons, to learn, for intimacy, and for pleasure.[36] While some reasons people pay for sex might fit the stereotypical paradigm (i.e., wanting to avoid emotional connection or dissatisfaction with their current partner), we also see reasons that foster healing and connection. If a relationship within sex work can foster such human connections, it is worth interrogating not only the dignity of the work and the necessity/value of the sex worker, but also the way sex work supports a societal goal for the common good. Let's turn to Catholic social thought as a frame for understanding a pastoral response to sex work and those who engage in it.

Catholic Social Thought and Sex Work

Catholic social thought is seen broadly as the theological and social reflections on issues within society, while Catholic social teaching refers to the official documents issued by the Roman Catholic Church.[37] Above, we considered both Catholic social teaching and thought. Christian Social Ethicist J. Milburn Thompson describes seven key principles that guide Catholic social teaching: human dignity, the common good, participation, solidarity, social sin, option for the poor, and human rights.[38] Much can be said about each of these principles in relation to sex work and what sex work scholars/activists have brought to the discussion over the years. After covering human dignity in the section above, we will take a brief look at the six remaining principles: common good, solidarity, social sin, option for the poor, participation, and human rights.

Common Good

The common good as described in the conciliar document *Gaudium et Spes* as "the sum of those conditions of social life which allow social groups and their individual members relatively thorough and ready access to their own fulfillment."[39] The common good is a goal toward which we should all work, allowing people and groups access to their own fulfillment. The concept of the common good is often applied to strenuous social conditions, such as poverty, as a foundational understanding for why we, as a society, should ensure these social stressors are eliminated in order for people to flourish.[40]

Concerning sex work, the concept of the common good helps us understand that we should take seriously the social conditions that make sex work dangerous, as the church oft suggests. This means within the purview of the common good are matters such as the social power difference between law enforcement and sex workers, undue economic constraints or social hierarchies within the sex industry, laws that criminalize sex work or will make it harder for sex workers to help those who are being trafficked, the criminalization of those who buy sex, institutionalized social and religious response to sex work, and much more. The concept of the common good also means taking seriously the ways in which sex work can bring about social good such as individual and communal healing. Understanding that we must work toward good in society means involving sex workers in making society a better place. With such a vast knowledge of the sex work community, sex workers often know best how to make the environment safer. If one of the primary goals of the common good involves the flourishing of all people and of the whole person, the autonomy of sex workers and the fulfillment of the work should not be discounted when discussing what a common good entails—something of which Augustine and Aquinas seemed to be aware.[41,42]

Solidarity

Moral theologian Thomas Massaro notes that solidarity calls attention to the "indisputable fact that people are interdependent; they rely upon each other for almost all their biological and social needs."[43] He goes on to explain that our interconnectedness is not only a fact but a positive value in the lives of humans. Noting our interdependence brings an understanding that sex workers and those who purchase sex are people deserving of support and care because, as a human community, we all participate in the relevant joys and pains. John Paul II notes in *Sollicitudo rei Socialis* that solidarity is not merely a "vague compassion" for or "shallow distress at the misfortunes" of others, but rather a determination to commit oneself to the common good (or good of all), stating that we all are responsible for all.[44] This means the violations of human dignity and rights that leave sex workers vulnerable to exploitation should be everyone's concern. We should also concern ourselves with the critical analysis of the goods that come from sex work to see how sexual healing and intimacy can benefit humanity on the societal level.

Social Sin

Social sin is also a useful concept when building a foundation for a pastoral response to sex work. Jesuit attorney, author, and activist Fred Kramer names social sin as the concept that humans structure sinfulness into social systems or institutions that, in turn, coercively shape the behaviors of individuals.[45] Theologians like Bryan Massingale and Megan McCabe describe how sin can be institutionalized in cultural or societal phenomena such as racism and rape culture.[46,47] Applying the concept of social or structural sin to the sex industry offers a theological frame for understanding the injustices suffered by sex workers at the hands of a society, including: a lack of safety precautions in the work, the criminalization of sex work that prevents reporting violence to the police, the social structures that put stress on people's ability to choose sex work as a profession, along with many other violations of human dignity and rights. One way John Paul II discusses social sin is "sin against justice in interpersonal relationship, committed...by the community against the individual."[48] Violations of sex workers' human rights can be seen as social sin of a community against individuals, allowing or even encouraging harm to come to people in the sex trade. When we understand social sin as a catalyst to harm the common good and our solidarity, we solidify a basis for a pastoral response that is not only to individuals but is systemic in its reach and holistic in its compassion.

Option for the Poor

In the spirit of human dignity and human rights, the preferential option for the poor encourages us to examine specifically the way in which our laws impact the poor and vulnerable. Thompson notes that a good society gives the poor and vulnerable privileged attention.[49] We see throughout Christian teaching that Jesus focuses on the poor in a way that attempts to change a culture that normalizes the ill treatment of those on the lowest economic rungs of society. The CST principle of preferential option for the poor must be considered here because, while not all sex workers are poor, poverty is inextricably linked to street sex work.[50] When societies pass laws that punish those in the sex trade, they are actively harming the economically vulnerable. Theologian Stephen Pope reminds us that this preferential option "appeals to an *expansion* rather than a *contraction* of love and wisdom." Pope Francis discusses the option for the poor as an ethical imperative in his encyclical *Laudato Si'*: "it demands before all else an appreciation of the immense dignity of the poor in the light of our deepest convictions as believers. We need only look around us to see that, today, this option is in fact an ethical imperative essential for effectively attaining the common good."[51] Here, the pope notes the interconnectedness of this principle with attaining the common good. In this way, many of our motivating questions are similar, but hold a particular focus on the poor and the forces that oppress them.

Within sex work, the preferential option for the poor encourages us to examine the conditions of economic scarcity that affect people in the sex trade. This involves an examination of the complex intersection of class with other points of oppression—how is our society addressing the needs of the poor and examining their causes before attempting to legislate or otherwise harm sex workers? Are we listening to the poor and marginalized when making laws intended to protect the vulnerable? How are the current legal practices affecting those in economic or socially vulnerable positions? These questions help us focus our attention on attaining the common good through consulting the poor, the vulnerable, and the marginalized. Without input from those activists and sex workers who best understand their experience, Catholics and Christians run the risk of ignoring this principle—one that Pope Francis urges is an ethical imperative—or worse, actively causing further harm to those in positions we are explicitly implored to uphold.

Participation

Strongly related to bringing about the common good is the principle of participation. This CST principle upholds participation in the social life of humanity as part of the human family. Thompson notes the goal of human rights is to uphold human dignity and "to allow and enable persons to participate in the community, create a good society, and thus to flourish as human beings."[52] This participation is often discussed in terms of politics as we see in papal encyclical *Pacem in Terris* (Peace on Earth). Pope John XXIII says as people participate in government, officials will "come into frequent contact with the citizens, and it is thus easier for them to learn what is really needed for the common good."[53] Working toward the common good is rooted in the expectation that all people are active in political life and the assumption that leaders will listen to those who participate. Humans are expected to participate in politics as well as economics—work and the distribution of wealth in society. More explicitly, we see calls for participation in political life to solve local problems, again from Pope Francis:

> Attempts to resolve all problems through uniform regulations or technical interventions can lead to overlooking the complexities of local problems which *demand the active participation of all members of the community*. New processes taking shape cannot always fit into frameworks imported from outside; they need to be based in the local culture itself.[54] [emphasis added]

Attempts to resolve problems require the participation and consultation of everyone in the community—paired with the preferential option for the poor, it is apt to say *especially* the input and participation of those who may be disadvantaged by the policies. While "local culture" may refer to geographic culture, sociologist and activist Gabriela Silva Leite notes sex work has created a culture of its own.[55] The principle of participation implores that attention be given to voices from within that culture.

When laws and economics create financial and power imbalances, the resulting restriction of participation constitutes a violation of human rights. The Synod of Bishops notes that "economic injustice and lack of social participation keep a [person] from attaining [their] basic human and civil rights."[56] When sex workers and advocates are excluded from political action, especially action that may cause further economic harm, society has failed to secure the participation of those most deeply affected by these changes.

The principle of participation is not only political, but "the full range of activities and institutions of social life."[57] Our duty to remove barriers that prevent people from participating in social life and their own human flourishing is firmly rooted in Catholic teaching. Regarding sex work, stigma that marginalizes and excludes people based on their profession is juxtaposed to the principle of participation. Stigmatizing sex work removes people from participation. As we examine our political and economic systems, we must also examine ways that sex workers are excluded from participation both in and outside our churches. In her book *I Heart Sex Workers: A Christian Response to People in the Sex Trade*, minister and activist Lia Claire Scholl subtitles Chapter 10 *Willing Participants in Their own Liberation*, offering practical recommendations to encourage such participation in economic life such as combating unjust hiring practices, resisting unjust wage differences, prioritizing child care, and career-learning opportunities.[58]

The CST principle of participation encourages us to examine ways in which we are complicit in a stigma-based exclusion of those in the sex industry. Massaro notes:

> "...anything that blocks full political...or economic participation...counts as a serious offense against human rights. A sincere regard for the common good will inspire concerned members of society to oppose such injustices and encourage full participation for all, regardless of differences or race, gender, or creed."[59]

In order to work toward the common good and avoid the violation of the human rights of others, we must protect the rights of sex workers to participate fully in the economic and social life of the human community.

Human Rights

The last principle of CST that we will consider, tightly bound to human dignity, is human rights. While this principle is scattered throughout Catholic doctrine, we see its clear presence in John XIII's encyclical *Peace on Earth*.[60] Thompson notes that the Catholic vision of human rights is inclusive of political rights and socio-economic rights.[61] The Christian understanding of human rights is communitarian—"the individual and the community give life to one another"—or "human dignity realized in community."[62] With regard to sex work, human rights exist in the political sphere with regard to decriminalization, or legal protections/exploitation. Human rights with social and economic rights include the ability to operate in an economy to meet one's social needs including ensuring social safety nets regarding housing, medical care, or economic misfortunes.[63] We must consider the ways in which the sex worker and the community give life to each other: what type of society do we create when we criminalize sex work? How can a community support those who buy and sell sex? Which human rights can we uphold for societal growth and which are we violating to societal detriment? The CST principle of human rights helps us focus on the ways in which communities can give to one another in a symbiotic relationship, minimizing potential injury to human dignity.

The disregard for the principle of human dignity constitutes a violation of human rights. Within sex work, we see issues of dignity arise in working conditions and pastoral care. The subtitle of Ward's paper is *What Sex Worker Advocates Can Teach Catholic Social Thought*. Through a discussion of CST's logic, she identifies that sex work is work even when it can be alienating as a result of social forces (i.e., capitalism, patriarchy, etc.). Ward notes that recognizing sex work as work forces society to see the dangers and disenfranchisements of sex work, violating workers' rights and human dignity.[64] In this way, human rights and solidarity work hand-in-hand. Just like with the variety of jobs outside of the sex industry, poor work conditions can violate a persons' dignity and autonomy—violations that should move us to address these conditions. Ward recognizes that sex worker advocates place themselves in solidarity, working for a change that upholds the dignity of all involved.

Pastoral care and the reduction of harm (or injury to human dignity) are ways of centering the principle of human rights. Nkiruka Okafor describes in Chapter 3 of this volume the type of pastoral care that can come from a theology of pastoral responses to sex work based in CST—she describes in more detail the acronym L.I.V.E: listen, introspection, validation, and emancipation. Both Okafor and Ward are describing what activists and healthcare professionals call harm reduction. Lia Claire Scholl ends her book *I Heart Sex Workers* with a chapter subtitled "Harm Reduction 101."[65] Harm reduction is an approach to issues of public health that focuses on reducing harmful consequences of behavior, as opposed to risk-reduction, which often starts with labeling a high-risk behavior as problematic.[66,67] Scholl sees the principles of harm reduction as guided by the overarching rule: "individuals are to be treated as adult agents in their own lives and with respect."[68]

To pose a question tied to human dignity and rights: What are you doing to show that the humanity of those involved in the sex trade matter? An answer to this question pertains not only to those who sell sex but also the consumers. Those who purchase sex are vilified in ways that may continue to isolate them. There are certainly people who purchase sex with ill intention or disregard for the other person or persons in the transaction. But there are also people who purchase sex for the opportunity to connect with someone, heal from trauma, or experience intimacy that may not otherwise be available to them. These people also exist in a matrix of social systems that stigmatize or alienate—a system that, moved by solidarity, we are also called to address.

Harm reduction gives us the language to name how Catholics and Christians can better support those in the sex trade while being oriented toward the justice emphasized in Catholic social thought. First, using the name "sex work" gives dignity to those in the industry and naming the role of sex work in society more clearly can give validation to the possible benefits that sex work brings to society. Second, focusing on the dignity of both sex worker and sex buyer can further clarify the fact that they are invaluable parts of the human family. Third, with the goal of human flourishing, we can all work together toward a common good that benefits individuals and communities on interpersonal, communal, and policy levels. Fourth, recognizing the interconnectedness (solidarity) of our life with the lives of those who buy and sell sex can help us understand the importance of ensuring safety for all, truly listening to their concerns, and addressing them because their pain affects us and is a reflection of the world in which we are allowing them to live and suffer. And fifth, we should always be aware of the social and structural sin that permeates the ideological and concrete institutions of our society, normalizing and excusing the harm that comes to those in the sex trade. The systemic disenfranchisement and legal pressures we enact on those in the sex trade either actively or passively must be named, eradicated, and reconciled to truly bring justice to this deeply human aspect of our society.

Morality, Proportionality, and Sex Work

Part of a compassionate pastoral response is understanding the complex moral components of the sex industry and our own judgments. I'd like to return for a moment to Augustine and Aquinas' discussion of sex work noted above. To thoroughly engage in a compassionate pastoral response, moving us past vague compassion or distress of the misfortunes of those in the sex industry, I'd like to look briefly at some of the moral components involved in transactions of sex. We see Augustine claim that sex work is necessary in a society or else it will be destroyed by lust.[69] Aquinas builds this further calling for sex work to be tolerated because of either a possible good or because it is avoiding another evil.[70] Quite a bit of literature has been written about the evils that can come from sex work.[71] People within the sex trade are aware that bad things can certainly exist in this landscape of work. Very little, however, has been written about the moral goods that can come from sex work. A traditional Catholic view of sex makes it difficult to address any type of good that comes from sex outside of marriage. The common thought process goes: if sex outside of marriage is a sin, no good is able to come from such a sin. There is, however, the theory of proportionality that might offer insight to the good that can come from sexual transactions.

For moral theologian Philip Keane, the sinfulness of an act can be mitigated for a proportionate reason rendering an act morally good.[72] Keane notes that something which may be considered a sinful act (i.e., sex outside of marriage) does not necessarily mean it should be judged to be objectively gravely morally evil.[73] In other words, for Keane, the sin of sex outside of marriage may have a proportionate reason to justify it morally.[74] I note proportionality in moral theology to identify that there is a school of thought in Catholic moral theology that looks at these acts in the context of the totality of an individual's life situation rather than as an act to be judged morally wrong based on a single criterion.

This discussion of morality is important when it comes to the sex industry because much of sexual ethics in sex work has been articulated in ways that (1) assume all sex workers are women, (2) those women are enslaved against their will, (3) all people who buy sex are men, and (4) they buy sex solely for reasons of sexual objectification. While a majority of sex workers are certainly cisgender women, the other three assumptions make for a problematic foundation when addressing the morality of sex work. When scenarios do fit these four assumptions—a woman who is enslaved against her will forced to have sex with men who only purchase sex to objectify and use her sexually—this constitutes trafficking, not consensual sex work. These assumptions fail to include the dynamics and goods that can come from engaging in sexual activity that gives one power or ownership over one's body (worker or consumer), sexual encounters that can help healing from sexual trauma, encounters that foster intimacy and human connection and that economically support individuals and families. In order to more proportionally address the morality of sex work, it is necessary to have an accurate understanding of as many components of the situation as possible. This accurate understanding is what moral theologians will call "seeing rightly" or "conceptual knowledge" when discerning if something is morally right or wrong.[75] In order for a society to act morally toward sex workers and the sex industry, it is necessary to have a correct view of the possible benefits sex work brings to the human community. This information can be gained from greater dialogue, empirical research, and listening seriously to the voices that make their needs known.[76]

Conclusion

Using Catholic social teaching, in the spirit of Catholic social thought, we have theological foundations for treating sex workers and consumers with dignity and respect. We have briefly covered the intersections of sex work and Catholicism in a number of ways. First, we examined the categorical inconsistency of sex work (prostitution) in official church documents, resulting in a conflation of consensual sex work with sex trafficking. We then covered the dignity of sex work as work, sex workers as free and responsible persons, and effects of sex work that can bring about healing and unity. After examining the principles of Catholic social thought and their application to sex work, we took a brief look at proportionality as one way of starting the conversation about goods that may come from sex work. However, theology is incomplete without more explicit pastoral considerations. In this same book, Okafor describes pastoral approaches in more detail grounded in Catholic frameworks that can help mitigate suffering in the sex industry to work toward a common good.

It is clear to church leaders, sex workers, and most of the general population that sex trafficking is wrong—the moral evil of forcing people into sexual labor is evident across these social groups. Recent church documents often consider the people who are non-consensually trafficked, forced against their will to partake in sex work. The condemnation of the trafficking of others is seen across all fields (sexuality and theology alike) as bad, harmful, and should be stopped. It is evident to those who listen to sex workers that the criminalization of sex work drives the ills of trafficking deeper underground, preventing the eradication of this evil and the rescue of those involved. Respecting sex workers means allowing those in the sex work community to organize and communicate to work toward the common goal of eliminating trafficking. Respecting sex workers means not only eradicating the laws that oppress and systemically disadvantage sex workers, but also working to implement policies that allow sex workers to thrive, giving autonomy to those in the sex trade, and working toward the betterment of society. In the frame of Catholic social thought, it is important to work in solidarity with sex workers to address the structures of sin that injure the human dignity of those within and around the sex industry. While many Catholics and Christians may feel a sense of moral superiority, or desire to look down on those who engage in sex work, it is important for the good of our society to name the harms caused by this approach. It is imperative, for the common good of humanity, to begin working for the support of sex workers because their misfortunes are not mere misfortunes of others, but are insults to the whole of humanity, the human family, the body of Christ. We should care, listen, help, and support because, in the words of John Paul II, we are all really responsible for all.[77]

Notes

1 Paul VI, "*Gaudium et Spes*: Pastoral Constitution on the Church in the Modern World," 1965, accessed http://www.vatican.va/archive/hist_councils/ii_vatican_council/documents/vat-ii_const_19651207_gaudium-et-spes_en.html. 27 "...whatever insults human dignity, such as subhuman living conditions, arbitrary imprisonment, deportation, slavery, prostitution, the selling of women and children; as well as disgraceful working conditions, where men are treated as mere tools for profit, rather than as free and responsible persons; all these things and others of their like are infamies indeed." It is important to note most of the references to prostitution as something that insults human dignity reference this document.

2 Pontifical Council for the Pastoral Care of the Migrants and Itinerant People, "International Meeting of Pastoral Care for the Liberation of Women of the Street," 2005, http://www.vatican.va/roman_curia/pontifical_councils/migrants/documents_1/rc_pc_migrants_doc_20210605_Iinc-past-don-strada-findoc_en.html.

3 Ibid. Conclusions 4.

4 *Catechism of the Catholic Church*, 2nd ed. (Citta del Vaticano: Libreria Editrice Vaticana, 2000). #2355.

5 Augustine of Hippo, *On Order [De Ordine]*, trans. Silvano Borruso (South Bend, IN: St. Augustine's Press, 2007). 2, 4. As Augustine describes prostitutes in one popular translation: "Remove prostitutes from the social order, however, and lust will destroy it. Let them rise to the same status as married women, and you will dishonor matrimony with an unseemly stain. This most unchaste lifestyle, therefore, places its practitioners at the very bottom of the social order." 65–67.

6 *Catechism of the Catholic Church*, #2355. Prostitution "usually involves women, but also men, children, and adolescents (The latter two cases involve the added sin of scandal.)."

7 Pontifical Council for the Pastoral Care of the Migrants and Itinerant People, "Women of the Street." 1.

8 Stop The Traffik, "Sex Trafficking VS Sex Work: Understanding the Difference," 24 September, 2018, https://www.stopthetraffik.org/sex-trafficking-vs-sex-work-understanding-difference/.

9 Pontifical Council for the Pastoral Care of the Migrants and Itinerant People, "Women of the Street." 1.

10 See references in Archbishop Bernardito Auza, "The Holy See And The Fight Against Human Trafficking," 2017, https://holyseemission.org/contents/statements/58ba091c820ab.php. Phrases like "sex slaves in prostitution," 2, "forced into prostitution," 4, and "subject to slavery in various forms...from prostitution to forced marriages," 5, indicate an equivalency of sex work with forced labor. See also United States Conference of Catholic Bishops Inc. and Conferencia del Episcopado Mexicano, "A Pastoral Letter Concerning Migration from the Catholic Bishops of Mexico and the United States," 2003, https://www.usccb.org/issues-and-action/human-life-and-dignity/immigration/strangers-no-longer-together-on-the-journey-of-hope. "Trafficking in persons...for the purposes of forced prostitution or labor" 90.

11 United States Conference of Catholic Bishops, "Strangers No Longer Together on the Journey of Hope," 2003, https://www.usccb.org/issues-and-action/human-life-and-dignity/immigration/strangers-no-longer-together-on-the-journey-of-hope. 90: "Trafficking in persons–in which men, women, and children from all over the globe are transported to other countries for the purposes of forced prostitution or labor–inherently rejects the dignity of the human person and exploits conditions of global poverty."

12 Migrants and Refugees Section of the Vatican, "Pastoral Orientations on Human Trafficking," 2019, https://migrants-refugees.va/documents/en/read/a4/pastoral-orientations-on-human-trafficking.pdf. Citing *Gaudium et Spes*, the Pastoral Orientations says: "At Vatican II the Catholic Church reaffirmed its historic concern about forced labour, stating that "slavery, prostitution, the selling of women and children; as well as disgraceful working conditions where men are treated as mere tools for profit rather than free and responsible persons [...] are infamies" (Gaudium et Spes, 27)." #6. Pairing this alongside treating people as "tools for profit rather than free and responsible persons" is an important component where we see the assumption of prostitution as never freely chosen.

13 Francis I, "Meeting With the Members of the General Assembly of the United Nations Organization," 2015, http://www.vatican.va/content/francesco/en/speeches/2015/september/documents/papa-francesco_20150925_onu-visita.html. 10.

14 Francis I, "Angelus," 30 July, 2017, para. 6, vatican.va/content/francesco/en/angelus/2017/documents/papa-francesco_angelus_20170730.html. "...today is the World Day against Trafficking in Persons, promoted by the United Nations. Each year thousands of innocent men, women and children are victims of exploitative labour and sexual abuse, and of organ trafficking, and it seems that we have become so accustomed to this, as to consider it a normal thing. This is deplorable; it is cruel; it is criminal!" Here we see the mention of exploitative sexual abuse named (sex trafficking) rather than using the term "prostitution."

15 Pontifical Council for Justice and Peace, "Compendium of the Social Doctrine of the Church," 2004, http://www.vatican.va/roman_curia/pontifical_councils/justpeace/documents/rc_pc_justpeace_doc_20060526_compendio-dott-soc_en.html. 158.

16 *Catechism of the Catholic Church*, #2355.

17 John Paul II, "Letter of John Paul II to Archbishop Jean-Louis Tauran on the Occasion of the International Conference Twenty-First Century Slavery - The Human Rights Dimension to Trafficking in Human Beings," 2002, http://www.vatican.va/content/john-paul-ii/en/letters/2002/documents/hf_jp-ii_let_20020515_tauran.html. 5.

18 Ibid. "The disturbing tendency to treat prostitution as a business or industry not only contributes to the trade in human beings, but is itself evidence of a growing tendency to detach freedom from the moral law and to reduce the rich mystery of human sexuality to a mere commodity."

19 Thomas Aquinas, *Summa Theologica*. trans. The Fathers of the English Dominican Province (1947), http://www.ccel.org/ccel/aquinas/summa.html. Question 10, article 11, Treatise on The Theological Virtues (QQ[1] - 46), citing Augustine in *De Ordine* (ii, 4), Aquinas writes: "human government also, those who are in authority, rightly tolerate certain evils, lest certain goods be lost, or certain greater evils be incurred: thus Augustine says (*De Ordine* ii, 4): 'If you do away with harlots, the world will be convulsed with lust.' Hence, though unbelievers sin in their rites, they may be tolerated, either on account of some good that ensues therefrom, or because of some evil avoided." Aquinas discusses sex work as either preventing the loss of some goods or avoiding some evil (adding to Augustine's claim that it is staving off more evil).

20 Pontifical Council for the Pastoral Care of the Migrants and Itinerant People, "Women of the Street." Para 1. For a discussion about the conundrum of agency referring to economic agency, see Boetumelo Julianne Nyasulu, "Coercion and Agency in Zimbabwean Sex Work," 2020, https://blogs.lse.ac.uk/gender/2020/07/13/coercion-and-agency-in-zimbabwean-sex-work/.

21 *Gaudium et Spes*, 28.

22 For a discussion of the consensual complexity between sex work, work, and capitalism see Cathy Reisenwitz, "Sex Work and the Spectrum of Coercion," 2020, https://www.liberalcurrents.com/sex-work-and-the-spectrum-of-coercion/.

23 Kate Lister, "Sex workers or prostitutes? Why words matter," 5 October, 2017, https://inews.co.uk/opinion/columnists/sex-workers-prostitutes-words-matter-95447.

24 James Martin, *Building a Bridge: How the Catholic Church and the LGBT Community Can Enter into a Relationship of Respect, Compassion, and Sensitivity* (New York, NY: HarperCollins Publishers, 2017). In this book, Fr. Jim Martin discusses the need for the Catholic Church to use the language of sexual identity (i.e., gay, lesbian) that gives dignity to those who hold these identities, rather than using the impersonal and largely biologically based "homosexual." 22.

25 Kate Ward. "Human and Alienating Work: What Sex Worker Advocates Can Teach Catholic Social Thought." *Journal of the Society of Christian Ethics 41, no.* 2 (2021): 261–78. https://doi.org/10.5840/jsce2021112952.

26 Clementine von Radics, "Foreward," in *A Whore's Manifesto: An Anthology of Writing and Artwork by Sex Workers*, ed. Kay Kassirer (Portland, OR: Thorntree Press, 2019). Para. 5.

27 Molly Smith and Juno Mac, *Revolting Prostitutes: The Fight for Sex Workers' Rights* (New York, NY: Verso, 2018). Chapter 2. For example, the authors critique the logic that sex work is "too awful" to be work, by identifying other jobs that are also considered awful or dangerous. They also rebut the concept of 'purchasing consent' by pointing out consent still exists in a commodified sexual transaction. Ward also expounds on this difference.

28 Daniel Finn, "Human Work in Catholic Social Thought," *American Journal of Economics and Sociology* 71, no. 4 (2012): 865, http://www.jstor.org/stable/41721429. 875.

29 John Paul II, "Laborem Exercens," 1981, http://www.vatican.va/content/john-paul-ii/en/encyclicals/documents/hf_jp-ii_enc_14091981_laborem-exercens.html. 6. When John Paul II writes "the basis for determining the value of human work is not primarily the kind of work being done but the fact that the one who is doing it is a person."

30 Amin R. Yacoub, "Consensual sex work: An overview of sex-workers' human dignity in law, philosophy, and Abrahamic religions," *Women's Studies International Forum* 76 (2019), https://doi.org/10.1016/j.wsif.2019.102274. 8.

31 Melissa Gira Grant, *Playing the Whore: The Work of Sex Work* (New York, NY: Verso, 2014). 4.

32 Yacoub, "Consensual Sex Work." 10.

33 *Gaudium et Spes*, 26.
34 Ibid., 28
35 Hilary Caldwell and John de Wit, "Women's experiences buying sex in Australia – Egalitarian powermoves," *Sexualities* (2020): 7, https://doi.org/10.1177/1363460719896972. Caldwell and de Wit describe these reasons, citing six different studies: Philip Birch, "Making sense of men's procurement of sexual services" (PhD thesis University of New South Wales, Australia, 2014); Elizabeth Bernstein, *Temporarily Yours: Intimacy, Authenticity, and the Commerce of Sex* (Chicago, IL: University of Chicago Press, 2010); Hilary J. Caldwell, "Long-Term Clients Who Access Commercial Sexual Services in Australia" (Master's thesis University of Sydney, Australia, 2011); Thomas J. Holt and Kristie R. Blevins, "Examining Sex Work from the Client's Perspective: Assessing Johns Using on-line Data," article, *Deviant Behavior* 28, no. 4 (2007); Marian K. Pitts et al., "Who Pays for Sex and Why? An Analysis of Social and Motivational Factors Associated With Male Clients of Sex Workers," *Archives of Sexual Behavior* 33, no. 4 (2004), https://doi.org/10.1023/B:ASEB.0000028888.48796.4f; Teela Sanders, "The politics of sexual citizenship: Commercial sex and disability," *Disability & Society* 22, no. 5 (2007), https://doi.org/10.1080/09687590701427479.
36 Ibid., 7–10.
37 J. Milburn Thompson, *Introducing Catholic Social Thought* (New York, NY: Orbis Books, 2010), 6–7.
38 Thompson, *Introducing Catholic Social Thought*, 58–64.
39 *Gaudium et Spes*, 26.
40 For a detailed example of the application of common good to poverty, see David Hollenbach, *The Common Good and Christian Ethics* (Cambridge: Cambridge University Press, 2002).
41 Martin Schlag, ed., *Handbook of Catholic Social Teaching: A Guide for Christians in the World Today* (Washington, D.C.: The Catholic University of America Press, 2017), 41. Schlag notes five characteristics of the common good: (1) that it is common, involving every member of society; (2) indivisible, not to be divided among members of society; (3) the flourishing of all people and the whole person, named a primary goal; (4) transcendental, through time and all of creation; and (5) that it is an arduous good, or difficult to attain because of the necessity of the constant ability to seek the good of others as your own.
42 See Endnote 19.
43 Thomas Massaro, *Living Justice: Catholic Social Teaching in Action* (Lanaham, MD: Rowman & Littlefield, 2008), 84.
44 John Paul II, "Sollicitudo rei Socialis," 1987, http://www.vatican.va/content/john-paul-ii/en/encyclicals/documents/hf_jp-ii_enc_30121987_sollicitudo-rei-socialis.html. 38.
45 Fred Kramer, *Doing Faithjustice: An Introduction to Catholic Social Thought* (New York, NY: Paulist Press, 2004), 107.
46 Bryan N. Massingale, *Racial Justice and the Catholic Church* (Maryknoll, NY: Orbis Books, 2010), 74–78.
47 Karen Ross, Megan K. McCabe, and Sara Wilhelm Garbers, "Christian Sexual Ethics and the #MeToo Movement: Three Moments of Reflection on Sexual Violence and Women's Bodies," *Journal for the Society of Christian Ethics* 39, no. 2 (2019): 346–51, https://doi.org/10.5840/jsce201939238.
48 John Paul II, "Reconciliation and Penance," 1984, http://www.vatican.va/content/john-paul-ii/en/apost_exhortations/documents/hf_jp-ii_exh_02121984_reconciliatio-et-paenitentia.html. 16.
49 Thompson, *Introducing Catholic Social Thought*. 63.
50 Jacquelyn Monroe, "Women in Street Prostitution: The Result of Poverty and the Brunt of Inequity," Article, *Journal of Poverty* 9, no. 3 (2005), https://doi.org/10.1300/J134v09n03_04.

51 Francis I, "Laudato Si'," 2015, http://www.vatican.va/content/francesco/en/encyclicals/documents/papa-francesco_20150524_enciclica-laudato-si.html. 158.
52 Thompson, *Introducing Catholic Social Thought*. 60.
53 John XXIII, "Pacem in Terris," 1963, http://www.vatican.va/content/john-xxiii/en/encyclicals/documents/hf_j-xxiii_enc_11041963_pacem.html. 74.
54 Francis I, "Laudato Si'." 144.
55 Gabriela Silva Leite, "The prostitute movement in Brazil: Culture and religiosity," *International Review of Mission* 85, no. 338 (1996). 425–426.
56 World Synod of Catholic Bishops, "Justice in the World," 1971, accessed https://www.cctwincities.org/wp-content/uploads/2015/10/Justicia-in-Mundo.pdf. 9.
57 Massaro, *Living Justice: Catholic Social Teaching in Action*. 86.
58 Lia Claire Scholl, *I Heart Sex Workers: A Christian Response to People in the Sex Trade* (Chalice Press, 2012). 114.
59 Massaro, *Living Justice: Catholic Social Teaching in Action*. 86.
60 John XXIII, "Pacem in Terris." 60–63. We see these paragraphs sit under headings like "*Responsibilities of the Public Authority, and Rights and Duties of Individuals,*" "*Reconciliation and Protection of Rights and Duties of Individuals,*" and "*Duty of Promoting the Rights of Individuals.*"
61 Thompson, *Introducing Catholic Social Thought*. 64.
62 Ibid.
63 John XXIII, "Pacem in Terris." 64.
64 Ward, "Human and Alienating Work," 277.
65 Scholl, *I Heart Sex Workers*, 143–161. In this chapter, Scholl offers many practical ways individuals and groups can offer support to those who trade sex. For more information on decriminalization and harm reduction, see also Positive Women's Network, "Harm Reduction Fact Sheet," 2019, https://www.pwn-usa.org/wp-content/uploads/2019/01/harm-reduction-factsheet-final.pdf.
66 Ibid., 143.
67 Joseph A. Catania, Susan M. Kegeles, and Thomas J. Coates, "Towards an Understanding of Risk Behavior: An AIDS Risk Reduction Model (ARRM)," *Health Education & Behavior* 17, no. 1 (1990): 57.
68 Scholl, *I Heart Sex Workers*, 144. Principles are generally described as respecting the rights of others, a commitment to evidence, a commitment to social justice, and the avoidance of stigma. See for more information: Harm Reduction International, "What is Harm Reduction?," 2021, https://www.hri.global/what-is-harm-reduction. In Catholic teaching, harm reduction falls within the principle of gradualism and the principle of lesser evil.
69 Augustine of Hippo, *On Order [De Ordine]*. II, 4.12.
70 Aquinas, *Summa Theologica*. (Q. 10, art. 11)
71 See, for example, Sascha Settegast, *Prostitution and the Good of Sex*, vol. 44 (2018). and David A. J. Richards, "Commercial Sex and th Rights of the Person: A Moral Argument for the Decriminalization of Prostitution," *University of Pennsylvania Law Review* 127, no. 5 (1979), https://core.ac.uk/download/pdf/195160739.pdf. sections II. C. and IV.
72 Philip S. Keane, *Sexual Morality: A Catholic Perspective* (New York, NY: Paulist Press, 1977), 46–51.
73 Keane, *Sexual Morality*, 181–82. What I have termed here "considered a sinful act" Keane describes as "the fact that significant ontic evil is present." 181.
74 Richard M. Gula, *Reason Informed by Faith: Foundations of Catholic Morality* (Mahaw, NJ: Paulist Press, 1989), 269. As the opposite of ontic evil, Gula describes premoral or ontic goods. "…all human actions contain some features which enhance our humanity and some features which restrict it. To the extent that these features enhance the potential for human goodness and growth, they are premoral or ontic goods."

75 See William C. Mattison, *Introducing Moral Theology: True Happiness and the Virtues* (Grand Rapids, MI: Brazos Press, 2008), 96. Mattison described the saying "we cannot act rightly if we do not see rightly." See also Gula, *Reason Informed by Faith*, 83. Gula describes conceptual knowledge as "the kind of knowledge we have when we have the right information and have mastered the facts."

76 There exist some unrealized theological avenues when discussing the moral or ethical implications of sex work. More theological attention beyond the scope of this work should be given to the moral components of sex work.

77 John Paul II, "Sollicitudo rei Socialis," 38.

Bibliography

Aquinas, Thomas. *Summa Theologica*. Translated by The Fathers of the English Dominican Province, 1947. http://www.ccel.org/ccel/aquinas/summa.html.

Augustine of Hippo. *On Order* [*De Ordine*]. Translated by Silvano Borruso. South Bend, IN: St. Augustine's Press, 2007.

Bernstein, Elizabeth. *Temporarily Yours: Intimacy, Authenticity, and the Commerce of Sex*. Chicago, IL: University of Chicago Press, 2010.

Birch, Philip. "Making Sense of Men's Procurement of Sexual Services." PhD thesis, University of New South Wales, Australia, 2014.

Caldwell, Hilary, and John de Wit. "Women's Experiences Buying Sex in Australia – Egalitarian Powermoves." *Sexualities* (2020): 1–25. https://doi.org/10.1177/1363460719896972.

Caldwell, Hilary J. "Long-Term Clients Who Access Commercial Sexual Services in Australia." Master's thesis, University of Sydney, Australia, 2011.

Catania, Joseph A., Susan M. Kegeles, and Thomas J. Coates. "Towards an Understanding of Risk Behavior: An Aids Risk Reduction Model (Arrm)." *Health Education & Behavior* 17, no. 1 (1990): 53–72.

Catechism of the Catholic Church. 2nd ed. Citta del Vaticano: Libreria Editrice Vaticana, 2000.

Finn, Daniel. "Human Work in Catholic Social Thought." *American Journal of Economics and Sociology* 71, no. 4 (2012): 874–885. http://www.jstor.org/stable/41721429.

Francis I. "Angelus." 30 July, 2017. vatican.va/content/francesco/en/angelus/2017/documents/papa-francesco_angelus_20170730.html.

Francis I. "Laudato Si'." 2015, http://www.vatican.va/content/francesco/en/encyclicals/documents/papa-francesco_20150524_enciclica-laudato-si.html.

Francis I. "Meeting with the Members of the General Assembly of the United Nations Organization." 2015, http://www.vatican.va/content/francesco/en/speeches/2015/september/documents/papa-francesco_20150925_onu-visita.html.

Grant, Melissa Gira. *Playing the Whore: The Work of Sex Work*. New York, NY: Verso, 2014.

Gula, Richard M. *Reason Informed by Faith: Foundations of Catholic Morality*. Mahaw, NJ: Paulist Press, 1989.

Harm Reduction International. "What Is Harm Reduction?", 2021, https://www.hri.global/what-is-harm-reduction.

Hollenbach, David. *The Common Good and Christian Ethics*. Cambridge: Cambridge University Press, 2002.

Holt, Thomas J., and Kristie R.Blevins. "Examining Sex Work from the Client's Perspective: Assessing Johns Using on-Line Data." *Deviant Behavior* 28, no. 4 (2007): 333–354.

John Paul II. "Laborem Exercens." 1981, http://www.vatican.va/content/john-paul-ii/en/encyclicals/documents/hf_jp-ii_enc_14091981_laborem-exercens.html.

John Paul II. "Letter of John Paul II to Archbishop Jean-Louis Tauran on the Occasion of the International Conference Twenty-First Century Slavery - the Human Rights Dimension to Trafficking in Human Beings." 2002, http://www.vatican.va/content/john-paul-ii/en/letters/2002/documents/hf_jp-ii_let_20020515_tauran.html.

John Paul II. "Reconciliation and Penance." 1984, http://www.vatican.va/content/john-paul-ii/en/apost_exhortations/documents/hf_jp-ii_exh_02121984_reconciliatio-et-paenitentia.html.

John Paul II. "Sollicitudo Rei Socialis." 1987, http://www.vatican.va/content/john-paul-ii/en/encyclicals/documents/hf_jp-ii_enc_30121987_sollicitudo-rei-socialis.html.

John XXIII. "Pacem in Terris." 1963, http://www.vatican.va/content/john-xxiii/en/encyclicals/documents/hf_j-xxiii_enc_11041963_pacem.html.

Keane, Philip S. *Sexual Morality: A Catholic Perspective*. New York, NY: Paulist Press, 1977.

Kramer, Fred. *Doing Faith Justice: An Introduction to Catholic Social Thought*. New York, NY: Paulist Press, 2004.

Leite, Gabriela Silva. "The Prostitute Movement in Brazil: Culture and Religiosity." *International Review of Mission* 85, no. 338 (1996): 417–426.

Lister, Kate. "Sex Workers or Prostitutes? Why Words Matter." 5 October, 2017. https://inews.co.uk/opinion/columnists/sex-workers-prostitutes-words-matter-95447.

Martin, James. *Building a Bridge: How the Catholic Church and the LGBT Community Can Enter into a Relationship of Respect, Compassion, and Sensitivity*. New York, NY: HarperCollins Publishers, 2017.

Massaro, Thomas. *Living Justice: Catholic social teaching in Action*. Lanaham, MD: Rowman & Littlefield, 2008.

Massingale, Bryan N. *Racial Justice and the Catholic Church*. Maryknoll, NY: Orbis Books, 2010.

Mattison, William C. *Introducing Moral Theology: True Happiness and the Virtues*. Grand Rapids, MI: Brazos Press, 2008.

Migrants and Refugees Section of the Vatican. "Pastoral Orientations on Human Trafficking." 2019, https://migrants-refugees.va/documents/en/read/a4/pastoral-orientations-on-human-trafficking.pdf.

Monroe, Jacquelyn. "Women in Street Prostitution: The Result of Poverty and the Brunt of Inequity." Article. *Journal of Poverty* 9, no. 3 (2005): 69–88. https://doi.org/10.1300/J134v09n03_04.

Nyasulu, Boetumelo Julianne. "Coercion and Agency in Zimbabwean Sex Work." 2020, https://blogs.lse.ac.uk/gender/2020/07/13/coercion-and-agency-in-zimbabwean-sex-work/.

Paul VI. "Gaudium Et Spes: Pastoral Constitution on the Church in the Modern World." 1965, accessed http://www.vatican.va/archive/hist_councils/ii_vatican_council/documents/vat-ii_const_19651207_gaudium-et-spes_en.html.

Pitts, Marian K., Anthony M. A. Smith, Jeffrey Grierson, Mary O'Brien, and Sebastian Misson. "Who Pays for Sex and Why? An Analysis of Social and Motivational Factors Associated with Male Clients of Sex Workers." *Archives of Sexual Behavior* 33, no. 4 (2004): 353–358. https://doi.org/10.1023/B:ASEB.0000028888.48796.4f.

Pontifical Council for Justice and Peace. "Compendium of the Social Doctrine of the Church." 2004, http://www.vatican.va/roman_curia/pontifical_councils/justpeace/documents/rc_pc_justpeace_doc_20060526_compendio-dott-soc_en.html.

Pontifical Council for the Pastoral Care of the Migrants and Itinerant People. "International Meeting of Pastoral Care for the Liberation of Women of the Street." 2005, http://www.vatican.va/roman_curia/pontifical_councils/migrants/documents_1/rc_pc_migrants_doc_20210605_Iinc-past-don-strada-findoc_en.html.

Positive Women's Network. "Harm Reduction Fact Sheet." 2019, https://www.pwn-usa.org/wp-content/uploads/2019/01/harm-reduction-factsheet-final.pdf.

Reisenwitz, Cathy. "Sex Work and the Spectrum of Coercion." 2020, https://www.liberalcurrents.com/sex-work-and-the-spectrum-of-coercion/.

Richards, David A. J. "Commercial Sex and The Rights of the Person: A Moral Argument for the Decriminalization of Prostitution." *University of Pennsylvania Law Review* 127, no. 5 (1979): 1195–1287. https://core.ac.uk/download/pdf/195160739.pdf.

Ross, Karen, Megan K. McCabe, and Sara Wilhelm Garbers. "Christian Sexual Ethics and the #Metoo Movement: Three Moments of Reflection on Sexual Violence and Women's Bodies." *Journal for the Society of Christian Ethics* 39, no. 2 (2019): 339–356. https://doi.org/10.5840/jsce201939238.

Sanders, Teela. "The Politics of Sexual Citizenship: Commercial Sex and Disability." *Disability & Society* 22, no. 5 (2007): 439–455. https://doi.org/10.1080/09687590701427479.

Schlag, Martin, ed. *Handbook of Catholic Social Teaching: A Guide for Christians in the World Today*. Washington, D.C.: The Catholic University of America Press, 2017.

Scholl, Lia Claire. *I Heart Sex Workers: A Christian Response to People in the Sex Trade*. Chalice Press: St Louis, MI, 2012.

Settegast, Sascha. *Prostitution and the Good of Sex*. Vol. 44, 2018. doi:10.5840/soctheorpract201862040.

Smith, Molly and Juno Mac. *Revolting Prostitutes: The Fight for Sex Workers' Rights*. New York, NY: Verso, 2018.

Stop The Traffik. "Sex Trafficking Vs Sex Work: Understanding the Difference." 24 September, 2018. https://www.stopthetraffik.org/sex-trafficking-vs-sex-work-understanding-difference/.

Thompson, J. Milburn. *Introducing Catholic Social Thought*. New York, NY: Orbis Books, 2010.

United States Conference of Catholic Bishops. "Strangers No Longer Together on the Journey of Hope." 2003, https://www.usccb.org/issues-and-action/human-life-and-dignity/immigration/strangers-no-longer-together-on-the-journey-of-hope.

United States Conference of Catholic Bishops Inc. and Conferencia del Episcopado Mexicano. "A Pastoral Letter Concerning Migration from the Catholic Bishops of Mexico and the United States." 2003, https://www.usccb.org/issues-and-action/human-life-and-dignity/immigration/strangers-no-longer-together-on-the-journey-of-hope.

von Radics, Clementine. "Foreward." In *A Whore's Manifesto: An Anthology of Writing and Artwork by Sex Workers*, edited by Kay Kassirer. Portland, OR: Thorntree Press, 2019.

Ward, Kate. "*Human and Alienating Work: What Sex Worker Advocates Can Teach Catholic social thought*." Paper presented at the Society for Christian Ethics Annual Meeting, Virtual,January 4–13, 2021.

Ward, Kate. "Human and Alienating Work: What Sex Worker Advocates Can Teach Catholic Social Thought." *Journal of the Society of Christian Ethics* 41, no. 2 (2021): 261–278. https://doi.org/10.5840/jsce2021112952.

World Synod of Catholic Bishops. "Justice in the World." 1971, https://www.cctwincities.org/wp-content/uploads/2015/10/Justicia-in-Mundo.pdf.

Yacoub, Amin R. "Consensual Sex Work: An Overview of Sex-Workers' Human Dignity in Law, Philosophy, and Abrahamic Religions." *Women's Studies International Forum* 76 (2019). https://doi.org/10.1016/j.wsif.2019.102274.

5 'A Catholic and an Agnostic Walk into a Homeless Camp…' Collaborating Across Religious Differences[1]

Yvonne C. Zimmerman

Introduction

Accounting for the ways that religion impacts efforts to end human trafficking is a complex endeavor, one which defies simplistic categorizations classifying the effect of religion as either inherently harmful or intrinsically beneficial. A decade ago in an article entitled "Sex, Secularism and Religious Influence in U. S. Politics," sociologist Elizabeth Bernstein and religious studies scholar Janet Jakobsen analyzed the impact of religion on antitrafficking activism in the U.S.[2] They identified a range of effects, positive and negative. The positive impacts they identified include the way that religious engagement with the issue of human trafficking—first by evangelical Christians, and now by a wide variety of religious groups—has contributed to the elevation of this issue to greater social, political and cultural prominence, as well as physical rescues of individuals from trafficking situations. While not everyone that would-be rescuers perceive as "trafficked" understand themselves in the same way, many individuals, nevertheless, expressed genuine gratitude for these groups' concern and efforts on their behalf.[3] The negative impacts they identified include the financial crises many peer-based sex worker projects have experienced as a result of refusing to capitulate to religiously backed anti-prostitution pledges that require, as a condition of continued funding, that organizations publicly repudiate sex work and prostitution; expanded initiatives to criminalise domestic sex workers and other participants who work consensually in the street-based sexual economy; the arrest and subsequent deportation of migrant sex workers, both documented and undocumented, who are apprehended in immigration enforcement stings, antitrafficking raids, and undercover prostitution busts; and the systematic funnelling of formerly trafficked persons who gain certification as victims of human trafficking into dead-end, minimum wage jobs.[4]

The range of the effects Bernstein and Jakobsen identify indicates that religion has multiple and even contradictory effects in the antitrafficking movement.[5] Indeed, their findings showed that, contrary to popular wisdom, it is not the case that religious antitrafficking policy, activism, advocacy and service provision is necessarily more conservative; nor that secular antitrafficking policy, activism, advocacy and service provision is necessarily more progressive.

DOI: 10.4324/9780429328824-6

The situation with religion is more complicated than that. A recent study investigating the roles of faith-based organizations in responses to human trafficking in the UK came to similar conclusions. Although the religious actors involved in antitrafficking work in the UK are mainly Christian, the study notes that "There is no one 'Christian response' to modern slavery. The picture is complex."[6]

For the past several years, my colleague, Letitia Campbell, and I have been working on a project in which we hope to confront a particular contradiction that faces progressive Christians who want to become active in the antitrafficking movement. The contradiction is this: We have observed that progressive Christians often come to the issue of human trafficking motivated by concerns about sexual violence, sexual and economic exploitation of women, or the vulnerability of particular groups, such as immigrants or LGBTQ youth. For progressive Christians, these are *religious* concerns that are rooted in and reflective of their religious values and spiritual practices. However, the most common antitrafficking rhetoric in the U.S.—and, notably, a rhetoric that has been widely embraced by religious and faith-based antitrafficking organizations and activists—frames sex work of all kinds as inherently oppressive and tends to reflect heteronormative ideas about gender and sexual respectability. Moreover, the policy positions that have become associated with this type of antitrafficking rhetoric tend to rely heavily on criminal justice approaches such as policing and incarceration to prevent and remedy trafficking. For example, antitrafficking measures often rely heavily on police surveillance of poor communities and communities of color, and of queer, trans and gender non-conforming people—approaches that have the unintended effect of expanding the criminalization of already-vulnerable communities and contributing to patterns of over-policing and mass incarceration. Similarly, in the name of "fighting trafficking," feminists who, in principle, reject the sexual double standard that exalts an ideal of sexual purity for women, may be persuaded to support policies and social service models that reflect the gendered politics of sexual respectability and evangelical Christian purity culture. Thus the core moral values and concerns that inspire progressive Christians to become involved in ending human trafficking do not find an easy landing place in the U.S. antitrafficking movement. In fact, being credibly or legibly "against trafficking" implies support for policies and practices that are significantly at odds with many of progressive Christianity's core moral commitments.

Our contention is that progressive Christians can and must respond to human trafficking in our communities and in the broader social and economic systems that shape our world, and must do so in ways that are reflective of and consistent with their deeply held commitments. We believe that human trafficking can be resisted in ways that are shaped by antiracist analysis and commitment; that support the rights and dignity of LGBTQ+ and gender non-conforming people; that work in conjunction with peer-based sex worker groups; and that build on decades of work to expand women's sexual agency and eliminate violence against women. We believe that no fight to end human trafficking will be successful without incorporating critiques of the economic system, of immigration policies, and of the traditions of white supremacy that continue to shape American life.

Believing that is possible to oppose human trafficking in ways that reflect progressive Christianity's core moral values, our research has taken us across the country to a variety of organizations doing innovative work to combat human trafficking and address its impact. We explore the commitments that guide these organizations and discuss lessons from their work that can inform progressive Christian communities and groups as they respond to the phenomenon of human trafficking, as well as to people affected by trafficking in their local communities.

This chapter draws on our research, but with a slightly different analytical focus. Here, I will explore what it means for secular antitrafficking organizations and religious or faith-based ones to partner together in common antitrafficking work. Specifically, I am interested in identifying factors that make such partnerships genuinely viable. This is not dispassionate or fully objective inquiry. In the U.S., as elsewhere, the issue of human trafficking has become deeply polarized, with the dominant, radical feminist perspective contending that all sex work is inherently oppressive and exploitative, while the more marginalized sex worker activist perspective counters that, although sex work is oppressive and exploitative under certain conditions and circumstances, it is not necessarily so and can be compatible with personal agency and individual freedom.[7] Debates between these sides are not only heated but, as Lauren McGrow notes, often downright hateful. The result is individuals and organizations virtually at war with each other as they fight for ground for their political perspective.[8] Critically important issues are at stake in these arguments; however, in their current form they are anything but life-giving and constructive for anyone involved. In what follows I chart a relational path through a very polarized issue that has resulted in constructive outcomes for both practitioners and clients. Minimally, this is an interesting case study about the development of a personal friendship that had public consequences. Or, perhaps what can be learned from this case study, and other similar collaborations, has the potential to point a way around the swamp of intractable debates toward safer ground that is practical and generative in its effects.

Case study: Prax(us) and the Denver Homeless Ministry

The specific partnership that is the focus of my case study is one between a small, community-based non-profit organization called Prax(us), an anti-human trafficking organization serving homeless youth and young adults, and the Denver Homeless Ministry, an initiative of the Catholic Arch Dioses of Denver that operates in connection with the Knights of Columbus to serve homeless people in downtown Denver.[9]

Despite the fact that each works with Denver's homeless population, which is a significant similarity, I want to emphasize how very different these organizations are. The Denver Homeless Ministry is a conventional Catholic charitable organization. Its mission statement reads:

> The mission of the DHM is to provide awareness to people of our community as well as provide opportunities for them to serve the homeless by seeing them as our equals and friends. All we do is guided by showing the love of the Lord to all we come in contact with, that the homeless may understand by our actions that we care for them because Christ cares for us. We are committed to being open to serving when and where needed. Sometimes we only get one chance to reach out to another human being to make a difference in their lives. We want that mission to be a positive experience for the person reaching out and the person whom we have the opportunity to reach out to.[10]

The Denver Homeless Ministry website describes how this vision is instantiated, explaining:

> The Denver Homeless Ministry is all about Outreach. Partnering with other ministries and non-profit organizations concerned about the homeless and the poor in the Denver area, DHM serves our street friends by ministering to them and by providing them with food, clothing, and toiletries.[11]

The ministry provides a weekly meal from its base at the Knights of Columbus building, and provides snacks, toiletries and small clothing items (like socks, underwear, gloves and hats) in Ziplock bags that it distributes at a nearby park that serves as a gathering spot for many of Denver's homeless community, and it maintains a free clothes closet of gently used clean clothes.

Prax(us) served trafficked youth and young adults living on Denver's streets–homeless, runaway, age-outs from the foster care system, etc. Their mission statement read:

> Prax(us) is dedicated to ending human trafficking. We address the root causes of exploitation by creating systemic change and providing direct services through a comprehensive street outreach program. We conduct street outreach through a harm-reduction lens that supports youth agency and facilitates access to resources. We achieve systemic change through community organizing, collaborative relationships, community education, and policy work.[12]

Through their street outreach program, Prax(us) built relationships with youth and young adults experiencing homelessness and human trafficking. Prax(us)'s executive director, Mary Landerholm, explained that street outreach involved "a lot of hands-on, one-on-one conversation and relationship-building with the folks most impacted by the crime [of human trafficking]." She described:

> "We sit out on the 16th Street Mall all the time with my backpack and we talk about other things, like the weather, the game, where are you from? How's it going? How many siblings do you have?" "What's important,"

> she continued, "is the culture of the relationship, and the ways that we build this out. It's gotten so institutionalized. Like, what happened to just sitting across the table and saying, 'Hey...'? [Or] running into somebody on the corner [and having a conversation]?"

In the first ten months of 2015, the organization connected with over 15,000 youth and young adults in the Denver metro area. It was Prax(us)'s consistent presence on the streets in particular that built their reputation and credibility in Denver's street community.

In addition to street outreach, advocacy was also a central piece of Prax(us)'s work. Recognizing that many of the services offered to vulnerable and exploited people either do not fit their needs or make manipulative or otherwise inappropriate demands of them, Prax(us) attempted to intervene in and shift the entire range of systems youth and young people navigate, including—and, indeed, often starting with—those that are designed to help, like the social services and the criminal justice systems. For instance, they would advocate on behalf of trans and gender non-conforming youth whose identities, bodies, and experiences do not fit binary gender categories that determine the accommodation most shelter services provide. Mary explained that Prax(us) would be the advocate who would speak with organizations about how they could shift the way they offered their services to better meet the needs of the youth using them. "Our aim," she said, was to "chang[e] the way that systems respond to better fit the need of the community."

Prax(us) also developed a peer mentorship leadership training that taught homeless youth community organization and advocacy skills, an initiative that turned out to be wildly popular with the youth. Mary recounted that she was initially sceptical about this component:

> "I didn't think it was going to work. I gave my board pushback on that, said, 'This isn't going to work. You can't get people to organize who are in the middle of the muck' because when you think from a social work perspective, it's like 'Oh, they need Maslow's hierarchy of needs before they can engage.' But that is not the truth. I was dead wrong. So wrong."

To Mary's surprise, the youth in the leadership training program threw themselves into local political issues they thought were important, like abolishing the city's urban camping ban and developing an initiative to create affordable transit with the city's light rail system. They also worked on national issues, like the "Ban the Box" campaign that seeks to remove questions about criminal conviction history from employment applications. The purpose of the program was to connect young people both to the movements and to leaders in and ancillary to the antitrafficking movement, in ways that strategically platformed their voices. Mary explained:

> "Prax(us) really wanted to be able to get the voices of those who are not able to access the system, raise those folks as leaders, and have them go

> out, as [Paulo Friere's] *Pedagogy of the Oppressed* talks about, using their experience as the springboard for their own liberation. We wanted to start to position and platform those folks [as experts and leaders] in the movement."

At this juncture it is important to note that I am describing Prax(us) in the past tense because the organization no longer exists. Prax(us) disbanded and has been closed since October 2015. One of the challenges Letitia and I faced in the course of our research was how frequently and abruptly the landscape of local social service provision for trafficking survivors changes. For example, in our study one of the organizations we wanted to include that focuses on supporting LGBTQ+ people held in immigration detention centers at the U.S.–Mexico border has paused operations for what was supposed to be six weeks, but is now over six months and counting. Another organization changed its name and has scaled back its activity significantly as a result of one of its primary partnering organizations losing its permit to hold weekly needle exchanges. Larger organizations, like Polaris, Free the Slaves, International Justice Mission, or Salvation Army seem to enjoy greater organizational stability. But these bigger players are not primarily the types of organizations we are exploring. We want to be able to point to local, grassroots examples of communities organizing to address human trafficking and Prax(us) fit this bill.

Further motivating our desire to include Prax(us) in our research is that application of harm reduction principles with youth and young people specifically is unusual in the U.S. Rooted in strong commitments to public health and human rights, the philosophy of harm reduction holds that building knowledge, agency and options are meaningful strategies for reducing the harmful consequences of high-risk behaviours, circumstances and situations.[13] Harm reduction has had an uphill battle for public acceptance and traction within the U.S. antitrafficking movement, where rescue and abstinence models of anti-trafficking intervention and rehabilitation dominate. Consequently, using harm reduction principles with youth is not a widely employed strategy in this country and, in fact, Prax(us) was the only human trafficking organization in the state of Colorado using harm reduction with youth.

All the same, we had the concerns one would expect in deciding to include an organization that technically no longer exists in our study. In the end, we decided to keep Prax(us) in our project because of the uniqueness of using harm reduction with youth, and because we thought that there might be something interesting to learn from studying an organization that did not make it. We were imagining that our analysis might focus on identifying the confluence of factors that led to Prax(us)'s closure in a sort of cautionary tale scenario. What we did not anticipate was happening upon one of the most fascinating case studies in religious–secular partnership that we have ever encountered.

Mary described to us the painful process of closing the organization. Dismantling took about three months, during which time she prioritized sharing as widely as possible all of Prax(us)'s materials and trainings with all their stakeholders and community partners. She also began to identify organizations who would pick up various pieces of Prax(us)'s programing so that, as much as possible, Prax(us)'s work would continue through other organizations. We were not surprised to hear that the local chapter of the Sex Workers Outreach Project (SWOP) picked up some of the street outreach Prax(us) did with sex workers; but we were very surprised to hear that the Denver Homeless Ministry also picked up some of this work. Further, the way that Mary spoke about their partnership in such glowing terms, and with such evident respect, amazed us even more.

The ways that faith-based organizations engage the issue of human trafficking, and how religious organizations use their values and moral frameworks, particularly around sex and sexuality, as a central platform for taking up antitrafficking work has long been of interest to me. I admit that my body and mind often cringe pre-emptively because it is so often done so manipulatively or insensitively. This collaboration was clearly not that. We decided we wanted to return for a second interview in which we would interview Mary and Denver Homeless Ministry executive director Tonya Cangelosi together about their collaboration and what makes it work. Mary generously facilitated an email introduction to Tonya, who agreed to an interview. Several months later, I was able to return to Denver, and we met at the Denver Homeless Ministry office and sat down together for a conversation, after which they took me along for some street outreach to show me how they work.

They began our conversation by describing how they met. At the time, Tonya was with another group, a secular organization called Stand Up for Kids which is a nationwide non-profit that works to end youth homelessness.[14] Part of their work was providing a weekly meal for street youth in a nearby church basement. Tonya served as a volunteer. Several other local organizations, including Prax(us), used the same church basement to serve free meals other days of the week. Tonya has long had a soft spot in her heart for youth living on the streets because of her own experience of homelessness as a young person. She recounted that she struggled with Standup for Kids, because they have a firm rule of serving only young people under the age of 25. Tonya had a hard a time with their practice of turning people away when they aged out. She recounted:

> "I couldn't give up on those guys. And I noticed that Prax(us) never turned people away; they talked to them, where Stand Up for Kids was like, 'Are we 25 and under? Let me see an ID.'"

So Tonya decided to start her own ministry and in 2011 launched the Denver Homeless Ministry.

As Tonya launched the organization, she would sometimes come along with Prax(us) for street outreach. Mary reflected, "We were serving the same people, so it was natural for us to be in the same space together." She also noted that Tonya and the Denver Homeless Ministry "started to model what they saw us do, and then to implement that." As Mary began the process of closing Prax (us), she approached Tonya more formally about doing street outreach with sex workers. Tonya's reply was immediately affirmative: "I was like, 'yeah, I wanna get into that, too!'"

Tonya faced a dilemma, though, which she described as follows: "[Prax(us) hand[ed] out condoms and harm reduction kits for drug users and stuff and I'm like, 'I'm Catholic! Anybody sees me doing that and I'm excommunicated!'" I want to be careful not to characterize Tonya as prudish or a holier-than-thou religious type, because she is neither. But she is a committed Catholic, even though she recognizes that the official teachings of the Catholic Church do not comport well with the realities of surviving on the streets. She explained:

> "I believe in teaching someone why you don't use [drugs], but I understand that on the streets you can't just say [that, or], 'Let me tell you why condoms aren't good, and why you should abstain [from sex].' Is that gonna work? Definitely not!"

The scope of their mission and religious orientation of their framework severely constricts the way the Denver Homeless Ministry can engage with sex workers and people who sell sex. Yet, Tonya said of Prax(us):

> "I love what they're doing, and I see people's lives changing.... One of the main things I learned from Prax(us) is the importance of giving people their power back, and that to do that you need to support people where they're at today, not where you want them to be."

Even though her religious commitments prevent her from distributing condoms personally, Tonya nevertheless recognizes the value of Prax(us)'s harm reduction approach.

The challenge Mary and Tonya faced was to figure out how they could serve together while respecting each other's lenses and commitments. Mary recalled:

> "[W]e both started asking, 'Okay, how do we do this together in a parallel way that's good for you and your organization in a way that keeps you looking good on Facebook and all the public facing stuff?' We decided that I would bring the harm reduction piece and hold the sex worker space in a way that's complementary, right alongside them."

In practice, this means that when they do outreach together, Tonya talks to people about the crisis services the Denver Homeless Ministry provides—things like clothes, hygiene items, baby formula, substance-abuse treatment, referrals to mental health providers—while Mary has conversations about harm reduction and safe sex. Each is clear about the types of needs she can address, and they give one another the space to work from their respective capabilities.

Tonya expressed appreciation that when they do street outreach together, Mary is mindful of her comfort zone:

> "Mary never made me nervous," she said. "When she's handing out condoms, she does it discretely. She's never, 'Hey, I've got condoms over here!' If somebody says 'Does anybody got any condoms?' Mary goes, 'I do. Come over here.' ...You know, we ...work together and respect each other. We respect each other's beliefs, and that's huge."

Tonya feels respected by Mary, and reciprocates that respect in kind. For her part, Tonya does not proselytize or advocate sexual abstinence when they do street outreach. Mary shared:

> "The fact that Tonya also was able to do the same back to me is so significant. Like, if you're going to want me to do this work with you, I can't have you breathing down my neck or having you spout a moralistic standpoint when we're out on the street...[because] people will shut down."

She went on to explain, "Religion has done a lot of harm to a lot of people, and some folks experiencing homelessness that we're running into have had some kind of struggle with religion." She added. "Tonya's been great with understanding that we can't lead with that." Tonya added that she teaches all of the Denver Homeless Ministry's volunteers that she trains: "You cannot go out and gangbust about your faith. If somebody asks you? That's one thing. Share your one-on-one relationship. But you do not go out and ask people to pray; you don't lay hands on them."

This is not to say that there have never been any moments of discomfort or tension. Tonya described a memorable incident in their working relationship:

> "I remember coming in once time, and Mary's group was putting piles of condoms on tables for dinner, and I'm like 'Man, we're serving a meal! Is that what happens when I come to your house for dinner? I can pick a condom I want?' It was awkward for me to walk in there and see all these condoms laying on the table—I mean, I'm Catholic! But they quit doing that. All I did was say something and it never happened again."

She turned to Mary and added, "That just amazed me that you guys listened to me, and respected me enough [to make a change when I was uncomfortable]."

Mary acknowledged that for their collaboration to work, "there's some humility that's required on both of our parts." She continued, "I just appreciate that Tonya understands her boundaries and has been able to be aware of her framework." Yet, even with clear boundaries, negotiating their differences is still sometimes challenging.

> "For us, it sometimes doesn't feel like a reciprocal relationship," Mary admitted. "But," she continued, "then I think about how I've come into contact with somebody on the street who needs something that I can't provide, and I know that I can always turn to [Tonya and the Denver

> Homeless Ministry]. There's this trusting relationship that I have with them. And it's different than other religious organization that we've funnelled referrals to.... This kind of respect and boundary maintenance—in my experience, we don't do that in organizational relationship often. And so I think that's what's made our relationship strong and makes it work.

Mary and Tonya disagree on a lot, and yet they still manage to collaborate closely. They are not unaware of the significance of their achievement. "Our partnership shows that collaboration can happen. You can find common ground with people who don't have the same institutional set up. It's doable," Mary reflected. She continued: "The question it raises for me is 'How do I replicate this?' For [Tonya], it just comes so naturally. She's like 'Let's go hand out stuff!' And I'm like 'I don't think you realize what's happening here.'"

Indeed, the collaboration and partnership between these two very different organizations is extraordinary, unlike any I've ever encountered. And, I should add that even though Prax(us) closed, Mary did not leave the Denver antitrafficking community. She took a position with another non-profit, the Laboratory to Combat Human Trafficking, the organization that operates the 24/7 human trafficking hotline for the state of Colorado.[15] Although street outreach was not an official part of her new job description, she continued to accompany Tonya regularly, explaining that she sees it as "part of our continual effort to make sure that folks understand where trafficking is embedded into the issue of homelessness, and how folks who are experiencing homelessness are highly vulnerable." Mary reported that she continues to keep in regular contact with between 40 and 50 of the youth Prax(us) served. When we expressed our amazement at hearing this, Mary's response was simply, "They're my community members. Why would I *not*?"

Discussion

Since these interviews, Mary's question concerning replication has stayed with me. Several themes emerge from these interviews that are relevant for organizations that maintain or are looking to develop partnerships and collaborations across religious-secular lines, or lines of religious difference. They are: friendship, mutual respect, trust, relational intelligence and boundaries.

Friendship

At the outset of my joint interview with Mary and Tonya, I explained that I wanted to talk with them together because I found their collaboration so unique and, frankly, unlikely. Tonya's immediate response was "Well, we're friends."

And, indeed, they are. According to Tonya, she and Mary "clicked from the beginning" when they met through Stand Up for Kids. Mary noted that they share a common background in that both of them experienced homelessness at earlier points in each of their lives. "[Because this is] embedded in our own personal experience....We're just comfortable being on the street, because we've spent time there. And I think it's made us uniquely qualified and accessible in some ways," Mary explained. "Any of the kids know our stories," Tonya added. Laughing, Mary concluded, "And they just think we're two crazy old people who won't go anywhere!"

The partnership works because of their friendship. It was because Tonya genuinely liked and connected with Mary—because, "they clicked" —that she accepted the invitation to join Prax(us) in street outreach with sex workers, and eventually took leadership around that—despite the challenge to her traditional Catholic views on sex. The friendship made this tension bearable.

Mutual Respect

I recognize that mutual respect could go in the same category as friendship, because no friendship is really solid without respect. However, because I'm not trying to identify what makes friendship work, but the factors that make this particular partnership viable, I think mutual respect stands as its own theme.[16]

Respecting each other's beliefs, frameworks and boundaries was a theme that emerged repeatedly in both interviews. They demonstrated respect for one another in three ways: through accepting one another—their beliefs, values and religious commitments; by not trying to change one another (including on the points where they disagreed); and by working actively to accommodate one another—again, not on the basis of "agreement" but on the basis of the skills, strengths and experiences the other brought.

So, for example, as Prax(us) faced closing, and Mary and Tonya started to figure out how the Denver Homeless Ministry could take over the component of street outreach with sex workers, that process was not a negotiation of trying to identify where and just how far each could bend on their values and frameworks. Rather, they focused on accommodating their respective needs. This meant trying to figure out how the Denver Homeless Ministry could be involved in street outreach with sex workers in ways that would parallel what Prax(us) was doing, and that would keep them in good standing with their religious constituencies. Meanwhile, Tonya and the Denver Homeless Ministry do not problematize, publicly critique or denigrate harm reduction. There is space for both in their relationship.

In other words, the space they have created together requires something from both parties. It is a two-way, not a one-way, street. It looks like Prax(us) figuring out a different way to distribute condoms besides placing them in a bowl at the dinner table; it looks like the Denver Homeless Ministry not making sexual abstinence or religious confession a condition of receiving the other services they provide.

Trust

Respect is the foundation of trust, the third characteristic that sustains their work. Mary and Tonya know that they have one another's backs. As Mary reflected, "I know that I can always turn to [the Denver Homeless Ministry because] there's this trusting relationship that I have with them." This is notable because trust is not a privilege Mary automatically extends to faith-based organizations. Mary's experience of homelessness earlier in her life also included experience with human trafficking.[17] The people who exploited her were religious people, and justified their actions in the name of religion. For this reason, Mary is not someone who assumes that religious people and organizations are naturally trustworthy or are automatic allies in the antitrafficking movement just because they are religious. But she noted that with the Denver Homeless Ministry "it's different than other religious organization that we've funnelled referrals to." I do not conclude that the nature of this difference is due to just one thing; but the respect she and Tonya have for one another, and the trust that respect fosters, is certainly one of the factors contributing to it. For example, Mary and Prax(us) frequently faced criticism from others in the Denver antitrafficking community about its harm reduction approach as "enabling." And Tonya is no stranger to the distrust from people in the social justice sector who call her a nun (she is not) and who make all kinds of assumptions about her because she is Catholic. They know they can trust the other to have her back, and not to trade in stereotypes.

Relational Intelligence

The fourth theme is relational intelligence, the meaning of which is similar to the way psychologists Peter Salovey and John Mayer define the concept of emotional intelligence in individuals as "the ability to monitor one's own and other people's emotions, to discriminate between different emotions and label them appropriately, and to use emotional information to guide thinking and behavior."[18] By relational intelligence, I mean awareness of organizational relationships, or the social ecology; the ability to read that ecology accurately and to navigate it effectively (where "effectively" means in accordance with one's own institutional mission, and in ways that legibly contribute to the common good); and the ability to build and maintain mutually beneficial relationships across differences. Put another way, relational intelligence refers to the ability to monitor how one's organization is functioning and the impact of its conduct and activities on others (individuals and organizations) around it. Mary and Tonya each demonstrated clear awareness that while their respective organizations occupied its own niche, they did so in the context of a wider, interconnected community so that the way any organization conducted itself impacted the rest.

For example, in the first interview Mary explained: "Prax(us) couldn't tell people…, 'Don't go to Tonya because Tonya's Catholic and won't give you condoms.' That wasn't ok." In the joint interview Tonya elaborated:

> "[W]e don't want the kids going back and bad mouthing the other groups, because then they're pitting everyone against each other. So if we maintain

> a friendship, and a love and a respect, then the kids are going to get that, too."

They both demonstrated awareness that, as Mary put it, "The people we're serving and we're loving are in relationships with *all* of us." Both grasped that the way their organization conducted itself in relation to others—including other organizations with whom they may struggle—would impact the kinds of relationships it would be possible to build with the people all of them sought to serve.

Relational intelligence is also evident in the manner in which Mary went about closing Prax(us). Through our conversations, it became clear to me that it is more than just a happy coincidence that she and Tonya began partnering. In the same way that Prax(us)'s peer mentorship program developed leadership and organizing skills in youth and young people, I realized that Mary did the same thing in her relationships with community partners. In building the relationship with Tonya, Prax(us) contributed to the expansion of the Denver Homeless Ministry's organizational capacity by bringing them into closer, more intentional relationship with the sex working community. Together they worked to build organizational relationships that would enhance services and increase options for the people they serve.

Boundaries

Finally, boundaries—awareness of boundaries and respecting boundaries—was a theme each emphasized as they described both how and what made their partnership work. In interpersonal relationships, practicing boundaries refers to understanding and managing where we end and another person begins.[19] Similarly, in institutional and organizational relationships, it means knowing and managing where our organization ends and another begins.

Mary reflected on how boundaries sustain their partnership: "I think our ability to work together like this came from our initial laying out of boundaries—we were each like, 'Here's my boundary. Here's your boundary.' But we can parallel and work alongside each other's stuff—and really sticking to that." She continued with an example:

> "So, I won't bring condoms into the church. But I'll have them in my car in the parking lot so if someone needs some, I can give them to them. I address needs that the ministry is not able to provide from their framework. And, I stick to it even when, for me, there were moments of really wanting to blow her boundaries; of 'Like, really? Come on! I'm just going to give these guys some condoms in your church!' So I've had to be clear with myself that 'No, I said I wasn't going to do that.'"

The following quotes are indicative of the way the crucial role of boundaries came up throughout the interviews:

- "I just appreciate that she understands her boundaries and has been able to be aware of her framework."
- "…[W]e have to do boundaries. Tonya talks about not holding bags of condoms [at meals]. I am sometimes on outreach where …I *am* holding up a bag of condoms and telling folks to come [take some]. But with Tonya, and when we're doing the work together and we're sharing the space, I know that she's uncomfortable [with that]. And why would I want to create that tension, when I could easily tap somebody and say, 'Hey, if you need anything…'? They know. And if they ask Tonya for something that she doesn't have or isn't willing to give them, she'll tell them, 'Go see Mary.'"
- "[T]he fact that we've been able to give that boundary to each other is, I think, what works. It's been pretty good, really good."

Practicing boundaries does not require similarity, agreement or approval. It is about awareness, respect and the ability to self-regulate. A common misnomer about boundaries is that their primary purpose is to maintain separation. This is certainly one of the things that boundaries do, but it actually is not their primary role. Their primary role is as ingredients in agency and empowerment.[20] Boundaries create the space in which an organization can carry out its mission with integrity.

Choosing a Better Subject

A noteworthy dimension of Mary and Tonya's working relationship is how they avoid the traps that could sink or ruin them. I have already noted how struggles over differing conceptions of *human trafficking* are extremely contentious and polarizing within the antitrafficking movement. Their respective views of sexual morality—Tonya's traditional Catholic view that objects to non-marital and contracepted sex, and Mary's modern liberal view that prioritizes consent—are often mapped directly onto different views about the morality of sex work and the relationship of sex work to human trafficking (is all sex work human trafficking? Or is sex work human trafficking only under certain conditions?). Yet, Mary and Tonya appear to have avoided the quagmire of these debates and struggles.

I could conclude that they have avoided becoming ensnared in the conflicts that have fractured (and continue to fracture) the antitrafficking movement, and that could well damage both their friendship and their working relationship, because they have dedicated themselves to studiously avoiding the conflict by agreeing to disagree. However, even though each possesses a well-practiced "live and let live" skillset, that is not the primary dynamic I observed between them. What I observed was less avoidance, and more of a refusal of the conventional terms by which *trafficking* is defined by the conflicting "sides" in trafficking debates, coupled with a skillful reframing of trafficking from its interpersonal dimensions as it plays out between individuals (e.g. a trafficker and trafficking victim) to its systemic dimensions, or the way it plays out in "patterned ways with respect to broad collectives—institutions, religious groups, eras in history, dimensions of culture, and within discourse itself."[21] For example, in the first interview Letitia and I conducted with Mary about her work with Prax(us), she responded to our question about how she defines and understands human trafficking—a question we asked of every organizational leader or spokesperson in our study—by asking *us* why *we* thought the language and framework of human trafficking was important: "Why do we need to handle that definition?" she asked. "Why is it important? Who is the term *trafficking* more important for: you or the individual? Why does it matter that an individual needs to identify in that perspective?" she probed.

Mary explained what has led her to begin pressing this set of questions, and the value she sees in them, recounting that many of the youth and young adults living on the streets who made up Prax(us)'s primary constituency did not see themselves as victims of human trafficking. "It was very hard for youth to identify that that [trafficking] was their experience," she told us. Young people would frequently say things to her like, "What do you mean I'm a trafficking survivor? I just traded sex for a place to stay. I don't get where you're coming from." Notably, it was not that young people did not identify as victims or survivors of human trafficking because of lack of familiarity with or education about sex trafficking; rather, they rejected this interpretive framework that did not resonate with how they understood their experiences. According to Mary, many young people pushed back on *her* for pushing a narrative that did not fit them. "Very few of the youth and young adults I worked with (and still do) have relationships with or identify with that definition," she said. The fact that the terminology and interpretive framework of human trafficking largely was not personally meaningful or empowering to the young people Prax(us) served led Mary to begin to ask herself, "Why is it important for me to label something? What is the reason behind that? Do I need to give that identity to trigger something or to get them something?"

Mary admitted that she rarely uses the term *human trafficking* anymore in her own speaking and teaching. But she found herself speaking about this term and its framework rather frequently with the youth and young people Prax(us) served because of how this term plays a key role in facilitating access to systems and services that are often otherwise closed off to, and even aggressively punitive towards, vulnerable young people. For instance, youth who admit to having engaged in survival sex will be positioned in the child welfare and criminal justice systems as victims of commercial sexual exploitation and even human trafficking, regardless of whether they see themselves as exploited or victimized. She explained that choosing not to resist these labels and characterizations, even if that is not how they understand their experiences, can be key in triggering access to a wide range of services and systemic responses (positive and negative). Mary reflected, "For us, it's about talking to youth and saying to them, 'This is where they're going to platform you or position you at [if you say or agree that you've experienced trafficking]: How do you feel about that? Is this the system that you want to enter?'" She continued:

> "You're telling someone…'This is the way you can access the system. Here's what that might look like. It might trigger law enforcement; it might trigger an insane exam; it might trigger them entering in your mental health background….' Whether they have to enter the system by choice or by system requirements, we need to have that conversation."

Human trafficking might not be a term that resonates *for the youth*, but it's one that is widely understood by and carries significant power in the systems that young people may decide to enter (or already be conscripted into).

Conversations with youth about the implications of the *human trafficking* label are necessary before those labels are applied to them by the system. Frequently, the systems that are designed to help and serve fail to deliver on those promises. Knowing what to expect and what kinds of options they will have, and the choices they will need to make, better equips vulnerable youth and young people to navigate those systems more successfully and with a greater sense of agency in the process.

Both the kinds of questions Mary asks about the necessity of labeling something as human trafficking and her insistence of talking frankly with young people about the kinds of effects that entering systems of services and support (and also surveillance) are likely to have for them signal her awareness of how *human trafficking* has become performative speech. By calling the language of human trafficking performative speech, I am highlighting that to label something as human trafficking not only *says* something; it also *does* something, both to the people who use this language, and to the people to whom the label of "trafficking victim" is willingly or unwillingly applied. Indeed, the series of questions Mary articulated throughout this portion of the interview—"Why do we need to handle that definition? Who is the definition more important for: you or the individual? Why does it matter that an individual needs to identify in that perspective [of human trafficking] Why is it important for me to label something? What is the reason behind that?"—directs critical attention away from familiar rhetorical contests that spar over what trafficking is or is not. It re-focuses attention on how the language of trafficking variously empowers and disempowers the social actors who are differently socially located in a conversation or situation. Her consistent priority is to build the power and agency of vulnerable people through increasing their options and choices, and enhancing their skills for navigating systems and structures, in ways that they experience as positive and empowering.

As an alternative to the language and framework of trafficking, Mary stated that she prefers the terms *exploitation* or *parallel human rights issues*. She explained that these terms facilitate the probing of root cause like homophobia, racism and gentrification in ways that notions of sex trafficking fail to adequately accommodate. She adamantly insisted that these social dynamics are the ones communities need to be discussing if they want to get a handle on ways that sex trafficking is manifesting in their communities. "These are the conversations," she declared. Mary consistently and skillfully highlighted the systemic dimensions of human trafficking that criminal justice frameworks, with their interpersonal focus on the dynamics of the relationship between individual traffickers and their victims, tend to minimize.

> "We're from a systems approach," she explained. "We understand that trafficking's happening because of oppression. This system [of oppression] is the root cause. We're trying to tap that [perspective] and get to that space where people can see not just the crime—because the crime's been happening forever; we've been exploiting people as long as we've been on the planet—[but that] the *system* continues to be part of that exploitation."

Shifting from an interpersonal to a systems perspective opens up understandings of wrongdoing and violation beyond the frameworks of crime, and the necessity of criminal conviction as the measure of public accountability and redress. Moreover, a systems approach acknowledges that the legal system does not exist in a pristine and uncontaminated space apart from dynamics of social power and violence but, in fact, is shot through with them. As Hilary Jerome Scarsella and Stephanie Krehbiel observe:

> "...the criminal justice system frequently both retraumatizes survivors who try to use it, and itself perpetuates sexual violence against those subject to its power, particularly people of color, members of the LGBTQIA+ community, and those detained or in prison. Further, white scholars and activists have often failed to respect that due to the racial injustices of police brutality, mass incarceration, and deportation, communities of color often cannot rely on the criminal justice system to be an ally in their pursuits of survival and wellbeing following sexual violence."[22]

In summary, by meticulously attending to the performativity of the language of human trafficking—that is, the work the language of trafficking does in particular spaces, situations and in situating particular people in institutional spaces—Mary is able to bring attention to important systemic dimensions of human trafficking, as well as successfully refuse the conventional terms by which trafficking is defined in polarizing debates. As relates to how all of this informs the working relationship between her and Tonya: they may not necessarily agree on where lines of criminality should be drawn—or maybe do they do, or would. In point of fact, they absolutely do not center the question of what is or should count as *trafficking*. What they do is share a broad conception of what systemic and social justice looks like and entails. Mary's ability to dodge—and in significant ways disarm—the traps that the politicization of "human trafficking" has laid is a crucial piece of what sets her up to work effectively with groups across the ideological spectrum.

Conclusion

Religious and ideological differences between organizations frequently function as barriers that either prevent collaboration and partnership in antitrafficking efforts, or that make such partnerships and collaborative ventures contentious and fraught. Those who bear the weight of such tensions and, essentially, pay the social price when actors cannot work together on projects that contribute to the common good are those who would be served by their success: people who are vulnerable to exploitation or who are experiencing human trafficking. The partnership described in this case study between Prax(us), the secular, harm reduction antitrafficking organization, and the Denver Homeless Ministry, the traditional Catholic charity, is indicative of the potential for strategic collaboration across significant organizational and personal differences. The collaboration worked because of the relationship of respect and trust the leaders developed. These qualities took root in and are nurtured by their friendship. Although friendship is not the only relational context that generates respect and trust, it is one that reliably does so. The boundaries Mary and Tonya practice in relation to one another maintain and further build the trust that this partnership requires to function effectively. They demonstrate remarkable relational intelligence through consistent awareness that the way that they conduct themselves personally and represent their organization professionally impacts the relational field of which they are a part, particularly to the people that they seek to serve and who they understand as members of their community. In conversations that replicate established dynamics of power, they reframe and choose a better subject.

Healthy, collaborative work among very differently oriented types of antitrafficking (or trafficking-adjacent) organizations is possible. Identifying factors that contribute to the viability and success of such partnerships can help organizations that wish to develop such partnerships as they consider the qualities, skills and commitments that such work requires.

Notes

1 I presented an earlier version of this chapter under the title "Reducing Harm, Practicing Faith and Building Relationships: Collaborating Across Religious Differences" as the keynote lecture for the Rights, Dignity and Religion: Responding to Modern Slavery conference at the University of Sheffield on January 25, 2020. I am grateful to Drs. Hannah Lewis, Gwyneth Lonergan, Rebecca Murray, Emma Tomalin, and Louise Waite for the invitation to speak at this conference, an important event that marked the culmination of a three-year research project conducted by the Universities of Leeds and Sheffield and funded by the Economic and Social Research Council. The report on the findings of this research project is entitled "Faith Responses to Modern Slavery" (January 2020) and is available at: http://faithantitrafficking.group.shef.ac.uk/wp-content/uploads/2020/01/Faith-reponses-to-modern-slavery-2020-Uni-Sheffield-and-Leeds_LowRes.pdf.

2 Elizabeth Bernstein and Janet R. Jakobsen, "Sex, Secularism and Religious Influence in US Politics" (2010) 31 *Third World Quarterly* 1023, at pp. 1035–1036.

3 Bernstein and Jakobsen, 1035.

4 Bernstein and Jakobsen, 1035–1036.
5 Bernstein and Jakobsen, 1035.
6 Hannah Lewis et al., Faith Responses to Modern Slavery (University of Sheffield and University of Leeds, 2020) 1. http://faithantitrafficking.group.shef.ac.uk/wp-content/uploads/2020/01/Faith-reponses-to-modern-slavery-2020-Uni-Sheffield-and-Leeds_LowRes.pdf (accessed 1/29/2020).
7 This characterization of struggles in the U.S. anti-trafficking movement over the definition of human trafficking, and between groups that understand what counts as "trafficking" differently, is greatly oversimplified. Not only is it simplified in depicting the choices for understanding the nature of commercial sex in binary terms (exploitation or personal freedom/individual agency), this characterization also utterly erases the problem of forced and exploited labor that pervades the global economy. Particularly attempting to resist the erasure of labor exploitation, the conceptualization of trafficking that guides my work is that human trafficking is an umbrella category referring to situations of exploited labor in which a person has lost control of their life and is paid nothing or next to nothing for their work, and cannot quit their job or leave their situation without fear of violence to themselves or someone else (Campbell and Zimmerman, 2017, 271). Be that as it may, my conception of trafficking is not the focus of this essay, and I intentionally background my own views in order to center and more clearly present those of the participants' in this study.
8 Lauren McGrow, email to Yvonne Zimmerman, June 17, 2020.
9 This study is based on two interviews with the leaders of Prax(us) and the Denver Homeless Ministry. The first interview with Mary Landerholm, former executive director of Prax(us), was conducted by Yvonne Zimmerman and Letitia Campbell on August 8, 2017 at the Laboratory to Combat Human Trafficking offices in Denver, CO. The second interview with both Mary Landerholm and Tonya Cangelosi, executive director of the Denver Homeless Ministry, was conducted by Yvonne Zimmerman on March 25, 2018 at the Denver Homeless Ministry offices in Denver, CO. The interviews were conducted in accordance with Human Subjects research protocols of the Methodist Theological School in Ohio, including informed consent forms signed by both parties. All quoted material by Mary and Tonya are from these two interviews.
10 The Denver Homeless Ministry, http://www.thedhms.org/ (accessed 11/5/2019).
11 The Denver Homeless Ministry, http://www.thedhms.org/ (accessed 11/5/2019).
12 Prax(us), https://www.linkedin.com/company/prax-us-/about/ (accessed 1/15/2020).
13 "What is Harm Reduction?" Harm Reduction International. https://www.hri.global/what-is-harm-reduction (accessed 4/27/2018).
14 StandUp For Kids, https://www.standupforkids.org/ (accessed 1/28/2020).
15 Laboratory to Combat Human Trafficking, https://combathumantrafficking.org/ (accessed 1/28/2020). Mary has since also left the Laboratory to Combat Human Trafficking to launch Collective Solutions, an anti-trafficking consulting business. Collective Solutions, https://www.facebook.com/Collective-Solutions-103111801070440/ (accessed 1/28/2020).
16 By the concept respect I mean acknowledging the equality, dignity and independence of others. (Sharon Welch, *A Feminist Ethic of Risk* (2000) 15.
17 Mary Landerholm, "I Survived Human Trafficking" (SoulPancake: June 28, 2018) https://www.youtube.com/watch?v=LKV-L_Sdd_Q&list=PLzvRx_johoA-cyirLMZznW8w9TMcm-sjL&index=4&t=0s (accessed 2/3/2020); Matt Watson, "Under Lock and Key: Nonprofit Fights to End Human Trafficking by Influencing Policy, Training Responders, Empowering Survivors and More" (Red: Denver, CO, July 19, 2018) https://red.msudenver.edu/2018/under-lock-and-key.html (accessed 2/3/2020).
18 "Emotional Intelligence" *Oxford Reference* (New York, NY: Oxford University Press, 2020) https://www.oxfordreference.com/view/10.1093/oi/authority.20110803095749954 (accessed 1/16/2020).

19 Metta Psychology Group, "What are Boundaries?" Columbus, OH, July 31, 2017 http://www.mettapsych.com/news/2017/7/31/what-are-boundaries (accessed 1/16/2020).
20 Jennifer Chesak "The No BS Guide to Protecting your Emotional Space" *Healthline* December 10, 2018. https://www.healthline.com/health/mental-health/set-boundaries (accessed 1/16/2020).
21 Hilary Jerome Scarsella and Stephanie Krehbiel, "Sexual Violence: Christian Theological Legacies and Responsibilities" *Religion Compass*; e12337. Available at https://doi.org/10.1111/rec3.12337 (accessed 6/29/2020).
22 Scarsella and Krehbiel, "Sexual Violence."

Bibliography

Bernstein, Elizabeth and Janet R. Jakobsen. "Sex, Secularism and Religious Influence in US Politics." *Third World Quarterly* 31, no. 6 (2010): 1023–1039.

Campbell, Letitia M. and Yvonne C. Zimmerman, "Forced Labor and the Movement to End Human Trafficking." In *A Companion to Public Theology*, edited by Sebastian Kim and Katie Day, 271–297. Boston, MA: Brill, 2017.

Chesak, Jennifer. "The No BS Guide to Protecting your Emotional Space." *Healthline*. December 10, 2018. https://www.healthline.com/health/mental-health/set-boundaries.

The Denver Homeless Ministry. AccessedJanuary 5, 2020. http://www.thedhms.org/.

Lewis, Hannahet al., "Faith Responses to Modern Slavery." University of Sheffield and University of Leeds, 2020. http://faithantitrafficking.group.shef.ac.uk/wp-content/uploads/2020/01/Faith-reponses-to-modern-slavery-2020-Uni-Sheffield-and-Leeds_LowRes.pdf.

Harm Reduction International. "What is Harm Reduction?" AccessedJanuary 5, 2022. https://www.hri.global/what-is-harm-reduction.

Laboratory to Combat Human Trafficking. AccessedJanuary 5, 2020. https://combathumantrafficking.org/.

Landerholm, Mary. "I Survived Human Trafficking." *SoulPancake*, June 28, 2018. https://www.youtube.com/watch?v=LKV-L_Sdd_Q&list=PLzvRx_johoA-cyirLMZznW8w9TMcm-sjL&index=4&t=0s.

Metta Psychology Group. "What are Boundaries?" July 31, 2017. http://www.mettapsych.com/news/2017/7/31/what-are-boundaries.

"Prax(us)." AccessedJanuary 5, 2022. https://www.linkedinA.com/company/prax-us-/about/.

Salovey, Peter and John Mayer. "Emotional Intelligence." *Oxford Reference*. Oxford: Oxford University Press, 2020. https://www.oxfordreference.com/view/10.1093/oi/authority.20110803095749954.

Scarsella, Hilary Jerome and Stephanie Krehbiel. "Sexual Violence: Christian Theological Legacies and Responsibilities." *Religion Compass* 13no. 9 (2019): 1–13.

StandUp For Kids. Accessed January 5, 2022. https://www.standupforkids.org/.

Watson, Matt. "Under Lock and Key: Nonprofit Fights to End Human Trafficking by Influencing Policy, Training Responders, Empowering Survivors and More." *MSU Denver Red*. July 19, 2018. https://red.msudenver.edu/2018/under-lock-and-key.html.

Welch, Sharon D. *A Feminist Ethic of Risk, Revised Edition*. Minneapolis, MN: Fortress Press, 2000.

6 Towards an Ethical Framework for Practice

Three "Touchstones" for Faith-based Organizations at the Margins

Lauren McGrow

Introduction: the work of FBOs

Faith-based organizations (FBOs) play a crucial role in delivering social justice outcomes for people in need. At their best they model a divine concern for humanity by demonstrating loving care through social action.[1] Church-based charities have been active in Australia for over a century, providing material goods and assistance with the twofold aim of spreading the gospel and working for the common good.[2] Historically, moral leaders and religious organizations have exerted strong influence on welfare policy in Australia.[3] Across the world FBOs continue to grow as neo-liberal governments outsource their social responsibilities and limit expenditure on welfare.

FBOs range from local churches to national organizations or international aid agencies working across multiple domains. They can be formally structured systems or informal groups invested in a local response to hardship. FBOs are defined as "any organisation that derives inspiration and guidance for its activities from the teachings and principles of the faith or from a particular interpretation or school of thought within the faith."[4] In Australia, they dominate social service delivery to a greater extent than other Western nations, with large organizations competing for hundreds of millions of dollars in core funding from federal and state governments to provide a vast array of programs.[5] There are also small, independent FBOs relying on volunteers and donations to fund their work. Most FBOs in Australia outreaching to sex workers come under this second category.

Religious organizations that focus on sex workers and trafficking survivors have had global influence on sex industry discourse and policy through networks of moral activism.[6] By way of example of their breadth of reach are the Christian women who visit strip clubs on a weekly basis; or faith-based homeless shelters for people in the sex industry; church groups that do street outreach in mega-cities; or international Pentecostal organizations raising awareness to abolish sex slavery, as discussed by Carly Daniel-Hughes in this volume.[7,8,9] There are also influential FBOs advocating at a political level to combat sex work and trafficking through changing international law.[10]

DOI: 10.4324/9780429328824-7

This is both a specialized and extensive operational context that has increased in influence over the last 20 years, bringing moral beliefs about the abuse of women through commercial sex into the public sphere to push back against progressive sexual politics.[11] Conservative religious actors are now able to confidently narrate and define the sex industry and have largely done so without the input of sex worker peer organizations and queer collectives.[12] Their representations are often framed by a victim discourse that omits agency, ambivalence, self-determination and pleasure.[13] FBOs, aligned with a radical feminist agenda to end sex work, are also more likely to discount socio-institutional structures (including religion) that give rise to generational race, gender, and class discriminations.[14]

Because of their growing influence, there is an urgent need for evidence-based analysis of their work: to understand the connections between gender oppression, religion, and the impact of social justice initiatives.[15] Comprehensive theoretical frameworks for analysing practice are needed.[16] It is my aim to help address this analysis gap by developing an ethical framework for best practice.

At the Margins

> But I would say that the street-based sex workers are the most marginalized. They've made a choice; they might be putting themselves in danger but they're choosing not to directly hurt other members of the community. They're not weak they are marginalized. The women we work with you know are often in vulnerable situations but they're not weak, they're extremely resilient and strong.[17]

Marginalization is a key reason FBOs work in this context, using outreach, practical assistance, and spiritual support, which is often combined with political advocacy and education.[18] But can their work increase marginalization? Many FBOs represent sex work as individual brokenness, highlighting stories of rescue and restoration. This sets up a victim / rescuer narrative that shields the power and impact of systemic abuse. Sex worker activists insist that legislative and economic change will reduce the risks associated with the sex industry and part of this change is contesting the idea that sex workers are those most in need of faith-based intervention.[19]

In *Sex at the Margins*, Laura Agustin posed a challenge for practitioners who want to rescue sex workers.[20] Agustin theorized that there is a great divide between the representation of sex work that helpers use, and the practicalities of sex work as named by people in the industry, especially migrant women.[21] FBOs often frame their perspective by constructing slavery and freedom in oppositional terms.[22] Women in the sex industry are enslaved while social helpers have a dynamic freedom that gives them social capital and power, and this becomes sanctified work – to restore others. Agustin challenged FBOs to listen to primary stakeholders and be realistic about what help can be provided. For example, in Western nations, migrants want citizenship rather than to be rescued from sex work.[23] Agustin offered a nuanced critique of social agencies that make life harder for sex workers by forcing solidarity and imposing help as they believe women are always victimized by commercial sex.

One way to develop rigor is to listen to this critique and reflect on the ethics of FBO practice. A well-developed ethical framework can help practitioners evaluate cultural and religious discourse about sex work, understanding the circumstances that give rise to oppression. Reflective thinking is crucial for knowledge building to inform best practice for the benefit of marginalized people.

Methodology

Using critical participatory action research, I've studied FBOs in Australia that work with sex workers for the past six years. The purpose is to build capacity for reflection through conversation about practice, defined as language, action, and relationships.[24] Often described as a spiral of self-reflection, critical participatory action research encompasses planning, acting, observing, and reflecting, then replanning, further action and reflection to increase knowledge and transform practice.[25] The process is not as neat as described.

In 2016 I conducted semi-structured interviews with five leaders of Australian FBOs. At the time, all were led by white, Evangelical Christian women, except for one organization, led by a white, Evangelical Christian man. Three interviews were with organizational founders. All leaders were between the ages of 35 and 65 and from a middle-class background. Two were former sex workers now converted to Christianity who started non-profits to help other women escape the sex industry.

Over the next two years, I visited four FBOs to observe their practice including at a social enterprise café; a social enterprise second-hand clothing shop; a night outreach visit to city brothels and three drop-in centers for sex workers. I collected secondary data including news articles, training and promotional materials, website information and videos produced by the organizations. These results were published in *Missionary Positions*.[26]

My researcher status is an insider to this cohort which gives an advantage that enables me to reflect on practice enmeshed in my own life and work.[27] In the 2000s I was the coordinator of one of these FBOs for five years. Before that time, I had sex industry experience as a young person in the 1990s. Since conducting interviews in 2016, I have maintained contact with each group and several other FBOs to provide expertise, reflective resources, and conversation, and in the process have learned more about their practice.

One key finding from the original study was that Australian FBOs who work with sex workers did not have a network of support with each other. I used action learning, an aspect of critical participatory action research, and facilitated a three-day symposium in 2018 for peer-based reflection, relationship building, and best-practice discussion. Twelve people from five organizations spent three days together, delivering formal presentations about their work, while making social connections.[28] Each presentation took between one and two hours with time for questions. As a participant observer I wrote summaries of their talks to critically reflect on the language, action, and relationships of practice.

As each group presented their work, I noted reoccurring themes of *stigma*, *complexity*, and *power*, and a new understanding began to emerge.[29] From my perspective these themes were latent and could be interlinked in a stronger way to build an ethical framework for their work. The touchstones for practice began to emerge. As a metaphor, a touchstone is a principle for judging quality or a reference point against which other things can be evaluated.[30] In the same way, FBOs can use ethical references to deeply comprehend and develop their practice at the margins.

Considering these emergent themes, I re-examined previous interviews and noted stigma, complexity, and power embedded in the conversation in a variety of ways. I recoded the data and mapped the symposium presentations against these concepts. How were the words stigma, complexity, and power defined and used? What were the actions that FBOs took in response and how were relationships formed as a result? These concepts, at the heart of practice, also resonated with my own experience of coordinating an FBO project for sex workers and further, with the type of respectful support I desired as a young person.

This ethical framework developed in conversation with Australian FBOs "is directed towards studying, reframing and reconstructing social practices."[31] The purpose is two-fold, first, so that practices are more rational, just, and inclusive and secondly, to assist FBOs in other parts of the world to learn about the Australian context and critically reflect on their own work.[32]

Touchstone One: Reducing Stigma through Safe Space

Erving Goffman's 1963 book *Stigma* is the starting point for reflection on stigma.[33] Stigma means a stain or spoiled identity – it is to be "not quite human."[34] Historically, the word stood for blemish, a physical sign of difference from "the normal" but it could also mean individual moral failing. People with disability, mental illness, viral contagion, drug addiction, and physical deformity experience stigma. This is carried individually, in the body, and is enacted structurally, as violence and oppression. Stigma is also made manifest through a power differential in interpersonal relationships.

Entire people groups are stigmatized due to ethnicity or class.[35] Sex workers, especially female and trans women, experience stigma because they have broken with the normative model of sexual virtue.[36] Stigma is performed relationally and isolates sex workers, who employ measures to protect their social identities and minimize risk. Results of stigma include harassment, state surveillance, public condemnation, othering, and violence at every level. Even FBO intervention in the lives of sex workers can be an outworking of social stigma, especially if voice and agency is not respected. This is because sex workers are often perceived by religious people as those who lack dignity: victims in need of forgiveness and rescue.[37]

Gayle Rubin notes that "sexuality in western societies has been structured within an extremely punitive social framework and has been subjected to very real formal and informal controls."[38] This social framework puts heteronormative, white, married, conservative people in a hierarchy above those who are sex workers. In conforming to that hierarchy, religious practitioners aren't always aware that their beliefs about gender conformity and sexual virtue intensify stigma.[39] On the contrary, religious authorities have a vested interest in maintaining the idea that sex work is deviance, therefore increasing stigma and shoring up an order of sexual purity and control.[40] This chaste/unchaste model took hold in early Christian communities where male leaders equated sexual modesty with belonging to Christ while the slave/prostitute was the epitome of depravity and death.[41] Belonging (and salvation) is coupled with conformity to a social, sexual order that remains foundational for many religious practitioners.

In the data, the concept of stigma was noted in conversation about the sex industry and included discussion of women breaking with heteronormative sexual roles and mitigation strategies. Each group approached the issue differently. One FBO respondent detailed how they try to connect with people in the industry through highlighting the dangers and shame they face, telling women:

> You're at high risk do you realise that you're at high risk ... Sometimes I go well is this really what you want to do with your life if you had three wishes what would they be if you didn't do prostitution and it just makes them feel like there's another life out there and they've got to think about it and that can upset them.[42]

Sex workers break with a purity model by being available for sex with many partners and using sexual ability to satisfy male lust.[43] Despite ambiguous and even positive accounts, this FBO leader said that degradation results from promiscuity:

> I believe that no woman is ever meant to have continuous like up to 12 men a day just using their bodies because it's soul destroying. ... Some go oh I have sex with many men and they just love me, some just lie with me and cuddle me for the hour, and you do get that [but] I still feel that there's a brokenness and it's not meant to be.[44]

The sex worker has a "spoiled identity" because of paid sex and the language used frames her as victim, no matter her lived experience. The FBO action is to reach out and visit brothels trying to connect with women, but it is no surprise that they have difficulty doing so because of the stigmatizing belief that drives language and action, resulting in disconnect. When I accompanied this FBO on night outreach, brothel reception was frosty at best. On three occasions sex workers would not open the door to the outreach team but did take the pretty gifts offered by the Christian ladies. Anti-trafficking and anti-sex work programs are often premised on the belief that "nonmarital sexual activity that involves the exchange of sex for money produces in and for the women involved a separation from God so profound as to constitute an affront to human dignity."[45] This ideology manifests in practice at the grassroots as language that reinforces stigma, with action to rescue women and relationships premised on women being harmed by commercial sex. Clients of sex workers are also stigmatized, along with the industry in general.

> It's a cruel industry and men seem to just think it's okay like so what she probably wants it anyway. When they go in and have sex with a girl that's saying please don't you're hurting me there's some predator or something inside of them that just goes I'm paying for it just shut up or whatever. They have no mercy on the girls and you just go what is that? They don't see the suffering or anything, so I don't know what to make of it all I know is that God wants to reach out to these women. Right now they're trying to decriminalize it here. So if they decriminalize it, it's just open slather. What happens is the underworld just goes more under and more under because once they start becoming legal they gotta pay taxes and all that sort of stuff, why would they want that? By decriminalizing you're saying that's alright we've got this secret underworld, men need sex so there you go we need something to keep them happy.[46]

Social stigma, experienced as exclusion and judgement, has wide-ranging impacts for sex workers such as mental and physical health issues, suicide risk, and drug misuse.[47] Stigma dehumanizes people in the sex industry. One Australian organization takes another approach by creating a space of acceptance where women can discuss impacts and how personal risk is managed through identity protection.

> Even if a woman wants to leave it means that she's isolated it means that she can't just freely tell the rest of the community oh yeah you know I was once a street-based sex worker. One woman said to me she's been fourteen years out of this scene she said you know I can tell anyone that I was a heroin addict I can tell anyone I went to gaol but as soon as I mention street-based sex work I can see the judgement in their eyes.[48]

Stigma is a form of social displacement that tells sex workers they are not at home in this world. Their belonging is undermined by legal frameworks that limit human rights; by traditional beliefs about sex; and by rejection from others. FBOs can participate in a spirit of homecoming with excluded people and do so with excellence. From a theological perspective, home is a place of safety characterized by receptivity at the deepest level. It is a place for belonging, celebration, nurture, and equality where character emerges. Symbolically, at home, masks of protection slip, and genuine connection becomes possible.

Homecoming as a faith-based practice is not primarily about helping but is more concerned with being, through welcoming each person with their hopes, dreams, and contradictions. Nourishment happens at home. It is physical, best represented by a shared cup of tea as life is embodied. Emotional sustenance also occurs through expression and validation of experience, in and out of sex work. Spiritual wellbeing occurs through relationships as a space opens for rest and safety.

Home has been an abusive or insecure place for many people, and the language of domestication has colonial underpinnings, so it is important to recognise the limits of this metaphor, but a model of care grounded in relationship, intimacy, and sense of place – neighbourhood – may lessen the impact of stigma.[49] At the symposium, three Australian FBOs reported how they create safe space, via drop-in centres that facilitate the things you do at home – washing, eating, connecting, cleaning, and creativity. Building on the principles of sex worker affirmative therapy that promotes healing from stigma, FBOs can take a structural approach to individual wellbeing by offering safe space.[50] A home is where people have a nourished identity, a place to build skills, have strengths affirmed, and be refreshed in body. This type of community building develops capacity for healthy coping strategies.[51]

Belonging in the world also means being able to confidently access justice. "Home is not a domestic space, but a public space of freedom" where people are not confined by the distortions of stigma.[52] A shift in the law and exclusionary power must occur and is beginning in Australia as three states have decriminalized sex work.[53] FBOs, alongside sex workers, can play a part by making room, acknowledging that safe space is reciprocal. "Space as an existential category means primarily to give room, more generally, to give way, to shrink back … to hold something, to have room to receive something."[54]

How appropriate are religious motifs that objectify sex workers as morally inferior symbols of death and destruction?[55] Ironically, creating safe space with sex workers can mean a leaving home experience for religious practitioners, whose beliefs and assumptions are subject to critique here.[56] Women tell nuanced stories about their experiences in the industry, and this must be acknowledged by FBOs at the margins. Theological beliefs that picture sex workers as typologies of sin must be cross examined. In doing so, a connection might be made with activists who resist sex and gender normativity as they advocate for human rights.[57] The invitation is for practitioners to do likewise with the understanding that making home (creating a hospitable space in the world) is in a "dual sense of welcoming the other *and* being a guest in their presence."[58]

One Australian FBO advocated for decriminalization at a governmental level, circumventing Evangelical beliefs about sex to center rights and respect, thereby leaving their traditional "home." Rather than taking an approach of strategic silence and neutrality, or advocating for punitive controls, the group supported decriminalization, resisting stigma at a structural level.[59,60]

> We got to participate in that government regulation to brothels last year. I guess what we said was really middle of the line in that we thought decriminalization was a really positive thing. That we understand that there are negatives associated with the sex industry but whatever changes to the law that they made, it wouldn't further marginalize or further make vulnerable women involved in street-based sex work. So really it was a middle of the road position saying, is this going to have an impact that actually might be a on flow effect to this group of women who already have a lot of marginalization?[61]

This FBO acknowledges that decriminalization helps sex workers live openly and safely. They have greater access to justice systems to reduce violence. Sex workers are no longer constructed as deviant, dirty, threatening of public order, or othered as promiscuous, less-than human beings.[62] This perspective and action affirms that people in the industry have a right to be at home in this world, and is a first step for minimizing stigma.[63] Belonging becomes a social and political space, where people are accepted.

> Tackling stigma in a way that positively impacts all sex workers requires shifting the narrative to one that acknowledges that sex workers represent a diverse population with differing histories and motivations, and that *all* sex workers deserve to be safe and respected.[64]

FBO participation at a strategic level can strengthen sex workers' human rights and is another way of making space. Through self-reflection to interrogate the impact of religious beliefs about sexual purity/impurity, FBOs can establish a more coherent foundation for practice. This includes holding safe space for stigma management, advocating for legal rights, and welcoming people into the neighbourhood. The metaphor of being at home speaks to a theological truth powerfully observed by Henri Nouwen in *The Return of the Prodigal Son*.[65] To be welcomed at the deepest level, no matter the circumstance, is the heart of a just response to marginalized people. Love is not conditional, and home is a place of surety.[66] This is why FBOs are operational and can be practiced with individuals and through structural advocacy.

Yet it is not a one-way street of faithful giver and needy receiver. A sense of home creates space for equality. "The act of welcoming others is what keeps our social fabric vibrant and diverse. The newcomer, the stranger brings a new insight into the world that we take for granted."[67] For Nouwen, this homecoming is undergirded by a spiritual maturity that understands "real joy and real fulfilment can only come from welcoming home those who have been hurt and wounded on their life's journey."[68] He describes this as a type of fruitful emptiness that enables people to live without condemnation or judgement while maintaining hope.[69] The touchstone of safe space, or homecoming, to reduce stigma provides rich resources for reflection on FBO practice that challenges language and action and is life-giving for relationship.

Touchstone Two: Playing with Complexity

People access FBO support when they are struggling with complexity and have specific social and material needs.[70] This can lead to public misconceptions about who sex workers are – always the traumatized or shattered ones.[71] But the problems are often structural. When sex workers are denied rights and resources and subject to stigma FBO relationships provide new opportunities.[72] FBO support can empower sex workers to advocate for change themselves. At the symposium, one practitioner spoke of being present with a woman who had been homeless for most of her life and yet was able to advocate on her own behalf at the Royal Commission into Institutional Responses to Child Sexual Abuse in Australia, in part gaining strength to do so through their supportive relationship.

People in the sex industry also draw upon FBOs because they have an experience of spirituality or want to be strengthened in faith. This is often named as a reason for exiting sex work.[73] The stereotype of fully realized agent or destitute victim fails to account for diverse identities, including inner psycho-spiritual experiences.[74] Complex conditions are the primary, rational motivator (rather than choice or coercion) for entering sex work.[75] This is something that practitioners learn as they come to know women as fully rounded individuals, embedded in intersecting communities, including faith communities. One practitioner noted that sex workers have a spiritual life:

> I think that's the thing that surprised me the most working here is how much they do want to have conversations about spirituality. I think I came with the assumption of you have probably been so judged by Christians, this is the last thing you'll ever want to talk about. But I have been surprised how many of the women have an active faith and an active spiritual life and engagement that often, you don't see under what we typically call traditional Christianity. It's something that's deeply important to them.[76]

One of the ways FBOs can be transformative is to limit damage-centred clinical practice that focuses on a specific outcome (usually exit from the industry or giving up drugs) and connect with people navigating complexity.[77] Complexity refers to "situations in which it is difficult to state exactly what is going on or to predict what will happen next."[78] This characterizes most human service work and is drawn from complex systems theory that questions the direct correlation between cause and effect in individual lives, instead highlighting relational subjectivity and the impact of systems.[79] Complexity means that there is no easy solution to the problems of gender bias, poverty, racism, ableism, and social exclusion lived out by people in sex work.

A dynamic encounter is required where practitioners understand that their ability to solve problems will be limited. Instead, they can play, or engage, in the co-creation of embodied relationship that opens moment by moment. Play seems a frivolous practice to use with people in complex circumstances, and it is, but it is also about making a collaborative space for imaginative living. It is the "creativity and spontaneous skill of professional work, and the value of knowledge that is co-produced with people in the situation rather than knowledge that is applied by experts to the situation" that is vital and characterizes play as practice.[80] This is also the realm where spirituality finds form through creativity, humour, and trust.

Clinical practice built on casework, trauma-informed care, harm minimization, counselling, anti-oppressive practice, and community development is crucial, but it is also crucial that play occurs. Not least because marginalized people are often great players, alluded to in one interview:

> They are so vulnerable but in that really strong beautiful way. They are fighters. They have wicked senses of humour. They have depth and they have dreams, they have complexity and they're really just the same as anyone.[81]

The language of practice used here is playful and respectful. Play is not easy to define because it is about liminal moments.[82] In concrete terms, it means playing games, making art and being creative. It is an activity that is spontaneous, creative, enjoyable, with no set goals to be achieved. Play is often paired in a binary relationship with work with the understanding that children play while adults work. Yet the two are not mutually exclusive.[83] People don't stop playing as adults, but it is often transformed into formal activities like surfing, tennis, or singing in a choir. Play also demands work, a game of backgammon requires skill, but the purpose is fun before achievement. For children, emotional and social worlds are created through play so that learning takes place. Theorists such as Erikson and Winnicott identify children's play with ego development that enhances the capacity of the self to "create a new world of hope that adults might emulate."[84]

Practitioners can inhabit a space of play by fostering possibility and experimentation in each relational moment. A type of exchange occurs in these encounters, that is, an expansive spirituality that goes beyond therapeutic interventions designed to turn people into compliant human beings.[85] Play gives people a space to cross thresholds in a creative, non-serious way, which makes for less risk. Life becomes an experiment for happiness, an opportunity for self-expression, and perhaps a moment to challenge the status quo. Theologian Michael Koppel defines play as "a means of cooperative and collaborative engagement within self and between self and others that seeks to heighten enjoyment of life experience by making space for the innovative within structured patterns of behaviour."[86] When you are living in complex situations or with stigma, this can help.

To play is to lose control and this is essential for practitioners who may have high specialization but lack the balance of vulnerability. Rather than a rescue and restore mindset, an attitude of play fosters creative expression of self with other.[87] The concept holds potential because "play does not teach us to cure, or to 'fix it,' but, instead, to care and to foster new growth."[88] Play helps people explore options and reframe complexity without a commitment to specific outcomes, while at the same time creating unique relationship with other players. "Play is active and participatory. It is a means of expression and communication. It is relational."[89] Play helps mitigate the embodied impacts of complexity through imaginative interactions with the world.[90] It is restorative, providing freedom from "real life" yet paradoxically can give rise to an intense, hyper-real experience called flow, which increases wellbeing.[91]

In March 2020 in New York, activists organised a Sex Worker Pop-Up on the Lower East Side. A gallery of floating red umbrellas (the symbol of sex worker rights), photographs of beautiful and vulnerable people in the industry, art, information, talks, and relationship building was on offer. This was a playful moment to encounter each other and build capacity for decriminalization in New York, just as the virus was taking hold.

In my experience, most Australian FBOs are unwilling to engage with the sex worker rights movement due to suspicion and judgement, and because activists take a sex positive approach to the industry. As Yvonne Zimmerman notes in

Figure 6.1 Floating red umbrellas at the Sex Worker Pop-Up in NYC, March 2020. Photo by author.

this volume, it takes relational and epistemic humility to work with people who have a radically different ideology. Opportunities to build mutual connection and increase human rights can be missed if FBOs refuse to openly engage in this type of playful activism.

Play is maligned in Western culture and religion while work and productivity are valued as the symbols of moral character.[92] Play can be dangerous as it builds capacity to resist domination.[93] The sex industry uses play as an advertising motif because sex is fun. Play is erotic. Sex work can be erotic also through dressing up, exploring the boundaries of pleasure, orgasm, touch, and bodily vulnerability. People in sex work embody a different level of "playing" with gender, bodies, and sexual expression.[94] They inhabit paradox where sex is work and work is play. Religious practitioners, habitually embedded in a discourse of sexual sin, might learn from sex workers in this regard; how to play and unravel an obsession with immorality.

Play is not rejected in the biblical text either. The Hebrew bible pictures God as one who plays, in a garden with humans at the end of the day (Gen. 3:9) and as the world was being fashioned, cavorting with a creative female consort called Wisdom (Prov. 8:30–31). In the Christian testament, Jesus is pictured as a wise fool hanging out with, and being intimately touched by, sex workers.[95] According to the poet Mary Oliver, "the spirit likes to dress up" because the metaphor of the body – fluids, flesh and imagination – is needed for sacred relationship: to stave off divine loneliness.[96] Could this theological insight help FBO practitioners take a sex positive approach, or at least be open to learning about playful moments in sex work? A play-centric attitude can initiate respectful conversation and care in unusual ways.

With this level of interpersonal intensity, the sex industry can be draining work, and particularly so for women of colour, trans women, im/migrants, women with disabilities, underage sex workers, street-based sex workers, drug addicted workers, and people surviving under punitive criminal frameworks. These are the people whom FBOs accompany and support. As noted earlier, complexity and suffering develop from oppression with psychological illness, trauma, and homelessness a daily reality. What does play have to offer people in these circumstances? Playing, like humour, eases pain.[97] And it is creative, a relational domain where life humiliations can be transformed into art, so the inherent beauty of people is seen and celebrated.

Play is a gift of exchange. An encounter recalled by one of the practitioners highlights this:

> I remember once one of the women who, I walk past her, to and from, every day and she is this beautiful woman. She's transgender, she has a lot of health issues. She would pop in every morning to have a coffee. I remember this one day she brought in an orchid, it was this beautiful orchid and she's like, you just look like you're having a bad day. You know that moment of like my life, like I have a house, I am not homeless, I haven't had all this trauma happen but you're the one that saw that I wasn't having a good day and you gave me something beautiful.[98]

Play is about paradox in that it is doing the work of supporting others without doing the work – playing instead – and this is where the concept is precarious because letting go is involved. A play approach acknowledges and embraces the wise fool.[99] This figure from pastoral theology draws upon creativity and radical openness to the world as a response to complexity. This is about practitioners becoming foolish so that they can see people with new eyes, noting the acumen of sex workers who make choices towards living, even while defying social norms, and suffering for it.

Play is a safe holding space for complexity to be reframed, not always for sex workers to make dramatic life changes but for FBO practitioners to respect sex workers as equal agents, as players, as givers and participators in the drama of life. Play is about accessing another part of our humanity not concerned with fixing but rather connection. When people play together something deep is revealed that can open possibilities for joy.

Touchstone Three: Sharing Power

FBO storytelling can obscure structural gender violence and represent sex workers as those without any recourse to power. Yet power is an unstable force and sex work is an ambiguous exchange.[100] Abolitionists most often frame commercial sex as the use and abuse of a woman's body to satisfy men's sexual desire. Yet in turning the tables, is sex work also "about the use of a man's desire by a woman for her own profit?"[101] Who wields power if the sex worker's economic needs are met? Sex work is subject to many interpretations that don't easily align. FBOs, in concert with radical feminists, usually portray women in the sex industry as injured to justify intervention, as noted earlier. The use of FBO authority to give meaning to sex work, framed from a position of traditional morality, is rarely acknowledged.

In 2018, a respected Australian minister gave a keynote address where he pictured a female sex worker as a sexualized, wounded woman while he was the law-abiding citizen doing good in the world.[102] She had been charged with loitering and requested representation as he was a lawyer and Baptist minister in the area. She thought she would go to gaol due to previous convictions. He got her off the charges and she did not pay for his counsel in court. Who wielded power in the situation? The minister had immense structural and moral authority behind him, yet the worker's immediate contextual need was met and exceeded without cost. Rather than a new reading of power or an examination of the structures at play in the relationship, in the keynote she became a trope for his purpose of loving, serving, and learning about "the other" in an edgy community.

This type of representation justifies FBO work while validating traditional sexual order by maintaining a power imbalance that is degrading for sex workers. This is an easier framework to embrace than challenging social structures. The real test is if practitioners can use their power to publicly question sex and gender categories in religion that do harm, and also give account for their helping projects in other ways. Power dynamics must be analysed in practice and continually reframed with ambiguity, gaps and contradictions acknowledged so that there is potential for organizational change and redistribution can occur. Abuse of power must also be addressed. It begins with recognizing the unequal power between practitioners and clients.

> The relationship between a case worker, a volunteer for an organization, or an outreach worker and a sex worker is not equal. The person with something to give has more power in the relationship than the person who is in need. Note that the relationship is not equal, but the people certainly are equal.[103]

One way that FBOs can shift the imbalance is by sharing structural power. Particularly for the projects that have developed social enterprise ventures, the expectation can be that women who access support will grow to mentor others, do paid work, and engage in publicity, making the separation between workers and practitioners redundant. One of the FBOs founded by a former sex worker, now converted to Christianity, stated that "we genuinely come alongside we don't lead, guide, direct, enforce. You know it's like we are a cheer squad and we encourage them in their own journey."[104]

This same ministry also reported strict conditions for accessing support, as women must agree not to contact other ministry recipients outside of the project. They name this as a safe boundary yet in doing so, trust in women and the cut and thrust of broader community is absent. Yet the goal is to empower women to do this type of religious mentoring work themselves:

> Because it's [a] community based support network they see one another grow and they're like you know they'll just kind of go we're doing this or I'm doing this and they basically mentor each other. Like peer support they just come alongside each other and I kind of sit there going my work here is done. I'm making myself redundant.[105]

The FBO becomes a shared space, and the power dynamic has the potential to shift. Those who access support may then influence future direction and have a real voice in operations, not as recipients but as leaders. FBO practitioners could become professional friends. But this practice (language, action, and relationship) needs to be modeled through policies on power sharing and there are risks involved, especially if women are outed and experience stigma and organizational pressure to perform salvific narratives for fundraising. That same FBO offers clients the opportunity to tell their stories and raise awareness and funds for the project. It is framed in this way:

> You know you've been exploited we're not into that so if you come to a place where you want to work at the café, you want to serve the ministry, you want to come with me to my school speaking engagements and stand

> alongside me I'll just introduce you as my friend, you're a part of the community, the same way I am. So I think it's that community and the belonging which is the power.[106]

If clients of the organization can have a real say in strategy, governance, supporting others, and FBO publicity this could shift power on a structural level, over the longer term. Considering this touchstone, future research and practice might focus on obtaining direct feedback from sex workers and sex trafficking survivors on their experience with religious organizations and how they may co-design operations. In interviews with Australian FBOs, a key finding was that recipients are rarely, if ever, consulted on the direction of programs. Yet best practice means that the voices of primary stakeholders are integral in formation, governance and strategy and careful thought needs to be given to accountability structures.

In a participatory action study from Chicago in 2012, institutional violence from law enforcement, the health and education system, and social services accounted for most complaints by sex workers.[107] This is a damning assessment. If FBOs can create authentic space to receive feedback and empower clients to make regular reviews of projects, this will help mitigate the potential for unchecked institutional violence that is often enacted against sexually marginalized people, as well as normalize the process of power sharing over time.

Theologically, power is a difficult concept both affirmed and repudiated in the biblical text. God is the one with all power (Ps. 62:11) yet as Jesus demonstrates, power is meant to be given away for the love of friends and neighbours (John 15:13). The power of the cross is foolishness (1 Cor. 1:18) yet in his name stands a global legacy of power abuse by religious institutions and missionaries over centuries.[108] Christianity's understanding of power is ambiguous at best and explicit recognition of this history is the best approach for developing safe practices with sex workers. A transformational understanding of power and marginalization is required if FBOs are to move beyond a charitable model that is based on benevolent giver and needy receiver.[109]

One approach is to reconceptualize *kenosis*, taking note of the critique and potential of this theological concept. *Kenosis* means self-emptying and comes from the hymn in Philippians 2: 5–8 NRSV:

> Let the same mind be in you that was in Christ Jesus,
> who, though he was in the form of God,
> did not regard equality with God
> as something to be exploited,
> but emptied himself,
> taking the form of a slave,
> being born in human likeness.
> And being found in human form,
> he humbled himself
> and became obedient to the point of death—
> even death on a cross.

This is not an example of power that maintains the status quo by upholding privilege at the cost of ongoing disempowerment of sex workers.[110] Neither is this a picture of "divine power as forceful obliteration" but there is an insistence here on not being the knowledgeable one who holds power.[111] Philippians 2 is a disputed text in feminist theology because the abandonment of self and unquestioning submission to death are poisonous concepts for women under patriarchy.[112]

Kenosis is not a paradigm to encourage self-abnegation, burnout, or victimization but can be an impetus for sharing power through vulnerability and openness in relationship. Christ's self-giving challenges paternalism and can bring all people into a greater sense of self in the community.[113] This is kenosis as resistance to the powers of this world. On this note, Anna Mercedes asks a pivotal question: "What if having followed the feminist call to come into ourselves, we find ourselves opening out, wanting to be there for others and with others: in the erotic embrace, in social justice, in acts of courage where we might lose it all?"[114]

Being vulnerable like this is an ethical way of being at the margins. One practitioner described the experience in a grounded way:

> I think so many of us who work here are in that category and if I can be extremely blunt I would describe a lot of us as fuck-ups really, which is a bit blunt but you know like we've all lived and made mistakes and I think that's served us well in the work that we're doing because for me it means I can't judge and I think that's a bonus.[115]

Statements like this honour the individual personhood of women while at the same time acknowledging the vulnerability of all people involved with the project. "When we embrace our vulnerability and allow it to be the place from which we form relationships, think critically, and live courageously, then we are living kenotically."[116] Interdependence is revealed through kenosis as flourishing becomes mutual.[117] This is a radical challenge for practitioners to leave the comfort and safety of service provision and affirm intersubjective encounters with people in the sex industry, sharing power as a touchstone for practice or, in the words of Jesus, losing your life to save it (Mark 8:35).

Conclusion: the Possibilities of Best Practice

An FBO by its nature is faith-based. In Australia, FBOs have diverged mainly in two ways – they overemphasize faith, transformation, and adherence to doctrine, forsaking the rigors of professional practice to be known as a Christian ministry, or, they move away from historic roots of charity to become a corporate body embracing social work practices, relegating faith to something unspoken, hidden, or flagged via a commitment to quasi-religious values.[118] These touchstones can provide an alternative space for FBOs to reflect upon their practice in an ethical way and avoid the binary stance of either super religious do-gooders (amateurs) or non-religious social workers (professionals).

In 2018, I conceptualized these touchstones into a training day for one of the stakeholder organizations, St Kilda Gatehouse in Melbourne, to help "make new connections and reconfigure existing knowledge into new forms."[119] Twelve staff and volunteers participated. One person's feedback indicated that taking time to reflect on ethics, framed as touchstones, helped them understand issues sex workers face and communicate this clearly to supporters.[120] The touchstones enabled another staff member to know how better to journey alongside women by making space for different perspectives about sex work and through a more informed understanding of what the organization is actually doing.[121] Another staff member requested a scholarly grounding, which is the rationale for this chapter.[122] This reflects a key purpose of critical participatory action research, learning together as a process of knowing how to go on.[123]

My aim has been to articulate an explanatory framework that both informs best practice and guides self-reflection towards this end.[124] This is not a definitive model but a unique beginning point to address the lack of rigorous evaluation of FBOs by noting how an ethical framework can strengthen the language, action, and relationship of practice. A robust ethical framework is vital for careful encounters with marginalized communities and ongoing organizational growth.[125] Reflecting on touchstones for practice can help FBOs increase the collective agency of very marginalized people and might enable religious groups to participate in diverse political coalitions with confidence.

An ethical framework, such as outlined here, may also help FBO practitioners to develop their practice and note change in their work. Are worker skills strengthened and client outcomes clearly defined if touchstones are incorporated into reflection on practice? How is success described in light of this framework? Further dialogue and research, especially with conservative religious groups outreaching to sex workers, may create mechanisms for good praxis and continuous quality improvement. As a result, surprising possibilities for practice affirmation are on offer as one participant noted when reflecting on her journey from detached professional to friend of sex workers; people who have slowly but surely transformed her self-understanding from good Christian girl to empowered woman.

> In the past we just blundered our way through, you know we were probably thought of as that little Christian organization down there. It's about going back and saying well hang on actually some of our practice is best practice.[126]

Notes

1 Brian E. Woolnough, "Christian NGOs in Relief and Development: One of the Church's Arms for Holistic Mission," *Transformation* 28/3 (2011), 196.

2 Brian Howe and Renate Howe, "The influence of faith-based organisations on Australian social policy," *Australian Journal of Social Issues* 47/3 (2012), 320–326.

3 Howe and Howe, "The influence of faith-based organisations," 326.
4 Gerard Clarke and Michael Jennings, "Introduction," in *Development, Civil Society and Faith-Based Organizations*, eds. Gerard Clarke and Michael Jennings (Hampshire: Palgrave McMillian, 2008), 6.
5 Howe and Howe, "The influence of faith-based organisations," 320.
6 Carly Daniel-Hughes, "Evangelical women are shaping public attitudes about sex work," *The Conversation* 4 January 2018, https://theconversation.com/evangelical-women-are-shaping-public-attitudes-about-sex-work-89129.
7 Betsy Coughlin, "More Than Clothes Coming Off: Approaching Feminist Theology from the Strip Club," in *Women, Religion, Revolution*, eds. Xochitl Alvizo and Gina Messina (Cambridge: Feminist Studies in Religion Books, 2017), loc. 1516 to 1619 of 2248, Kindle.
8 Susan Dewey, Jennifer Hankel and Kyria Brown, "Transitional Housing Facilities for Women Leaving the Sex Industry: Informed by Evidence or Ideology?" *Sexuality and Culture* 21 (2017), 74–95.
9 "Partnership Organisations," International Christian Alliance on Prostitution, accessed August 31, 2021, https://www.icapglobal.org/partnershiporganizations.
10 "102 Organizations and Advocates Wrote to the House of Representatives' Leaders in Support of Legislation to Fight Online Sex Trafficking," National Center on Sexual Exploitation, accessed August 31, 2021, https://endsexualexploitation.org/articles/102-organizations-advocates-wrote-house-representatives-leaders-support-legislation-fight-online-sex-trafficking/.
11 Elizabeth Bernstein, *Brokered Subjects: Sex, Trafficking and the Politics of Freedom* (Chicago: The University of Chicago Press, 2018), Chapter 3.
12 Letitia M. Campbell and Yvonne C. Zimmerman, "Christian Ethics and Human Trafficking Activism: Progressive Christianity and Social Critique," *Journal of the Society of Christian Ethics* 34/1 (2014), 146.
13 Nicole F. Bromfield, "Sex Slavery and Sex Trafficking of Women in the United States: Historical and Contemporary Parallels, Policies, and Perspectives in Social Work," *Affilia: Journal of Women and Social Work* 31/1 (2016), 130.
14 Bernstein, *Brokered Subjects*, Chapter 3.
15 Elena Fiddian-Qasmiyeh, "Engendering Understandings of Faith-Based Organisations: Intersections between religion and gender in development and humanitarian interventions," in *Routledge Handbook of Gender and Developmen*t eds. Anne Coles, Leslie Gray and Janet Momsen (London: Routledge, 2015), 560.
16 Emma Tomalin, "Thinking about faith-based organisations in development: where have we got to and what next?" *Development in Practice* 22/5–6 (2012), 700.
17 Interview with FBO practitioner, July 06, 2016.
18 Lia Claire Scholl, *I Heart Sex Workers: A Christian Response to People in the Sex Trade* (St. Louis, MI: Chalice Press, 2012), 141.
19 Molly Smith and Juno Mac, *Revolting Prostitutes: The Fight for Sex Workers' Rights* (London: Verso, 2018), loc. 3893 of 6669, Kindle.
20 Laura Maria Agustin, *Sex at the Margins: Migration, Labour Markets and the Rescue Industry* (London: Zed Books, 2007).
21 Agustin, *Sex at the Margins*, 191–192.
22 Gretchen Soderlund, "Running from the Rescuers: New U.S. Crusades Against Sex Trafficking and the Rhetoric of Abolition," *National Women's Studies Association Journal* 17/3 (2005), 65.
23 Agustin, *Sex at the Margins*, 192.
24 Stephen Kemmis, Robin McTaggart and Rhonda Nixon, *The Action Research Planner: Doing Critical Participatory Action Research* (Singapore: Springer, 2014), 59.
25 Kemmis, McTaggart and Nixon, *The Action Research Planner*, 89.
26 Lauren McGrow, *Missionary Positions: A Postcolonial Perspective on Sex Work and Faith-Based Outreach from Australia* (Leiden: Brill, 2017).

27 Kemmis, McTaggart and Nixon, *The Action Research Planner*, 5.
28 My thanks to the Australian Research and Theology Foundation Inc. for funding this symposium.
29 Jean McNiff, *Action Research: Principles and Practice* (New York: Routledge, 2013), 29–30.
30 "Touchstone," *Cambridge Dictionary*, accessed September 7, 2021, https://dictionary.cambridge.org/dictionary/english/touchstone.
31 Kemmis, McTaggart and Nixon, *The Action Research Planner*, 20.
32 Kemmis, McTaggart and Nixon, *The Action Research Planner*, 35.
33 Erving Goffman, *Stigma: Notes on the Management of Spoiled Identity* (New York: Simon and Schuster, 1963).
34 Goffman, *Stigma*, loc. 116 of 2740, Kindle.
35 Goffman, *Stigma*, loc 110 of 2740, Kindle.
36 Melissa Gira Grant, *Playing the Whore: The Work of Sex Work* (London: Verso, 2014), loc. 916 of 1670, Kindle.
37 "Alabaster Jar 2020 Prayer Diary," Alabaster Jar, accessed March 21, 2020, https://alabasterjar.de/.
38 Gayle S. Rubin, "Thinking sex: Notes for a radical theory of the politics of sexuality," in *Culture, Society and Sexuality: A Reader* eds. Richard Parker and Peter Aggleton (London: Routledge, 2006), 150.
39 Rubin, "Thinking sex," 151.
40 Ronald Weitzer, "Resistance to Sex Work Stigma," *Sexualities* 21/5–6 (2018), 725.
41 Carly Daniel-Hughes, "Prostitution," in *The Oxford Handbook of New Testament, Gender and Sexuality*, ed. Benjamin H. Dunning (New York: Oxford University Press), 652.
42 Interview with FBO practitioner, June 3, 2016.
43 Gail Pheterson, "The Whore Stigma: Female Dishonor and Male Unworthiness," *Social Text* 37 (Winter 1993), 46.
44 Interview with FBO practitioner, June 3, 2016.
45 Yvonne C. Zimmerman, *Other Dreams of Freedom: Religion, Sex, and Human Trafficking* (Oxford: Oxford University Press, 2013), 78.
46 Interview with FBO practitioner, June 3, 2016.
47 Katie Bloomquist and Eric Sprankle, "Sex Worker Affirmative Therapy: Conceptualization and Case Study," *Sexual and Relationship Therapy* 34/3 (2019), 393.
48 Interview with FBO practitioner, July 6, 2016.
49 Susannah Cornwall, "Home and Hiddenness: Queer Theology, Domestication and Institutions," *Theology and Sexuality* 23/1–2 (2017), 43.
50 For outline of the guidelines see Katie Bloomquist and Eric Sprankle, "Sex Worker Affirmative Therapy: Conceptualization and Case Study," *Sexual and Relationship Therapy* 34/3 (2019): 392–408.
51 Bloomquist and Sprankle, "Sex Worker Affirmative Therapy," 395.
52 Daniel L. Louw, "*Ekhaya*: Human displacement and the yearning for familial homecoming. From Throne (Cathedra) to Home (*Oikos*) in a grassroots ecclesiology of place and space: *Fides Quaerens Domum et Locum* [Faith Seeking Home and Space]," *Theological Studies* 73/4 (2017), 4.
53 New South Wales decriminalized sex work in 1995, the Northern Territory in 2019 and Victoria is in the process of decriminalizing sex work to take effect in 2022.
54 Louw, "*Ekhaya*," 6.
55 Daniel-Hughes, "Prostitution," 652.
56 Daniel Fleming and Terence Lovat, "Learning as Leaving Home: Fear, Empathy, and Hospitality in the Theology and Religion Classroom," *Teaching Theology and Religion* 18/3 (July 2015), 208.
57 Cornwall, "Home and Hiddenness," 39.
58 Fleming and Lovat, "Learning as Leaving Home," 209.

59 Sharon Oselin and Ronald Weitzer, "Organizations working on behalf of prostitutes: An analysis of goals, practices and strategies," *Sexualities* 16/3–4 (2013), 449–450.
60 Oselin and Weitzer, "Organizations working on behalf," 451–452.
61 Interview with FBO practitioner, July 7, 2016.
62 Lynzi Armstrong, "Stigma, decriminalisation, and violence against street-based sex workers: Changing the narrative," *Sexualities* 22/7–8 (2019), 1289.
63 Armstrong, "Stigma, decriminalisation, and violence," 1293.
64 Armstrong, "Stigma, decriminalisation, and violence," 1302.
65 Henri Nouwen, *The Return of the Prodigal Son: A Story of Homecoming* (New York: Doubleday, 1994).
66 Nouwen, *The Return*, 52.
67 Monica Y. E. Chi, "Faith-inspired praxis of love: a framework for helping," *Journal of Religion and Spirituality in Social Work: Social Thought* 37/4 (2018), 427.
68 Nouwen, *The Return*, 132.
69 Nouwen, *The Return*, 132–133.
70 Beth R. Crisp, *Social Work and Faith-Based Organizations* (London: Routledge, 2014), Chapter 2.
71 Bloomquist and Sprankle, "Sex Worker Affirmative Therapy," 392.
72 Sharon S. Oselin, "Weighing the Consequences of a Deviant Career: Factors Leading to an Exit from Prostitution," *Sociological Perspectives* 53/4 (Winter 2010), 546.
73 Oselin, "Weighing the Consequences," 532–533.
74 Katie Hail-Jares, Corey S. Shdaimah and Chrysanthi S. Leon, "Introduction," in *Challenging Perspectives on Street-based Sex Work*, eds. Katie Hail-Jares, Corey S. Shdaimah and Chrysanthi S. Leon (Philadelphia: Temple University Press, 2017), loc. 184 of 6607, Kindle.
75 Mira Baylson, "Victim or Criminal? Street-level Prostitutes and the Criminal Justice System," in *Challenging Perspectives on Street-based Sex Work*, eds. Katie Hail-Jares, Corey S. Shdaimah and Chrysanthi S. Leon (Philadelphia: Temple University Press, 2017), loc. 3013 of 6607, Kindle.
76 Interview with FBO practitioner, July 7, 2016.
77 Hail-Jares, Shdaimah and Leon, "Introduction," loc. 257 of 6607, Kindle.
78 Rick Hood, *Complexity in Social Work* (London: SAGE, 2018), loc. 108 of 6016, Kindle.
79 Hood, *Complexity*, loc. 108 of 6016, Kindle.
80 Hood, *Complexity*, loc. 1743 0f 6016, Kindle.
81 Interview with FBO practitioner, July 7, 2016.
82 Bonnie J. Miller-McLemore, "The Royal Road: Children, Play, and the Religious Life," *Pastoral Psychology* 58 (2009), 506.
83 Miller-McLemore, "The Royal Road," 506.
84 Miller-McLemore, "The Royal Road," 510.
85 D. W. Winnicott, *Playing and Reality* (London: Routledge, 1971), 65.
86 Michael S. Koppel, "Playing Church: Toward Critically Creative Pastoral Practices," *Pastoral Psychology* 54 (2007), 431.
87 Babette Davis Reeves, "A Theology of Play," *Journal of Health Care Chaplaincy* 2/2 (1989), 20.
88 Reeves, "A Theology of Play," 25.
89 Reeves, "A Theology of Play," 20.
90 Reeves, "A Theology of Play," 21.
91 Mihaly Csikszentmihalyi, *Finding Flow: The Psychology of Engagement with Everyday Life* (New York: Hachette, 1997).
92 Zimmerman, *Other Dreams of Freedom*, 133.
93 Miller-McLemore, "The Royal Road," 516.
94 Kate Holden, *In My Skin* (Edinburgh: Canongate, 2006), 1–3.

95 McGrow, *Missionary Positions*, 155–156.
96 Mary Oliver, *Devotions: The Selected Poems of Mary Oliver* (New York: Penguin, 2017), 351.
97 Donald Capps, *Humor Us: An Appeal for the Gospel of Relaxation* (Eugene: Cascade Books, 2016), Chapter 2.
98 Interview with FBO practitioner, July 7, 2016.
99 Miller-McLemore, "The Royal Road," 515.
100 Carisa R. Showden, *Choices Women Make: Agency in Domestic Violence, Assisted Reproduction, and Sex Work* (Minneapolis, MN: University of Minnesota Press, 2011), 162.
101 Showden, *Choices Women Make*, 162.
102 "Tim Costello at Neighbourhood Houses Tasmania conference 2018," Neighbourhood Houses Tasmania YouTube Channel, accessed July 4, 2020, https://www.youtube.com/watch?v=gJ29PCeCsjo&list=LL&index=297&ab_channel=NeighbourhoodHousesTasmania.
103 Scholl, *I Heart Sex Workers*, 145.
104 Interview with FBO practitioner, August 2, 2016.
105 Interview with FBO practitioner, August 02, 2016.
106 Interview with FBO practitioner, August 02, 2016.
107 C. Angel Torres and Naima Paz, "Bad Encounter Line 2012: A Participatory Action Research Project" Young Women's Empowerment Project, accessed November 19, 2021, http://ywepchicago.files.wordpress.com/2012/09/bad-encounter-line-report-2012.pdf.
108 For a complex reading of power misused by nuns caring for female sex workers in Ireland over the last two centuries, see for instance: James M. Smith, *Ireland's Magdalen Laundries and the Nation's Architecture of Containment* (Manchester: Manchester University Press, 2007).
109 Nadine Bowers Du Toit, "The elephant in the room: The need to re-discover the intersection between poverty, powerlessness and power in 'Theology and Development' praxis," *HTS Teologiese Studies/Theological Studies* 72/4 (2016), 1.
110 Bowers Du Toit, "The elephant in the room," 7.
111 Sarah Coakley, "Kenōsis and Subversion: on the repression of 'vulnerability' in Christian feminist writing," in *Powers and Submissions: Spirituality, Philosophy and Gender* (Malden, MA: Blackwell, 2002), 16.
112 Coakley, "Kenōsis and Subversion," 6.
113 Rosemary Radford Ruether, *Sexism and God Talk: Towards a Feminist Theology* (Boston, MA: Beacon Press 1993), 137.
114 Anna Mercedes, *Power For: Feminism and Christ's Self-Giving* (London: Bloomsbury, 2011), loc. 90 of 4937, Kindle.
115 Interview with FBO practitioner, July 6, 2016.
116 Emily M. Stetler, "Poured Out Like an Offering: Toward an Anthropology of Kenosis," (PhD dissertation, University of Notre Dame, 2012), 8.
117 Stetler, "Poured Out Like an Offering," 10.
118 Howe and Howe, "The influence of faith-based organisations," 327–328.
119 McNiff, *Action Research*, 30.
120 FBO practitioner, email message to author, September 11, 2018.
121 FBO practitioner, email message to author, September 6, 2018.
122 FBO practitioner, email message to author, October 11, 2018.
123 Kemmis, McTaggart and Nixon, *The Action Research Planner*, 53.
124 McNiff, *Action Research*, 6.
125 McNiff, *Action Research*, 4.
126 Interview with FBO practitioner, July 6, 2016.

Bibliography

Agustin, Laura Maria. *Sex at the Margins: Migration, Labour Markets and the Rescue Industry*. London: Zed Books, 2007.

Alabaster Jar. "Alabaster Jar 2020 Prayer Diary." Accessed March 21, 2020. https://alabasterjar.de/.

Armstrong, Lynzi. "Stigma, decriminalisation, and violence against street-based sex workers: Changing the narrative." *Sexualities* 227/8 (2019): 1288–1308.

Baylson, Mira. "Victim or Criminal? Street-level Prostitutes and the Criminal Justice System." In *Challenging Perspectives on Street-based Sex Work*, edited by Katie Hail-Jares, Corey S. Shdaimah and Chrysanthi S. Leon, 136–151. Philadelphia, PA: Temple University Press, 2017.

Bernstein, Elizabeth. *Brokered Subjects: Sex, Trafficking and the Politics of Freedom*. Chicago: The University of Chicago Press, 2018.

Bloomquist, Katie and Eric Sprankle. "Sex Worker Affirmative Therapy: Conceptualization and Case Study." *Sexual and Relationship Therapy* 34/3 (2019): 392–408.

Bowers Du Toit, Nadine. "The elephant in the room: The need to re-discover the intersection between poverty, powerlessness and power in 'Theology and Development' praxis." *HTS Teologiese Studies/Theological Studies*72/4 (2016): 1–9.

Bromfield, Nicole F. "Sex Slavery and Sex Trafficking of Women in the United States: Historical and Contemporary Parallels, Policies, and Perspectives in Social Work." *Affilia: Journal of Women and Social Work* 31/1 (2016): 129–139.

C. Angel Torres and Naima Paz. "Bad Encounter Line 2012: A Participatory Action Research Project."Young Women's Empowerment Project. Accessed November 19, 2021. http://ywepchicago.files.wordpress.com/2012/09/bad-encounter-line-report-2012.pdf.

Campbell, Letitia M. and Yvonne C. Zimmerman. "Christian Ethics and Human Trafficking Activism: Progressive Christianity and Social Critique." *Journal of the Society of Christian Ethics* 34/1 (2014): 145–172.

Capps, Donald. *Humor Us: An Appeal for the Gospel of Relaxation*. Eugene, OR: Cascade Books, 2016.

Chi, Monica Y. E. "Faith-inspired praxis of love: a framework for helping." *Journal of Religion and Spirituality in Social Work: Social Thought* 37/4 (2018): 414–435.

Clarke, Gerard, and Michael Jennings. "Introduction." In *Development, Civil Society and Faith-Based Organizations*, edited by Gerard Clarke and Michael Jennings, 1–16. Hampshire: Palgrave McMillian, 2008.

Coakley, Sarah. "Kenōsis and Subversion: on the repression of 'vulnerability' in Christian feminist writing." In *Powers and Submissions: Spirituality, Philosophy and Gender*. Malden, MA: Blackwell, 2002.

Cornwall, Susannah. "Home and Hiddenness: Queer Theology, Domestication and Institutions." *Theology and Sexuality* 23/1–2 (2017): 31–47.

Coughlin, Betsy. "More Than Clothes Coming Off: Approaching Feminist Theology from the Strip Club." In *Women, Religion, Revolution*, edited by Xochitl Alvizo and Gina Messina, chapter 12, Kindle. Cambridge: Feminist Studies in Religion Books, 2017.

Crisp, Beth R. *Social Work and Faith-Based Organizations*. London: Routledge, 2014.

Csikszentmihalyi, Mihaly. *Finding Flow: The Psychology of Engagement with Everyday Life*. New York: Hachette, 1997.

Daniel-Hughes, Carly. "Evangelical women are shaping public attitudes about sex work." *The Conversation*, 4 January 2018. https://theconversation.com/evangelical-women-are-shaping-public-attitudes-about-sex-work-89129.

Daniel-Hughes, Carly. "Prostitution." In *The Oxford Handbook of New Testament, Gender and Sexuality*, edited by Benjamin H. Dunning, 645–660. New York: Oxford University Press.

Davis Reeves, Babette. "A Theology of Play." *Journal of Health Care Chaplaincy* 2/2 (1989): 17–26.

Dewey, Susan, Jennifer Hankel and Kyria Brown. "Transitional Housing Facilities for Women Leaving the Sex Industry: Informed by Evidence or Ideology?" *Sexuality and Culture* 21 (2017): 74–95.

Fiddian-Qasmiyeh, Elena. "Engendering Understandings of Faith-Based Organisations: Intersections between religion and gender in development and humanitarian interventions." In *Routledge Handbook of Gender and Development* edited by Anne Coles, Leslie Gray and Janet Momsen, 560–570. London: Routledge, 2015.

Fleming, Daniel, and Terence Lovat. "Learning as Leaving Home: Fear, Empathy, and Hospitality in the Theology and Religion Classroom." *Teaching Theology and Religion* 18/3 (July 2015): 207–223.

Gira Grant, Melissa. *Playing the Whore: The Work of Sex Work*. London: Verso, 2014.

Goffman, Erving. *Stigma: Notes on the Management of Spoiled Identity*. New York: Simon and Schuster, 1963.

Hail-Jares, Katie, Corey S. Shdaimah and Chrysanthi S. Leon. "Introduction." In *Challenging Perspectives on Street-based Sex Work*, edited by Katie Hail-Jares, Corey S. Shdaimah and Chrysanthi S. Leon, 1–14. Philadelphia, PA: Temple University Press, 2017.

Holden, Kate. *In My Skin*. Edinburgh: Canongate, 2006.

Hood, Rick. *Complexity in Social Work*. London: SAGE, 2018.

Howe, Brian, and Renate Howe. "The influence of faith-based organisations on Australian social policy." *Australian Journal of Social Issues* 47/3 (2012): 319–333.

International Christian Alliance on Prostitution. "Partnership Organisations." Accessed August 31, 2021. https://www.icapglobal.org/partnershiporganizations.

Kemmis, Stephen, Robin McTaggart and Rhonda Nixon. *The Action Research Planner: Doing Critical Participatory Action Research*. Singapore: Springer, 2014.

Koppel, Michael S. "Playing Church: Toward Critically Creative Pastoral Practices." *Pastoral Psychology* 54 (2007): 431–440.

Louw, Daniel L. "Ekhaya: Human displacement and the yearning for familial homecoming. From Throne (Cathedra) to Home (Oikos) in a grassroots ecclesiology of place and space: Fides Quaerens Domum et Locum [Faith Seeking Home and Space]." *Theological Studies* 73/4 (2017): 1–11.

McGrow, Lauren. *Missionary Positions: A Postcolonial Perspective on Sex Work and Faith-Based Outreach from Australia*. Leiden: Brill, 2017.

McNiff, Jean. *Action Research: Principles and Practice*. New York: Routledge, 2013.

Mercedes, Anna. *Power For: Feminism and Christ's Self-Giving*. London: Bloomsbury, 2011.

Miller-McLemore, Bonnie J. "The Royal Road: Children, Play, and the Religious Life." *Pastoral Psychology* 58 (2009): 505–519.

National Center on Sexual Exploitation. "102 Organizations and Advocates Wrote to the House of Representatives' Leaders in Support of Legislation to Fight Online Sex Trafficking." Accessed August 31, 2021. https://endsexualexploitation.org/articles/102-organizations-advocates-wrote-house-representatives-leaders-support-legislation-fight-online-sex-trafficking/.

Neighbourhood Houses Tasmania YouTube Channel. "Tim Costello at Neighbourhood Houses Tasmania conference 2018." Accessed July 4, 2020. https://www.youtube.com/

watch?v=gJ29PCeCsjo&list=LL&index=297&ab_channel=NeighbourhoodHousesTasmania.

Nouwen, Henri. *The Return of the Prodigal Son: A Story of Homecoming*. New York: Doubleday, 1994.

Oliver, Mary. *Devotions: The Selected Poems of Mary Oliver*. New York: Penguin, 2017.

Oselin, Sharon S. "Weighing the Consequences of a Deviant Career: Factors Leading to an Exit from Prostitution." *Sociological Perspectives* 53/4 (Winter 2010): 527–550.

Oselin, Sharon and Ronald Weitzer. "Organizations working on behalf of prostitutes: An analysis of goals, practices and strategies." *Sexualities* 163/4 (2013): 445–466.

Pheterson, Gail. "The Whore Stigma: Female Dishonor and Male Unworthiness." *Social Text* 37 (Winter 1993): 39–64.

Rubin, Gayle S. "Thinking sex: Notes for a radical theory of the politics of sexuality." In *Culture, Society and Sexuality: A Reader*, edited by Richard Parker and Peter Aggleton, 143–178. London: Routledge, 2006.

Ruether, Rosemary Radford. *Sexism and God Talk: Towards a Feminist Theology*. Boston, MA: Beacon Press, 1993.

Scholl, Lia Claire. *I Heart Sex Workers: A Christian Response to People in the Sex Trade*. St. Louis, MI: Chalice Press, 2012.

Showden, Carisa R. *Choices Women Make: Agency in Domestic Violence, Assisted Reproduction, and Sex Work*. Minneapolis, MN: University of Minnesota Press, 2011.

Smith, James M. *Ireland's Magdalen Laundries and the Nation's Architecture of Containment*. Manchester: Manchester University Press, 2007.

Smith, Molly and Juno Mac. *Revolting Prostitutes: The Fight for Sex Workers' Rights*. London: Verso, 2018.

Soderlund, Gretchen. "Running from the Rescuers: New U.S. Crusades Against Sex Trafficking and the Rhetoric of Abolition." *National Women's Studies Association Journal* 17/3 (2005): 64–87.

Stetler, Emily M. *Poured Out Like an Offering: Toward an Anthropology of Kenosis*. PhD dissertation, University of Notre Dame, 2012.

Tomalin, Emma. "Thinking about faith-based organisations in development: where have we got to and what next?" *Development in Practice* 22/5–6 (2012): 689–703.

Weitzer, Ronald. "Resistance to Sex Work Stigma." *Sexualities* 21, 5–6 (2018): 717–729.

Woolnough, Brian E. "Christian NGOs in Relief and Development: One of the Church's Arms for Holistic Mission." *Transformation* 28/3 (2011): 195–205.

Zimmerman, Yvonne C. *Other Dreams of Freedom: Religion, Sex, and Human Trafficking*. Oxford: Oxford University Press, 2013.

7 Jesus Ate With Pras

Christianity and Commercial Sex Work in the Caribbean

Anna Kasafi Perkins and Dane C. Lewis

> The Church is supposed to be a sanctuary for anyone who walks in. There should be a level of comfort and understanding for the 'whosoever will' who come seeking solace. However, when it comes on to certain walk-ins such as prostitutes, 'loose' women and homosexuals, there appears to be a sort of disdain exhibited by some members.[1]

Introduction

Prostitution or sex work is the provision of sexual services in exchange for some form of payment.[2] James Nelson notes that affection and emotional investment tend to be absent or minimal in such engagements with the selection of sexual partners being relatively indiscriminate.[3] Judaism and Christianity appear to have always had prohibitions against such "disorderly" sexual activity, although there is evidence in the Hebrew scriptures of tolerance of female prostitution in spite of general condemnation. Similarly, the Christian Church has condemned "prostitution while tolerating it as a lesser evil, especially in the Middle Ages."[4] With the Protestant Reformation there was a clearer prohibition against sex work and the state was urged to supress it; even so, sex work has persisted and been treated as a significant social problem in many societies.

This chapter traces the contemporary conversation on commercial sex work as it has unfolded in the Caribbean region. The discussion focuses on the example of Jamaica by exploring the role of certain highly vocal segments of the Christian Church, who are key interlocutors in the conversation on recognising, legalising, and protecting the rights of marginalized groups, including sex workers. Indeed, such Christian groups are often opposed to sex work based on theological perspectives on the role and purpose of sex as well as notions of sin and sinfulness, including structural sin.[5] As such, faith-based activism on behalf of sex workers in the region has been rather muted while sex worker organisations have been reasonably vocal. Where there has been support it has been on a personal or individual church level rather than a denominational or general Christian response. Even so, such Christian responses have been largely around rescuing or rejecting sex workers.[6] The question of sex

DOI: 10.4324/9780429328824-8

work in the Caribbean is further complicated by several factors, including the transactional nature of sex in the wider population which leads to a blurring in distinguishing practice; patriarchy, which favours the usually male procurer of sex, whose socialization has encouraged him to regard sex as a commodity to be purchased; the unacknowledged presence of gender minority participants, such as transgender women, and men who have sex with men; and the issue of HIV transmission and/or prevention continues to lurk in the shadows of the conversation.[7] Of course, a central question always in the background is whether those whose livelihood is sex work are really free to do so. This question is further complexified since sex work has been recently "reshaped under the trafficking paradigm."[8] (The timing of this conversation is particularly resonant in the current global pandemic as sex workers continue to be seen as immoral, criminal vectors of disease. This negative perception was evident during the heights of the HIV and AIDS pandemic but is no less so during the COVID-19 crisis.[9])

In addition, noted sex work researcher Kamala Kempadoo maintains that sexual–economic relations and subjectivities have been marginalized in Caribbean daily life; more troubling is that they have not been given the level of attention in scholarship and research that LGBTQ rights and advocacy has received over the last several decades. (And this is in spite of the fact that many LGBTQ individuals support themselves through sex work and even engage actively in leadership of sex work organisations.) In Kempadoo's view, this slighting of the sexual economy has caused "an important part of the conversation about Caribbean sexuality and...sexual justice for the region" to be missing.[10] Concomitantly, there is a slighting of the value of those employed in the sexual economy and their contribution in other spaces may be disregarded or even refused.[11]

Furthermore, given that Christianity has played a significant role in defining the contours of sex work, the discussion is framed using a contemporary interpretation of stories in the Gospels that show that Jesus may have shared the intimacy of meals with sinners, among whom were to be found prostitutes or "pras," as they would be called colloquially in Jamaica. Jesus is often presented as saying to those outcast as public sinners, "Go forth and sin no more." What could this mean for the Church's current opposition to sex work and its indifference to and continued misinformation on the lives of sex workers? In asking such questions, the conversation takes a "liberative" approach to Christian ethics. "Because a Christian theological notion of liberation has to be rooted in the practices of Jesus, so must the definition of terms in liberative Christian ethics."[12] Indeed, as African-American ethicist Traci C. West maintains:

> Any ethical examination of how differing moral concerns are linked must be approached in a way that reflects the gospel stories about how Jesus challenged specific social practices and attitudes in his radical social and spiritual engagement of people. Therefore, attention to practical realities of this world is not optional but at the crux of liberative Christian social ethics.[13]

The call is therefore to confront as Jesus did whatever thwarts the ability of human beings to live fully, personally, and communally, to defy all which denies personal and communal well-being in solidarity.

A Word about Words

Roland Stringfellow, an African-American, queer, Protestant theologian, alerts us to important distinctions among the various words that are used to label sex workers.[14] Women who are – either by force or choice – engaged in sex work are called "prostitute," "whore," "harlot." These terms are gendered in essence as they are referents to a female person, albeit a transgressive, outlaw female. Each of these words has varying weight in terms of the opprobrium heaped upon the woman, with "harlot" perhaps being the most freighted because of its biblical resonances. (These words are also used against women who have many sexual partners without monetary compensation. Similarly, the term harlot can be deployed against a woman who has not been promiscuous as a form of punishment.) In the North American context, "hooker" generally indicates those who have sex for money or other compensation while "slut" generally refers to those who "give it away for free." In the Jamaican context, a woman who is sexually promiscuous would be styled a "skettel,"[15] whether she charges for it or not. "Whore," which is used for a woman who sells sexual services, can also be a term of derision and condemnation. "Pras," which is used in the title of this chapter, captures the local referent for prostitute, which perhaps does not carry the same opprobrium as "whore" while averting to engagement in sex work. Jamaican sex workers refer to themselves as "pras" as the Jamaican short form for prastichuut (prostitute) – a kind of self-chosen name that owns self and practice while allowing the notion of prostitution with its biblical reference to remain present.

As journalist Cecilia Campbell-Livingston reports, some churches do not see a difference between prostitutes and women who have had multiple sexual partners.[16] Yet, there is a complex dynamic between sex, pleasure, and economics in the lives of Caribbean women that is not significantly interrogated.[17] Theologian James Nelson is therefore pointed in his refusal of the term "prostitute" for women who sell sex as he rejects the negative moral connotation of the term.[18] He uses sex worker as a means of focussing on sex work and that use highlights the nature of the interaction, which is driven by commerce "rather than low or aberrant morality."[19] Similarly, the recognition that commerce is the driving force behind sex work "rather than low or aberrant morality is more likely to lead to the development and widespread implementation of effective intervention and control strategies [for HIV/AIDS]."[20] This chapter also uses the term commercial sex work in order to focus on the commercial nature of the interactions and reject the stigma associated with the activity.[21] The term "pras" is also deployed interchangeably, from time to time, for both its cultural and biblical relevance.

The Caribbean and Christianity

The Caribbean is not just the archipelago of islands in the Caribbean Sea; it includes thirteen independent or sovereign states and nine island groupings that remain dependencies with some mainland territories in the south and west, namely Suriname and Guyana in South America, and Belize in Central America. The Caribbean has a rich, complex history. It is a history interrupted by the transatlantic trade in Africans, coloured by indentureship, and shaped and reshaped by European colonisation during which some territories changed hands multiple times, resulting in a post-colonial identity that is still finding its maturity through independence. Haiti is the oldest sovereign nation, having wrested independence from France some 200 plus years ago; the youngest Anglophone states have been independent for 37 years or so.

European colonialism generated a Caribbean complex of ethnicities, religions, and laws. Religion is "a crossroads of a sort where varying religious expressions both imported and indigenous meet."[22] Nonetheless, in the Caribbean, Christianity is hegemonic, even in multi-faith and multi-ethnic countries such as Trinidad and Tobago, and Guyana. Christianity supplies explanations for how to live well in this life and the next, particularly, significant matters of sex and sexuality.[23]

Caribbean Christians tend to be increasingly affiliated to Conservative/evangelical/fundamentalist/Pentecostal groups, as demonstrated, for example, in the most recent Belize, Trinidad and Tobago, and Jamaica censuses.[24] As Anna Kasafi Perkins demonstrates, while such Christian groups are "somewhat indigenised," they have strong transnational administrative, financial, and personnel ties with so-called sister churches in the United States of America.[25] Perkins maintains that this shift towards such conservative Christian affiliation is a reflection of the increased presence and influence of these North American church groups, which often have an expressed moral mandate "to defend religious freedom from attack"; the particular freedom claimed is to maintain laws aimed at preserving traditional ways of characterising family and family life. These local conservative Christian groups, like their overseas counterparts, are powerful and are given much attention as the voice of the Church in the public square. Their mobilisation in attempts to influence processes of law reforms relating to sex and sexuality is important.[26] These mobilisations have attempted to shape not only public discourses around issues relating to gender, sexuality, and human rights, but also formal discussions and implementations during constitutional and other legal reform processes.[27]

Sex Work in the Caribbean

Sex work in the Caribbean is multifaceted, covering a range of activities and spaces, including brothel, massage parlour, club, tourist-oriented, street-based, exotic dancing, and escort services. Significant sex work takes place within the tourist industry. Most sex work activities are viewed by the public as stigmatizing and degrading for those who provide the services, and the majority constitute acts that have been made illegal or criminal. "Sex work" and "sex workers" are not legal terms in any Caribbean country.[28] The term prostitution continues to be used to describe "sexual acts, including those which do not actually involve copulation, habitually performed by individuals with other individuals of their own or opposite sex, for a consideration which is non-sexual..."[29]

However, as Kempadoo, who is Guyanese by descent, indicates, over the past two decades, the term "prostitution," which, as discussed previously, carries a stigma, and is often used to denigrate women, has been replaced by the concept of "sex work." This new term is understood as necessary to protect practitioners "from [the] stigma, abuse, and marginalization that comes with the perception of prostitutes as [being] against moral, sexual and behavioural norms of society."[30] "Sex worker" was first introduced in the Caribbean in the early 1990s by El Centro de Orientación e Investigación Integral (COIN) in the Dominican Republic and the Maxi Linder Association in Suriname, which used the terms *trabajadoras sexuales* and *sekswerkers*, respectively, in their outreach and empowerment work. Sex work is therefore widely utilised by Caribbean human rights organizations, NGOs working on HIV/AIDS, and researchers on issues of gender and sexuality. These new terms explicitly identified sex work as an income-generating activity or as "informal and unregulated labor."[31] This usage follows from the idea that "work" in the Caribbean stands for all activities, except for leisure, "which contribute to human welfare, and not merely those which are linked to a particular form of economic accounting" and that:

> "Caribbean women employ many different strategies to harness the resources they need to sustain themselves and their families and that all of these together constitute what might be classed their "'sources of livelihood.'"[32]

Of course, colloquially, in the Caribbean, wok/work also refers to sexual intercourse as in the connotative phrase "haad wok"/hard work.[33] It is also used connotatively in Barbados for styles of dancing that simulate sex; these are referred to "wokin op."

Debates on sex work in Christian-influenced spaces like the Caribbean are usually shaped by value conflicts related to questions such as whether it should be viewed as immoral/sinful and the extent to which it affects gender equity or undermines women's rights and status in society.[34] The Church in particular considers sex work as sinful and against the divine will for sex; feminists and members of various women's movements and groups are also divided as some consider sex work as a manifestation of patriarchy and therefore a threat to the dignity and value of women; others regard it as work and therefore requiring improved working conditions and various protections.[35] What is clear, however, is that any sex work policy is inevitably a kind of "morality policy" that has been shown to have significant impact on the economic growth of a society, particularly in countries where there is a recognised and regulated sex industry.[36]

Currently, Caribbean states largely deal with sex work using the prohibitive model where it is seen as having generally negative implications for public morals and is therefore criminalised.[37] In such approaches, it is usually only the sex worker who is punished not the client or the pimps or brothel owners.[38] This does not put an end to sex work, however; rather it increases sex worker vulnerability to police harassment, drives sex work underground, increases the power of pimps, "and contributes to the psychology of violence against women."[39]

Sex Workers Organising Across the Region

As a community, sex workers often operate in collectives to protect one another, but this does not prevent turf war over workspace and boundaries, especially among the street-based pras. A particularly vulnerable group among pras is transgender women, however, research on sex work among transgender women in the Caribbean, including Jamaica, where transgender women report pervasive violence, has been scanty.[40] As recently as January 2020, several sex workers operating in Montego Bay and its environs were lobbying to form their own organised local group which they call "MoBay Commercial Sex Workers Association."[41] The mainly female group believe it is in their best interest to form "a uniformed group," so they could be better able to protect each other. Through a spokeswoman, Pinky, the women, who work in a cluster, tell of being constantly abused, robbed, beaten, raped, and even sometimes killed by male customers; on many occasions, these male customers refuse to pay for the sex services after they had received them.

> "We a woman an wi face nuff danger a nighttime a sell sex to man, but still yet the police inna MoBay not even wudda tek we inna consideration. Dem jus mek the man dem a tek advantage a wi every night…A jus wha day a tour bus driver tek a girl from bottom road and bring har go pon a corner a Salt Spring. When she fi get har money, him an sum a him fren dem beat har up, an run out pon the street inna the night. She even a fi run lef har shoes."[42]
>
> [We as women face a lot of danger in the night when we sell sex to men yet the police in MoBay do not even look out for us. The police allow the men to abuse us every night. Just the other day, a tour bus driver took a girl from Bottom Road to a corner at Salt Spring. When she asked for her money, the driver and some of his friends beat her up. She had to run out into the street in the night. She even left her shoes behind.]

The women lament it was futile to report the events to the police who take no action, beyond saying come and make a report. As a result, the women have all taken matters into their own hands, including arming themselves.

Such localized efforts have borne fruit over the last several decades in the rise of national sex worker rights organisation. Perhaps unsurprisingly, the sex worker rights movement in Latin America and the Caribbean emerged organically and so has an independent and distinct history from the labour movement in the region.[43] Many national groups emerged out of the need to advocate on behalf of sex workers and have their roots in NGOs doing HIV and AIDS prevention and care work.[44] In Jamaica, there is the Sex Workers Association of Jamaica (SWAJ). Similarly, the Guyana Sex Work Coalition (GSWC) has been in operation since 2008, promoting the rights of male, female, trans, and migrant sex workers.

According to Miriam Haughton, current spokesperson, "[SWAJ is] an organization that is run by sex workers for sex workers." The mission is to advocate for and preserve the fundamental human and workers' rights of sex workers in Jamaica whilst empowering sex workers through creating and sustaining an enabling environment.[45] Ms Haughton notes that their current work is around forming linkages for increased testing of sex workers in the field, training field officers in human rights advocacy to engage sex workers to report instances of abuse and the hosting of a safe house for trans and MSM sex workers.

Haughton noted that COVID has had a significant impact on sex workers, in particular street-based sex workers. They still go out as many are the main breadwinners for their family. Even though some clubs are still operating clandestinely, many pras prefer to be street-based to avoid the kind of exploitation many experience in brothels.[46] During the pandemic, they are most vulnerable to abuse and violence, from both pimps and their domestic partners. There has been a rise in domestic abuse, which is why the safe house was established.

These national groups have formed a larger regional Caribbean Sex Work Coalition (CSWC) facilitated through the regional coalition of Caribbean Vulnerable Communities (CVC), which currently works with sex workers in Guyana, Jamaica, Suriname, Trinidad, Antigua, Grenada, and the Dominican Republic. CSWC aims to advocate for the decriminalization of sex work, zero tolerance of the sexual exploitation of children, the prevention of sex trafficking, and improved health care for sex workers. The profile of the CSWC has been enhanced by its official inclusion in the Regional Coordinating Mechanism (RCM) of CARICOM, the regional multi-sectoral body with a mandate to provide oversight to the PANCAP Global Fund grants, which is a requirement of the Fund. Notably, in July 2020, the Caribbean Public Health Agency (CARPHA) published Guidelines for Sex Work during the COVID-19 pandemic, even as sex work remains prohibited across the region.

These sex worker organisations "have worked to challenge the 'forced' versus 'voluntary' dichotomy, and other moralising discourses, through public campaigns calling for rights and protection, while also working to support sex workers across the region."[47] Angelique Nixon maintains that the forced vs voluntary false dichotomy does not truly capture what happens in the sex trade in the region. Of note is that due to the tireless organizing and advocacy by sex workers and their allies, the HIV and AIDS pandemic that initially decimated the sex worker population has been slowed.[48] Grassroots organizations like J-

FLAG provided care and support services by and for sex workers and are disseminating information about HIV prevention, care, and support. While J-FLAG does not serve the sex worker population directly, it does undertake advocacy on behalf of its members, among whom are transwomen, many of whom are involved in sex work.[49] In working with various partners such as the Open Society Foundation, J-FLAG has put out several social media posts in 2020 advocating on behalf of sex workers in order to reduce shame and broaden the public's understanding of sex work. According to Elton Johnson, Equality Jamaica's Communications Officer, many transwomen find sex work to be a source of economic and personal empowerment as they are often unable to find employment in traditional spaces. The media posts support the decriminalization of sex work as the best way to protect the health and human rights of sex workers. They make a clear distinction between human trafficking as a human rights violation and sex work as a consensual transaction between adults.

One post lists four reasons persons may choose to do sex work; yet another notes that, like other workers, some sex workers may dislike their work but find it is the best option for making a living; some sex workers enjoy their work and find it rewarding and fun; others are okay with their work but find it offers flexibility or good pay. It is clearly a complex phenomenon.

The Law and Its Implications

The most comprehensive study of the laws governing sex work in the Caribbean region was commissioned in 2009 by PANCAP, *Prostitution, Sex Work and Transactional Sex in the English-, Dutch- and French-speaking Caribbean: A Literature Review of Definitions, Laws and Research*. This excellent desk study is the main source for the discussion of the laws on sex work and sex workers, which, incidentally, are not legal terms in any Caribbean country, undertaken below. The most common terms used in the law are "prostitution" and "prostitutes." Laws that date to the late nineteenth and early twentieth century define a prostitute as "a woman who engages in common lewdness." However, these have been for the most part replaced by new laws (such as in Trinidad and Tobago, and Antigua and Barbuda) in the 1990s which define prostitution as "the offering of the body by a person of either sex for the purpose of arousing or gratifying the sexual desire of another for payment in return."[50]

In Jamaica, the Dutch Caribbean, Grenada, Guyana, St. Lucia, and St. Vincent the prostitute is still defined in the law as a woman, with procurers and clients most defined as men. Even in circumstances where the law defines prostitute in more gender-neutral terms, there are sometimes slippages where the law starts out by defining prostitution as a non-gendered practice but then slips back into references to a prostitute as "woman" or "she" or to a brothel keeper as "he." Clearly, these laws fail in completely dispelling long-standing hetero-patriarchal ideas that it is women who provide sexual services, and men who organize, profit from, and pay for those services, as "pimps," procurers, brothel-owners, and johns. Yet, the experiences on the ground show otherwise.

Specifically, in the Anglophone Caribbean, most activities undertaken by sex workers – male and female – are criminalised. These include aiding and procuring for the purposes of prostitution; soliciting in a public place for purposes of prostitution; the use of premises as a brothel; living off the earnings of prostitution; buggery and gross indecency. Vagrancy laws in Antigua and Barbuda, Belize, and Guyana, for example, which can be traced to colonial vagrancy laws identify as a prostitute any person in a public place "who gives no satisfactory account of him or herself."[51] Immigration law in countries such as Trinidad and Tobago and the Bahamas prohibits prostitutes, those who organise prostitution, or those that live off the proceeds of prostitution from entry. In Jamaica, sex work is prohibited by the Sexual Offences Act, the Offences Against the Person Act, and the Towns and Communities Act. Section 23 of the Sexual Offences Act states:

> "...every person who knowingly lives wholly or in part on the earnings of prostitution or who or in any place, whether public or private, persistently solicits or importunes for immoral purposes, commits an offence, can be fined up to $500,000 or imprisoned for up to three years if convicted in a Resident Magistrate's Court. If convicted in a Circuit Court, offenders can either be fined or be imprisoned for up to 10 years."[52]

The Act also states:

> "...if there is a reason to suspect that any house or any part of a house is being used for the purposes of prostitution and that any person residing in or frequenting the house is living wholly or in part on the earnings of prostitution, the Resident Magistrate or Judge may issue a warrant authorising any constable to enter and search the house and to arrest that person."[53]

Netherlandophone Caribbean countries such as Curacao and Aruba do not criminalise sex work; rather they focus on the activities of third parties who profit from and manage the prostitution of another person – brothel owners, pimps, johns. Nonetheless, local governments in Curacao, St. Martin, Bonaire, and Aruba have ignored or suspended these laws permitting some brothels to operate under hotel licences. Sex work is regulated in various ways, including the prohibition of street walking, the need for registration with the police and regular health checks. Even so, discrimination against sex workers still exists within the Dutch Caribbean. Similarly, the former French colony of Haiti does not criminalise prostitution.

Guadeloupe, Martinique, St. Martin, and French Guyana – as departments of France in the Americas – are governed by French Law. Various amendments to French Law in the twenty-first century have more broadly criminalised soliciting for, procuring, and facilitating prostitution within a framework that also criminalises human trafficking. "The inclusion of passive and active soliciting for prostitution in this most recent law [2000] effectively makes most acts of prostitution in France and its overseas departments a crime."[54]

Of course, these laws are reinforced and interpreted through specific cultural and religious ideological perspectives, which, as noted, condemn mainly women engaging in sex work.

Christian Discourse on Prostitution in Jamaica

Rhoda Reddock, a Caribbean gender researcher, has maintained that religion is a site of cultural contestations on gender ideologies.[55] Religious fundamentalism – Christian and non-Christian – has surged in response to the threat of global hegemony from Euro-America. Reddock maintains that these fundamentalisms may pose a threat to women's liberatory movements as two dichotomous processes regarding women's sexuality and identity have emerged. The first of these is the commodification of both men's and women's bodies through the expansion of pornography, the sex-work industry, and the beauty-contest industry. Second is the increased visibility of fundamentalism worked out on women's bodies such as the move towards veiling among Muslims, even for pre-pubescent girls, which was never the tradition in the Caribbean. In the realm of Christianity, US Christian ideology is overwhelmingly present in the Caribbean as demonstrated by radio and cable programming.[56] Such Christian ideology emphasises a return to Christianity that supports the submission of women, men's headship and domination, homophobia, and religious intolerance.[57]

The Christian community in Jamaica has been reasonably vocal around matters of sex and sexuality in national life, often supported by confreres in the USA.[58] This has been assisted by the Government's call for submissions for the 2009 review of the Sexual Offences Act, which, as noted previously, criminalises sex work, living from the proceeds of prostitution, and other practices such as anal sex (buggery). As Patrick Lalor, then Chair of Sex Workers Association of Jamaica (SWAJ) noted:

> "This [criminalising] has serious implications for the children of sex workers and the elderly parents of sex workers who are taken care of by the proceeds of these activities."[59]

Lalor expressed particular concern that groups like JASL (and the Church) who offer services to sex workers are themselves in danger given Section 23, subsection 3 of the Act, which speaks to "habitually being in the company of a prostitute." Lalor maintains that JASL workers have been able to produce IDs when accosted by the police while doing their duty. However, the law gives the police the right to arrest, and some officers subject these workers and their suspected sex worker clients to harassment.[60] Sex workers report that they are also subject to extortion of money and sexual favours at the hands of law enforcement officials. Laws dealing with consensual sex between men and illegal immigration also lead to severe consequences for sex workers, often leaving them vulnerable to violence, discrimination, and abuse from law enforcement and clientele.[61] In the face of all this, there has been an increase in organisation among sex workers, who are particularly vulnerable in the face of the global HIV and AIDS pandemic and remain without protections against the violation of their rights. There is still a long way to go regarding decreasing sex worker vulnerability while giving full protection to their human rights.

In responding specifically to sex work, the Churches have been outspoken on several related issues as can be seen by media coverage over the last five years, for example, some churches have joined forces with the police in attempting to stamp out prostitution in Montego Bay, Jamaica's tourist capital.[62] Others have been vocal in the discussions about revising the Sexual Offences Act. Many continue to undertake ministry to sex workers that shames and condemns them.[63] Overall, the perspectives presented do not support sex work as an occupation but run the gamut from outright condemnation of the activity to a kind of compassion towards pras who have reformed. Indeed, as McGrow demonstrates, many Christians who minister to prostitutes take a problem and solution approach to these women. The women who are working in the sex industry are framed as the problem – victims of a horrendous system, which sucks them dry and from which they need to be rescued by well-meaning Christians. "Many groups believe that acceptance of Jesus Christ as personal saviour is the means by which radical lifestyle change will occur so that women are healed, restored and returned to live normal lives."[64]

Nonetheless, as Miriam Haughton, spokesperson for SWAJ, noted, sex workers still go to church even though they face a lot of discrimination. Miriam herself has experienced discrimination in her community and church because of the work she does with the SWAJ. Even taxi drivers refuse to carry her. Persons who may visit her are faced with the same issue as they are labelled pras by association.[65] The condemnatory perspective is strong in the pronouncements by Jamaica CAUSE (Churches Action Uniting Society for Emancipation); an ad-hoc coalition of religious groups, Jamaica CAUSE organized mass rallies against the so-called "homosexual agenda" and repealing the buggery law.[66] Tied in with this is the rejection of so-called anti-family lifestyles, including adultery, same-sex marriage, and prostitution. LGBTQ persons are involved in sex work and so their safety and protection continue to be compromised by the approaches of such religious groups.

Definition can be Tricky

Among the matters dealt with by some churches is how to define a prostitute. Darren McKoy, a Christian pastor, and national youth director of the Church of God in Jamaica, cautions that using the biblical definition of a harlot "can become tricky, and you may just end up finding prostitutes in the Church."[67]

McKoy captures the idea of transactional sexuality, which was discussed previously:

> If we were to go strictly based on the idea that giving sex in exchange for money makes you a prostitute, then I would say we can easily find them any and everywhere. Using that definition can make some businesswomen prostitutes, it could make wives prostitutes (depending on their purpose in the marriage), so many women could have been placed in the category.[68]

McKoy is clear that being a prostitute is much more than a sex-for-cash exchange as he points out that it goes to the level of consecration for the tasks; he attempts to make this point through referencing the so-called temple prostitutes of Paul's Letter to the Corinthians. This, in his estimation, rules out Church women from being considered prostitutes. However, as biblical scholar Jennifer Wright Knust and others maintain, the mythical "cult prostitute" did not exist and were perhaps part of the standard pejorative accusations made against the adversaries of Christians and Israelites.[69] So, even as the attempt at biblical condemnation via temple prostitutes may be mythical, the implications of the condemnation remain and are played out in the moral stigma attached to the process and internalised by many sex workers as has been continually on display throughout this discussion.

Legitimacy for Sex Workers

In 2013, with the news that Zurich in Switzerland had created a secured compound for sex workers, sex workers in western Jamaica called again for the decriminalization of the trade and the establishment of red-light districts. In calling upon the Jamaican government to provide protection for them, including from being objects of scorn in the society, sex workers represented by Angella Brown, a Negril-based pras claimed:

> We need better protection from the Government because we are legitimately trying to earn a living to support ourselves and our children. Just like everyone else, we have bills to pay.[70]

Once again the bid for legitimacy drew rejection from the Church, as detailed by Reverend Conrad H. Pitkin, pastor of the Montego-Bay-based Faith Temple Assemblies of God: "The Church remains in opposition to the legalization of prostitution in Jamaica…Firstly, from a moral perspective, we believe it is not appropriate, and secondly, we cannot open the nation and our young children to that sort of conduct."[71] Individual Christians have written to the editors of the dailies setting out contrary positions. One such, Lipton Matthews, makes a Christian case for legalising prostitution based on the arguments of theologians Augustine and Thomas Aquinas, who reasoned from the perspective of the lesser of two evils. Matthews further tied together several pragmatic and justice perspectives:

> Additionally, under normal circumstances these women would not choose to be prostitutes. When such women are punished no mercy is exhibited by the state. Admittedly, legalising prostitution is about liberating women, thus prostitutes will be empowered to conduct their business without interference from the state. Hence the Jamaican government should legalise prostitution, but this must not be guided by the intention to collect taxes.[72]

There is a tendency across the arguments of sex workers, Church respondents, and others like Matthews to confuse or use decriminalization and legalization interchangeably. Sex workers globally have tended to campaign for their work to be decriminalised, allowing them to enjoy the same basic freedoms and levels of safety enjoyed by non-sex workers. Decriminalization differs from legalization as it attempts to get specific laws concerning sex work to be removed from the books. Legalization would mean that sex workers could apply for licences to operate, which would involve some form of state control, bringing, of course, its own set of concerns.

The Churches Respond

In 2017, in a response to the government's request for submissions on current legislation relating to sexual offences, a group of churches and the lobby group, Jamaica Coalition for a Healthy Society (JCHS), rejected any legalization of sex work and proposed that laws be passed to punish persons who buy sex.[73] In defending their submission, the JCHS spokeswoman Phillipa Davies argued "prostitution degrades and demeans women and girls and facilitates their abuse" and that "a law against prostitution is a reminder that sex is not a commodity."[74] JCHS went further in their lobbying and suggested that the Parliament link the punishing of buyers of sex work to human trafficking. They reject outright the call by JASL for legalization. JASL was not calling for legalization, however, but rather decriminalization.

In response, Lalor argued that:

> …the laws, as they stand, drive them [pras] underground, limits their ability to negotiate safe sex, limits their ability to have sex in safe places, exposes them to increased levels of violence that is not reported to the police – because they are participating in an illegal activity – and as a result, increase their risk of contracting HIV and sexually transmitted infections.[75]

Lalor was calling for decriminalization. He directly challenged the hypocrisy of the Church, "I said to the Church in an interview, when I raised this [issue] some time ago, that there are husbands of the wives in the Church who do business with sex workers, so if you heed our call, we are ensuring that these husbands take nothing home to their wives."[76]

Ministering to Sex Workers

Even where the Church is more open to ministering to sex workers, especially those who have seen the errors of their ways, they maintain gendered notions of pras, which make them unable to minister to the full community of persons represented among sex workers. McKoy asks the Church to "abandon its stand-offish attitude and be more active in reaching out" and calls for outreach "to these women."[77]

> The reality, however, is that many churches are not at that place. There are a few I know that do engage prostitutes as a part of their ministry, but interestingly, this is in the minority. Contrary to popular belief, prostitutes are people, too, and they do deserve the same salvation experience that we preach about at crusades ... Going to the highways and byways is not just preaching from a distance about salvation, but meeting people where they are. These prostitutes are at Ripon Road, "back road," New Kingston, etc. That's where we should be.[78]

The Ekklesia Bible Fellowship, in the parish of St Andrew, was highly critical of the general church response to the plight of vulnerable groups like pras and drug-addicted people. Their senior pastor, Barrington Hall, was critical of the actions of the Church, "The Church offers no real alternative. We are good at condemning. We condemn people who commit abortion, we condemn the prostitutes and the drug users, but what is the alternative that we offer?"[79] The call for the church to do something in the face of such hardship is rooted in a reading of the story of the feeding of the five thousand in the Gospels (Mt 14.13–21; Mk 6.3–44; Lk 9.10–12; Jn 6.1–5). According to Hall:

> The story of the feeding of five thousand, for example, do we think Jesus did it because He wanted another miracle to be recorded in the Bible, or was He trying to teach His disciples the importance of caring for one another? Even with the little, trust God to do something, but do something.[80]

The alternative response that Ekklesia Bible Fellowship proposes is a haven for vulnerable persons; and to this end, they have acquired land in the parish of St Mary and are actively seeking funding to build a centre.

Others such as the Joy Town Community Development Foundation (JTCD) undertake social-intervention projects with sex workers. Representatives from JTCDF often visit the red-light districts and offer free HIV testing and counselling to sex workers. In addition to this, they also recruit girls to send them back to school and pay them a stipend to encourage them to stay. More than 35 sex workers have been sent back to school under this project.[81]

These approaches illustrate the prostitution as problem perspective taken by many Christians who minister to sex workers.[82] In problematizing these approaches to prostitution, the underlying assumptions that frame the perspective of rescue need to be challenged. Are women who do sex work coerced victims who are significantly harmed by it? Are they in need of rescue by powerful Christians, who uphold unquestioned and unquestionable conventional perspectives on sexuality? Indeed, such Christians perpetuate the belief that the unchastity of sex workers is played out on their bodies so they must be rescued and returned to purity.[83] In so doing, they blame sex workers for the dangers experienced in their profession due to a lack of protections. Such approaches also silence sex workers, whose complex life experiences and often sex positive perspectives to their profession is muted.

Jesus Ate With Pras

Early Christian writers, starting with Paul, customarily repeated, rather than challenged, the image of the female prostitute as debased and abject, which was a feature of elite male Roman discourse, and bore not only gender biases but also class and ethnic ones.[84] In fact, Paul shaped the figurative use of the prostitute in early Christian circles (1 Cor 5–7). His focus on sexual virtue was part of his attempt to demarcate "gentiles-in-Christ" from all others by deploying Israelite polemics against foreign cults and peoples; such polemics cast gentiles as especially sexually perverse. However, prostitution during Roman times was largely a feature of enslavement; slaves were subject to the sexual impulses of their masters, which included the possibility of being sold into prostitution. Paul's admonitions against prostitution would certainly have forbidden prostitutes from becoming members of Christ-believing communities; many slaves, subject to the desires of their masters, would also have been "unable to embody the sexual virtue that he outlines stringently."[85] Carly Daniel-Hughes argues, however, that while the prostitute was located outside of the borders of the early Christian community, the social realities of prostitutes and vulnerable slaves who associated with Christ-believing communities was more complex than is often appreciated. She points to Jesus's saying in the Gospel of Matthew, "Truly I tell you, the tax collectors and the prostitutes are going into the kingdom of God ahead of you" (Matt 21:31).[86]

Coogan argues that although Jesus is thought to have associated with prostitutes, the biblical text does not say this explicitly.[87] Tax collectors and "sinners" were a part of Jesus's following, and he ate meals with them much to the distaste of the Jewish leaders and others in society. The reference to "sinners" is often taken to mean such public sinners as prostitutes, many of whom were apparently among the followers of John the Baptist. Jesus used food and drink as a means of uniting himself with all – holy and unholy, the righteous and public sinners.[88] So central was this breaking of bread with sinners that he was accused of being a glutton and a winebibber (Lk 7.34).

Indeed, in the Gospels, Jesus Christ presents a sympathetic approach to pras and other public sinners such as tax collectors. Christ describes such repentant sinners as like a son who refused to do his father's will but then did it. For that reason, they are better than the Jewish leadership who condemned them as public sinners. He told the leaders:

> Amen, I say to you, tax collectors and prostitutes are entering the kingdom of God before you. When John [the Baptister] came to you in the way of righteousness, you did not believe him; but tax collectors and prostitutes did. Yet even when you saw that, you did not later change your minds and believe him. (Mt 21.31–32).
>
> Jesus was not here endorsing the validity of prostitution as a lifestyle—indeed the power of the saying depends upon the undesirability of prostitution (even they are ahead of you!) But he was implicitly rejecting the idea that prostitutes were inherently lewd and was welcoming repentant prostitutes into the kingdom of God.[89]

This open approach is reinforced by the story of Jesus' attitude to the woman, who many believe was a pras (although the text does not say this explicitly) (Lk 7.36–50); she washed his feet with her tears and wiped them with her hair before anointing them with ointment. She is also known as the "Anointing Woman," who displayed love and hospitality beyond what was expected. Jesus evinced no horror at being touched by such a person, welcoming her ministrations as an example of a truly forgiven person. Stringfellow, however, asks a controversial question: "Did Jesus require this woman to repent of her 'whoring' ways?"[90] (Stringfellow assumes with the traditional interpretations that she was a prostitute.) He maintains that Jesus forgives the "Anointing Woman" of her sins but does not tell her to stop her line of work (prostitution?). Continuing his perspective that she is a pras, Stringfellow argues that everyone needs to be forgiven from their sin and the shame they carry, however, this case is different, because unlike the tax collectors Matthew or Zacchaeus, who were told or prompted to "stop their cheating ways," this unnamed woman is not. Of course, it is possible to argue that this expectation is implied in the forgiveness of her sins. This is possible, as in another story in Luke's Gospel, a widow in Nain, whose son had died and was brought back to life by Jesus, so that she was potentially spared a life as a reluctant pras.

The pras turns a mirror towards the heteronormativity, which is at the heart of the Christian tradition, that rewards one type of female – "the ordered woman – sweet, demure and sexually controlled."[91] She can and does function as an important corrective "because she unmasks our abhorrence of sexually assertive, powerful women, [who could choose sex work as a viable, enjoyable and economically worthwhile endeavour]."[92]

Changes We Want to See

Considering the foregoing overview of sex work in the Caribbean, the Church's response, and a biblical perspective that highlights Jesus's liberative ethics in eating with pras and other sinners, we would like to conclude with some reflections on where we would like to see change happen for pras in the Caribbean. Our perspective is in line with Angelique Nixon, who makes clear that:

> [T]he future of Caribbean feminist and sexual minority work relies upon our ability to prioritize decolonization that is centered upon sexual freedom and the rights of sex workers, sexual outlaws, women, domestic workers, migrants, and sexual minorities to determine livelihood and live freely with the rights and protections deserved by all people.[93]

By prioritising decolonisation centred on sexual freedom and rights of pras, intersections, and commonalities as well as differences would need to be engaged; this would allow the unrecognised diversity of experiences among sex workers, who are too often viewed as immoral promiscuous females, to be interrogated and taken cognizance of. Pras are by no means a homogenous group, yet sex work continues to be seen as a female endeavour. Less attention is paid to gender and sexual minorities who are involved in sex work and the peculiarities of the challenges they face.

Not to be forgotten in the decolonization of sexual freedom and the rights of sex workers is the interpretation of scriptural texts that lead and give support to their oppression. Certain interpretations of scripture reinforce patriarchal perspectives that dehumanise women, especially women who challenge the expectations of demure womanhood. As this discussion of pras in the Caribbean context has shown, the metaphors, teachings, and interpretations serve to legitimate the lack of freedoms and protections for sex workers in a male dominated and Christian hegemonic space. In contrast, there is much food for thought in interpretations of Jesus's approach to the poor and outcasts, especially tax collectors and public sinners among whom were to be counted pras, with whom he ate and shared fellowship without demanding that they leave their sex work behind. Daniel-Hughes makes clear that such stories indicate the significant presence of women among Jesus's disciples; she questions, however, the attempt by some feminist scholars to distance Jesus's female disciples from the charge of prostitution, which may be implied in their freedom to follow and support Christ. Daniel-Hughes maintains that some feminist biblical scholars have themselves bought into negative attitudes to prostitution and women's autonomy in a fashion that continues to inform feminist discourse today.

Like Kempadoo and others, we maintain that it is important to challenge the perspective that those who engage in sex work are coerced and/or are victims of sex trafficking; rather, sex work is an intelligible response to the historical, socio-economic, and cultural realities of our Caribbean region. Yet hegemonic interventions of the Global North and the direction of international law and policy continues to frame sex work based on trafficking, forcing nations of the Caribbean to focus on sex work as a soft target for meeting reporting requirements and rankings. This must be challenged. So too, the widely accepted ideas that pras are victims in need of rescue, immoral women in need of conversion, or criminals in need of reform must be interrupted and space be made for the voices of pras to facilitate better understanding of their realities.

The continued marginalization and delegitimization of the voices of pras, despite their years of calling for recognition as equal citizens, demonstrates that they are still not being considered in framing the laws and policies that affect them. Some voices, particularly those of a very vocal minority claiming to represent "the church," continue to dominate and influence how law makers legislate bodies and limit diversity. Yet pras communities are vocal in demanding that no policy or law should be put in place without their full participation. We support their call for decriminalization, which will facilitate reporting abuses as well as address discrimination, particularly from the security forces. They also need resources to conduct peer educational programmes as well as access to comprehensive, quality, user-friendly healthcare services.[94] At the end of it all, pras are real people – mothers, sisters, brothers, and fathers – trying to make a living to support their families in the ways they know best.

Notes

1 Cecilia Campbell-Livingston, "Prostitutes, harlots and the Church," *The Jamaica Gleaner*, Saturday May 20, 2017.
2 Robin Parry, "Prostitution," in *Dictionary of Scripture and Ethics*, eds. Joel B. Green, J. Lapsley, R. Miles, and A. Verhey (Grand Rapids: Baker, 2011), 639.
3 James B. Nelson, "Prostitution," in *The Westminster Dictionary of Christian Ethics*, eds. James Childress and John Macquarrie (Philadelphia, PA: The Westminster Press), 513.
4 Nelson, "Prostitution," 513.
5 Lauren McGrow, "Doing It (Feminist Theology and Faith-Based Outreach) With Sex Workers – Beyond Christian Rescue and the Problem-Solving Approach," *Feminist Theology* 25, no. 2 (2017): 150–169.
6 McGrow, "Doing It."
7 Pan Caribbean Partnership against HIV and AIDS [PANCAP], *Prostitution, Sex Work and Transactional Sex in the English-, Dutch- and French-speaking Caribbean: A Literature Review of Definitions, Laws and Research* (Georgetown, Guyana: PANCAP, 2009).
8 Leticia Sabsay, "The ruse of sexual freedom: Neoliberalism, self-ownership and commercial sex," in *Global Justice and Desire: Queering Economy*, eds. Nikita Dhawan, Antke Engel, Christoph H.E. Holzhey, and Volker Woltersdorff (London: Routledge, 2015), 181. See also Angelique Nixon, "Sex/Trade/Work in the Caribbean – Challenging Discourses of Human Trafficking," *Social and Economic Studies* 65, no. 4 (2016): 83–91 and Kamala Kempadoo, "The War on Humans: Anti-trafficking in the Caribbean," *Social and Economic Studies* 65, no. 4 (2016): 5–32.
9 The Caribbean Vulnerable Communities Coalition (CVC) and El Centro de Orientación e Investigación Integral (COIN) (CVC/COIN), *From Tolerance to Rights: HIV and Sex Work Programs in the Caribbean - Effective Models and Opportunities for Scale Up* (The Caribbean Vulnerable Communities Coalition (CVC), El Centro de Orientación e Investigación Integral (COIN), Pan Caribbean Partnership Against HIV and AIDS (PANCAP), CARICOM Community Secretariat, March 2012).
10 Kamala Kempadoo, "Caribbean Feminisms: Interventions in Scholarship, Art, and Activism across the Region," *The Scholar and Feminist Online* 16, no. 1 (2020).

11 See the story of sex worker Natalee Garwood, who put herself up to run for Member of Parliament in Bridgetown, Barbados, in 2018. *Jamaica Observer,* "Sex worker gets support in her bid for Barbados Parliament," Saturday, March 17, 2018.
12 Traci C. West, *Disruptive Christian Ethics: When Racism and Women's Lives Matter* (Louisville, KY: Westminster John Knox Press, 2006), 49.
13 West, *Disruptive Christian Ethics*, 49.
14 Roland Stringfellow, "Denouncing the Real Villains of Sex Work: Towards a Compassionate Theology for Sex Workers," *Religión e incidencia pública. Revista de investigación de GEMRIP 2* (2014).
15 Ben Rolfe, Joanne Hemmings, Tricia Anne Morris, and Veronica Samuels-Dixon, *'she sweet up the boopsy and him nuh get nuh wine' - Young women and sexual relationships in Kingston, Jamaica: A PEER study* (Options Consultancy Services and Hope Enterprises Ltd., July 2007).
16 Campbell-Livingston, "Prostitutes."
17 Anna K. Perkins, "'Oh, Daddy, that's my G-Spot': Women and Sexual Pleasure in Jamaican Dancehall Music," in *Handbook on Sexuality: Perspectives, Issues and Role in Society*, eds. Nicholas E. Peterson and Whitney Campbell (Nova Science Publishers, Inc., 2012).
18 Nelson, "Prostitution," 196.
19 Nelson, "Prostitution," 196.
20 Kenrad E. Nelson and David D. Celentano, "Why Isn't a Commercial Sex Worker a Prostitute?", *JAMA* 271, no. 3 (1994):196.
21 In an email exchange with Dane Lewis, Cariflags noted that they had stopped using the "commercial" part of the title for several years now.
22 Anna Kasafi Perkins, "Introduction," in *Justice and Peace in a Renewed Caribbean: Contemporary Catholic Reflections*, eds. Anna Kasafi Perkins, Donald Chambers and Jacqueline Porter (New York: Palgrave Mcmillan, 2012), 18.
23 Anna Kasafi Perkins, "More than Words: Evangelicals, the Rhetoric of Battle and the Fight over Gay Rights in the Caribbean," *Journal of Eastern Caribbean Studies* 41, no. 1 (April 2016): 13–46.
24 Jamaica 2010; Belize 2011; Trinidad and Tobago 2010.
25 Perkins, "More than Words," 16.
26 Latoya Lazarus, "Enacting citizenship, debating sex and sexuality: conservative Christians' participation in legal processes in Jamaica and Belize," *Commonwealth & Comparative Politics* 58, no. 3 (2020): 366–386. https://doi.org/10.1080/14662043.2020.1773115
27 Lazarus, "Enacting citizenship".
28 Kamala Kempadoo, "Caribbean Sexuality: Mapping the Field," *CRGS: Caribbean Review of Gender Studies* 3 (2009): 1–44.
29 Henriques (1961, 17) in Kempadoo, "Caribbean Sexuality", 9.
30 CAFRA, *Situation Analysis of Commercial Sex Work in Trinidad and Tobago: Addressing a Vulnerable Group in Trinidad and Tobago* (Trinidad: UNAIDS, 2004) in Pan Caribbean Partnership against HIV and AIDS [PANCAP], *Prostitution, Sex Work and Transactional Sex in the English-, Dutch- and French-speaking Caribbean: A Literature Review of Definitions, Laws and Research* (Georgetown, Guyana: CARICOM Secretariat, PANCAP, 2009).
31 Christel C.F. Antonius-Smits et al., "Gold and Commercial Sex: Exploring the link between Small-scale Gold Mining and Commercial Sex in the Rainforest of Suriname," in *Sun, Sex, and Gold: Tourism and Sex Work in the Caribbean*, ed. Kamala Kempadoo (Lanham: Rowman and Littlefield, 1999), 241.
32 Senior quoted in Kamala Kempadoo, *Sexing the Caribbean: Gender, Race and Sexual Labor* (London: Routledge, 2004), 64.
33 Listen to Soca artistes like Allison Hinds, "Wuk & Run," *Sugar Stick Riddim* (2020). https://www.youtube.com/watch?v=ybLYKGdLJTo; Machel Montano, "Gyal Wuk," *The Whistle Riddim* (2012). https://www.youtube.com/watch?v=ON-YPfFPRtA

34 Eva-Marie Euchner and Christoph Knill, "Prostitution: Sin, unavoidable evil, or recognized profession?", in *On the road to permissiveness?: Change and convergence of moral regulation in Europe*, eds. Christoph Knill, Christian Adam and Steffen Hurka. (Oxford: Oxford University Press, 2016), 129–156.

35 Jacqueline Comte, "Decriminalising Sex Work," *Sexuality & Culture: An Interdisciplinary Quarterly* 18 (2014): 196–217. DOI: 10.1007/s12119–013–9174–5.

36 Wagenaar Hendrik and Sietske Altin, "Prostitution as Morality Politics or Why It Is Exceedingly Difficult to Design and Sustain Effective Prostitution Policy", *Sex Res Soc Policy* 9 (2012): 279–292.

37 This has not always been the case as detailed in Brian Moore and Michele A. Johnson, "'Fallen Sisters'? Attitudes to Female Prostitution in Jamaica at the Turn of the Twentieth Century," *The Journal of Caribbean History* 34, nos. 1&2 (2000): 46–70.

38 Sweden outlawed sex purchasing in 1999, followed by Norway and Iceland (2009), Canada (2014), Northern Ireland (2015), France (2016), the Republic of Ireland (2017), and Israel (2018). According to Annalee Lepp and Borislav Gerasimov,"'Editorial: Gains and Challenges in the Global Movement for Sex Workers' Rights", "[T]here has been mounting evidence that the Swedish model exacerbates the stigma against sex workers and forces them to engage in more dangerous activities, and increases the risk of HIV and STIs, and violence from clients and the police" (p. 1).

39 Laura Reandra, "Prostitution as a Human Rights Question: Problems and Prospects of United Nations Action," *Human Rights Quarterly* 13, no. 2 (1991), 203.

40 Carmen H. Logie, Ashley Lacombe-Duncan, Kathleen S. Kenny, Kandasi Levermore, Nicolette Jones, Annecka Marshall and Peter A. Newman, "Associations between Police Harassment and HIV Vulnerabilities among Men Who Have Sex with Men and Transgender Women in Jamaica," *Health and Human Rights Journal* 19, no. 2 (December 2017): 147–154.

41 Hopeton Bucknor, "MoBay sex workers want to form association." *The Star*, March 10, 2020.

42 Bucknor, "MoBay."

43 Lepp and Geramisov, "Editorial."

44 Christine Barrow, "Sexuality Research, Sexual Politics and Sexual Rights in the Anglophone Caribbean", *SexPolitics: Trends & Tensions in the 21st Century* 2 (April 2019): 41–71.

45 Interview with Dane Lewis, November 16, 2020.

46 Wilson, "Sacrilege."

47 Nixon, "Sex/Trade/Work," 24–25.

48 CVC/COIN, *From Tolerance.*

49 Anna Kasafi Perkins interview with Elton Johnson, November 16, 2020.

50 PANCAP, *Prostitution.*"

51 PANCAP, *Prostitution*, 16. The document also contains a comprehensive listing of relevant laws related to sex work in the English-, Dutch- and French-speaking Caribbean.

52 Okoye Henry, "No traction for prostitution out west," *Jamaica Gleaner*, Tuesday February 2, 2016.

53 Henry, "No traction."

54 PANCAP, *Prostitution*, 33.

55 Rhoda Reddock, "Caribbean Masculinities and Femininities: The Impact of Globalisation on Cultural Representation," in *Gender in the 21st Century: Caribbean Perspectives, Visions and Possibilities*, eds. Barbara Bailey and Elsa Leo-Rhynie (Kingston: Ian Randle, 2004), 179–216.

56 Perkins, "Evangelical Christianity."

57 Perkins, "Evangelical Christianity."

58 Perkins, "Evangelical Christianity."

59 Edmond Campbell, "Make it legal," *Jamaica Gleaner*, Friday June 9, 2017 http://jamaica-gleaner.com/article/news/20170609/make-it-legal-group-says-law-drives-prostitutes-underground
60 Campbell, "Make it legal".
61 Caribbean Vulnerable Communities and Jamaica AIDS Support for Life (CVC/JASL), *Position Paper on Decriminalizing Sex Work* (CVC and JASL, 2016).
62 Henry, "No traction."
63 Stabroek News, "Jamaica: 'Back Road' sex workers suspend usual activities for open-air church service", *Stabroek News*, May 28, 2019.
64 McGrow, "Doing It," 151.
65 Interview with Dane Lewis, November 16, 2020.
66 Human Rights Watch, *Not Safe at Home: Violence and Discrimination against LGBT people in Jamaica* (Human Rights Watch, 2014).
67 Campbell-Livingston, "Prostitutes".
68 Campbell-Livingston, "Prostitutes."
69 Jennifer Wright Knust, *Unprotected Texts: The Bible's surprising contradictions about sex and desire* (New York: HarperCollins, 2011).
70 Karrie Williams, "MoBay prostitutes want legitimacy; Church says no", *The Jamaica Daily Gleaner*, Tuesday September 3, 2013.
71 Williams, "MoBay prostitutes".
72 Lipton Matthews, "Christian case for legalizing prostitution," Letter to the Editor, *Jamaica Observer*, Tuesday March 10, 2020.
73 Campbell, "Make it legal." JCHS is a group composed of the Jamaica Association of Full Gospel Churches, the Jamaica Union of Seventh Day Adventists, the Jamaica Evangelical Alliance, the Church of God in Jamaica, Independent Churches of Jamaica, and the Pentecostal Union.
74 Campbell, "Make it legal."
75 Campbell, "Make it legal".
76 Campbell-Livingston, "Prostitutes".
77 Campbell-Livingston, "Prostitutes".
78 Campbell-Livingston, "Prostitutes".
79 Jodi-Ann Gilpin, "Church moves to save prostitutes and 'druggists'", *Sunday Gleaner*, Sunday October 22, 2017.
80 Gilpin, "Church moves'".
81 Wilson, "Reformed".
82 McGrow, "Doing It."
83 McGrow, "Doing It."
84 Carly Daniel-Hughes, "Prostitution", in *The Oxford Handbook of the New Testament, Gender and Sexuality*, ed. Benjamin H. Dunning (Oxford: Oxford University Press, 2019).
85 Daniel-Hughes, "Prostitution," 564.
86 Daniel-Hughes, "Prostitution," 654.
87 Michael Coogan, *God & Sex: What the Bible Really Says* (New York: Twelve, 2010).
88 Robert J. Karris, "The Gospel According to Luke," in *The New Jerome Biblical Commentary*, eds. Raymond E. Brown, Joseph A. Fitzmeyer and Roland E. Murphy (London: Geoffrey Chapman, 1990), 675–721.
89 Parry, "Prostitution", 640.
90 Stringfellow, "Denouncing," 190.
91 McGrow, "Doing it," 163.
92 McGrow, "Doing it," 163.
93 Nixon, "Sex/Trade/Work," 90.
94 CVC, *Position Paper.*

Bibliography

Antonius-Smits, Christel C.F. et al. "Gold and Commercial Sex: Exploring the link between Small-scale Gold Mining and Commercial Sex in the Rainforest of Suriname." In *Sun, Sex, and Gold: Tourism and Sex Work in the Caribbean*, edited by Kamala Kempadoo, 237–259. Lanham, MD: Rowman and Littlefield, 1999.

Barrow, Christine. "Sexuality Research, Sexual Politics and Sexual Rights in the Anglophone Caribbean." *SexPolitics: Trends & Tensions in the 21st Century* 2 (April 2019). https://sxpolitics.org/trendsandtensions/uploads/capitulos/2-caribbean.pdf.

Bucknor, Hopeton. "MoBay sex workers want to form association." *The Star*, March 10, 2020. http://web3.jamaica-gleaner.com/article/news/20200310/mobay-sex-workers-want-form-association.

Campbell, Edmond. "Make it legal." *Jamaica Gleaner*, Friday June 9, 2017 http://jamaica-gleaner.com/article/news/20170609/make-it-legal-group-says-law-drives-prostitutes-underground.

Campbell-Livingston, Cecelia. "Prostitutes, harlots and the Church". *The Jamaica Gleaner*, Saturday May 20, 2017. http://jamaica-gleaner.com/article/news/20170520/prostitutes-harlots-and-church.

Caribbean Vulnerable Communities and Jamaica AIDS Support for Life (CVC/JASL). *Position Paper on Decriminalizing Sex Work*. CVC and JASL, 2016.

Caribbean Vulnerable Communities and El Centro de Orientación e Investigación Integral Vulnerabilised Groups Project (CVC/COIN). *From Tolerance to Rights: HIV and Sex Work Programs in the Caribbean - Effective Models and Opportunities for Scale Up*. CVC/COIN. March 2012.

Comte, Jacqueline. "Decriminalising Sex Work" *Sexuality & Culture: An Interdisciplinary Quarterly* 18 (2014): 196–217. doi:10.1007/s12119-013-9174-.

Coogan, Michael. *God & Sex: What the Bible Really Says*. New York: Twelve, 2010.

Daniel-Hughes, Carly. "Prostitution". In *The Oxford Handbook of the New Testament, Gender and Sexuality*, edited by Benjamin H. Dunning, 645–660. Oxford: Oxford University Press, 2019.

Eldemire-Shearer, Denise and Althea Bailey. "Determinants of Risk Behaviour of Sex-workers in Jamaica: A Qualitative Approach." *West Indian Medical Journal* 57, no. 5 (2008): 450–455.

Euchner, Eva-Marie and Christoph Knill. "Prostitution: Sin, unavoidable evil, or recognized profession?" In *On the road to permissiveness?: Change and convergence of moral regulation in Europe*, edited by Christoph Knill, Christian Adam, and Steffen Hurka, 129–156. Oxford: Oxford University Press, 2016.

Fairchild, Halford H. "Frantz Fanon's *The Wretched of the Earth* in Contemporary Perspective." *Journal of Black Studies* 25, no. 2 (December 1994): 191–199.

Gilpin, Jodi-Ann. "Church moves to save prostitutes and 'druggists'." *Jamaica Sunday Gleaner*, Sunday October 22, 2017. http://jamaica-gleaner.com/article/news/20171022/religion-culture-church-moves-save-prostitutes-and-druggists.

Hendrik, Wagenaar and Sietske Altink. "Prostitution as Morality Politics or Why It Is Exceedingly Difficult to Design and Sustain Effective Prostitution Policy". *Sex Research Social Policy* 9 (2012): 279–292. doi:10.1007/s13178-012-0095-0.

Henry, Okoye. "No traction for prostitution out west." *Jamaica Gleaner*, February 2, 2016. http://jamaica-gleaner.com/article/western-focus/20160202/no-traction-prostitution-out-west.

Human Rights Watch. *Not Safe at Home: Violence and Discrimination against LGBT people in Jamaica*. Human Rights Watch, 2014.

"Jamaica: 'Back Road' sex workers suspend usual activities for open-air church service." *Stabroek News*, May 28, 2019. https://www.stabroeknews.com/2019/05/28/news/regional/jamaica/jamaica-back-road-sex-workers-suspend-usual-activities-for-open-air-church-service/.

Jamaica Daily Gleaner. "It is all about survival – MoBay prostitutes." February 2, 2016. http://jamaica-gleaner.com/article/western-focus/20160202/it-all-about-survival-mobay-prostitutes.

Jamaica Observer. "*Sex worker gets support in her bid for Barbados Parliament*." March 17, 2018. http://www.jamaicaobserver.com/latestnews/sex_worker_gets_support_in_her_bid_for_barbados_parliament.

Karris, Robert J. "The Gospel According to Luke." In *The New Jerome Biblical Commentary*, edited by Raymond E. Brown, Joseph A. Fitzmeyer and Roland E.Murphy, 675–721. London: Geoffrey Chapman, 1990.

Kempadoo, Kamala. "Caribbean Feminisms: Interventions in Scholarship, Art, and Activism across the Region". *The Scholar and Feminist Online* 16, no. 1 (2020).

Kempadoo, Kamala. "Women of Color and the Global Sex Trade: Transnational Feminist Perspective." *Meridians: feminism, race, transnationalism* 1, no. 2, (Spring 2001): 28–51. doi:10.1353/mer.2001.0011.

Kempadoo, Kamala. "The War on Humans: Anti-trafficking in the Caribbean." *Social and Economic Studies* 65, no. 4 (2016): 5–32.

Kempadoo, Kamala. "Caribbean Sexuality: Mapping the Field". *CRGS: Caribbean Review of Gender Studies* 3 (2009): 1–44.

Kempadoo, Kamala. *Sexing the Caribbean: Gender, Race and Sexual Labor*. London: Routledge, 2004.

Knust, Jennifer Wright. *Unprotected Texts: The Bible's surprising contradictions about sex and desire*. New York: HarperCollins, 2011.

Lazarus, Latoya. "Enacting citizenship, debating sex and sexuality: conservative Christians' participation in legal processes in Jamaica and Belize," *Commonwealth & Comparative Politics* 58, no. 3 (2020): 366–386. https://doi.org/10.1080/14662043.2020.1773115.

Lepp, Annalee and Borislav Gerasimov. "Editorial: Gains and Challenges in the Global Movement for Sex Workers' Rights." *Anti-Trafficking Review* 12 (2019): 1–13. www.antitraffickingreview.org.

Lewis, Linden. "Masculinity, the Political Economy of the Body, Patriarchal Power in the Caribbean." In *Gender in the 21st Century: Caribbean Perspectives, Visions and Possibilities*, edited by Barbara Bailey and Elsa Leo-Rhynie, 236–261. Kingston: Ian Randle, 2004.

Logie, Carmen H., Ashley Lacombe-Duncan, Kathleen S. Kenny, Kandasi Levermore, Nicolette Jones, Annecka Marshall and Peter A. Newman. "Associations between Police Harassment and HIV Vulnerabilities among Men Who Have Sex with Men and Transgender Women in Jamaica." *Health and Human Rights Journal* 19, no. 2 (December 2017): 147–154.

Matthews, Lipton. "Christian case for legalising prostitution." *Jamaica Daily Gleaner*, March 11, 2020. http://jamaica-gleaner.com/article/commentary/20200311/lipton-matthews-christian-case-legalising-prostitution.

Meszaros, Julia and Christina Bazzaroni, "From Taboo to Tourist Industry: The Construction of Interracial Intimacies between Black Men and White Women in Colonial and Contemporary Times." *Sociology Compass* 8, no. 11 (2014): 1256–1268.

Moore, Brian, and Michele A. Johnson. "'Fallen Sisters'? Attitudes to Female Prostitution in Jamaica at the Turn of the Twentieth Century." *The Journal of Caribbean History* 34, nos. 1&2 (2000): 46–70.

Nelson, Kenrad E. and David D. Celentano. "Why Isn't a Commercial Sex Worker a Prostitute?" Letters-Reply. *JAMA* 271, no. 3 (1994): 196. doi:10.1001/jama.1994.03510270042035.

Nelson, James B. "Prostitution". In *The Westminster Dictionary of Christian Ethics*, edited by James Childress and John Macquarrie, 196. Philadelphia, PA: The Westminster Press, 1996.

Nixon, Angelique. "Sex/ Trade/ Work in the Caribbean – Challenging Discourses of Human Trafficking". *Social and Economic Studies* 65, no. 4 (2016): 83–91.

Pan Caribbean Partnership against HIV and AIDS (PANCAP). *Prostitution, Sex Work and Transactional Sex in the English-, Dutch- and French-speaking Caribbean: A Literature Review of Definitions, Laws and Research*. Georgetown, Guyana: CARICOM Secretariat/PANCAP, 2009.

Parry, Robin. "Prostitution." In *Dictionary of Scripture and Ethics*, edited by Joel B. Green, J.Lapsley, R.Miles, and A. Verhey, 639–641. Grand Rapids, MI: Baker, 2011. https://www.academia.edu/8342687/_Prostitution_and_Biblical_Ethics_.

Perkins, Anna Kasafi. "More than Words: Evangelicals, the Rhetoric of Battle and the Fight over Gay Rights in the Caribbean." *Journal of Eastern Caribbean Studies* 41, no. 1 (April 2016): 13–46.

Perkins, Anna Kasafi. "Introduction." In *Justice and Peace in a Renewed Caribbean: Contemporary Catholic Reflections*, editors Anna Kasafi Perkins, Donald Chambers and Jacqueline Porter, 1–40. New York: Palgrave Macmillan, 2012.

Perkins, Anna Kasafi. "'Oh, Daddy, that's my G-spot': Women and Sexual Pleasure in Jamaican Dancehall Music." *Handbook on Sexuality: Perspectives, Issues and Role in Society*, edited by Nicholas E. Peterson and Whitney Campbell, 137–152. Hauppauge, NY: Nova Science Publishers, 2012.

Reddock, Rhoda. "Caribbean Masculinities and Femininities: The Impact of Globalisation on Cultural Representation." In *Gender in the 21st Century: Caribbean Perspectives, Visions and Possibilities*, edited by Barbara Bailey and Elsa Leo-Rhynie, 179–216. Kingston: Ian Randle, 2004.

Reandra, Laura. "Prostitution as a Human Rights Question: Problems and Prospects of United Nations Action." *Human Rights Quarterly* 13, no. 2 (1991): 202–228.

Rolfe, Ben, Joanne Hemmings, Tricia Anne Morris, and Veronica Samuels-Dixon, "'she sweet up the boopsy and him nuh get nuh wine'" – Young women and sexual relationships in Kingston, Jamaica: A PEER study." Options Consultancy Services and Hope Enterprises Ltd., July 2007.

Sabsay, Leticia. "The ruse of sexual freedom: neoliberalism, self ownership and commercial sex". In *Global Justice and Desire: Queering Economy*, edited by Nikiat Dhawan, AntkeEngel, Christoph F.E.Holzhey and Volker Wolterstoff, 180–194. London: Routledge, 2015.

Stringfellow, Roland. "Denouncing the Real Villains of Sex Work: Towards a Compassionate Theology for Sex Workers." *Religión e incidencia pública. Revista de investigación de GEMRIP2* (2014): 171–196. [Revista digital]. http://www.gemrip.com.ar.

West, Traci C. *Disruptive Christian Ethics: When Racism and Women's Lives Matter*. Louisville, KY: Westminster John Knox Press, 2006.

Williams, Andre. "It's all for you, son, says sex worker." *Jamaica Daily Gleaner*, July 6, 2020. http://jamaica-gleaner.com/article/lead-stories/20200706/its-all-you-son-says-sex-worker.

Williams, Andre. "COVID cleanness hard in a dirty business." *Jamaica Daily Gleaner*, July 6, 2020. http://jamaica-gleaner.com/article/lead-stories/20200706/covid-cleanness-hard-dirty-business.

Williams, Bianca C. *The Pursuit of Happiness: Black Women, Diasporic Dreams and the Politics of Emotional Transnationalism*. London: Duke University Press, 2018.

Williams, Karrie. "MoBay prostitutes want legitimacy; Church says no." *The Jamaica Daily Gleaner*, September 3, 2013. http://jamaica-gleaner.com/gleaner/20130903/lead/lead5.html.

Williams, Ros. "Postcolonial Discourses and 'Sex Tourism'." *E-International Relations* (August 15, 2011): 1–9. https://www.e-ir.info/2011/08/15/postcolonial-discourses-and-sex-tourism/.

Wilson, Nadine. "Sacrilege – Seedy sex shop blooms next to sacred sanctuary." *Jamaica Sunday Gleaner*, July 27, 2014. http://jamaica-gleaner.com/gleaner/20140727/lead/lead1.html.

Wilson, Nadine. "Reformed sex worker vows never again." *Jamaica Sunday Gleaner*, August 10, 2014. http://jamaica-gleaner.com/gleaner/20140810/news/news4.html.

8 When Survival Precedes Faith

Decolonial Perspectives on the Ethical Dilemma Confronting Female Christian Sex Workers in Africa

Beatrice Dedaa Okyere-Manu, Margaret Ssebunya and Sophia Chirongoma

Introduction

Sex work is one of the oldest professions in the world. It is believed to have been in existence since the recordings of history.[1] Be that as it may, sex work around the world remains a very contentious issue that has prompted intense and profound debate about morality, autonomy, equality, poverty and public safety in both political and religious spaces. Many sex workers in Africa believe that they have no other recourse apart from commoditizing their bodies as a means of survival. The need for survival has also led many sex workers, both males and females, to move beyond limited teaching of the Church which does not have much relevance to their daily lives. For example, one perspective of the Christian moral teaching on sex is that it should be confined within marriage.

As such, most sex workers find themselves trapped in a quagmire if they are religious. However, women in this trade see sex work as "work" which has the capacity to improve their economic lives. The moral dilemma that they grapple with is that socio-economic realities force them to overlook their Christian moral responsibility on the sacredness of sex and sexual relations. For them, survival takes precedence even though the survival strategy at their disposal clashes with their faith. For instance, a study by Wanyenze et al. on the experiences and perceptions of sex workers in Kampala, showed that a majority of the participants recruited in the study were practicing Christians with about 38 percent being Catholics and 31 percent Anglicans.[2] Because of the high presence of Christianity in our four study areas, the probability of the majority of study participants professing Christianity is high which poses a real dilemma for the Church.

Steeped in agency theory, whilst drawing insights from decolonial and postcolonial frameworks, the crux of this chapter is that if religious leaders are to engage ethically in ministry whilst genuinely exercising critical solidarity and compassionate care for marginalized people in their pursuit of a just society, then conversations that challenge and reconstruct approaches to sex work are desperately needed. Such conversations are intended to provide a springboard for non-discriminatory and non-judgemental attitudes and to proffer ways in

DOI: 10.4324/9780429328824-9

which religious leaders can affirm sex workers' agency to jointly explore alternative and humanizing livelihood strategies with them. Additionally, the chapter beckons Christian leaders to affirm the agency that sex workers already exhibit in choosing sex work – to accept them as they are rather than pressure women to find alternative sources of income, to offer them unconditional positive regard and to see what sex workers want.

Methodology and Theoretical Framework

Using the narrative method, this chapter presents the narratives of female sex workers from the selected study areas. The study was conducted among commercial female sex workers in four African countries (Ghana, South Africa, Uganda and Zimbabwe) in the cities of Accra, Pietermaritzburg, Kampala and Harare respectively. Selection of these sites was based on the place of origin and residence of the authors. The cities were particularly selected because they are among the hotspots for commercial sex work in the respective countries. The study was cross-sectional in nature and it employed qualitative data collection methods using focus group discussion guides. Eight focus group discussions (two groups in each city) were conducted with a total of 100 female sex workers over a period of two years (2017–2019). In each city, 25 female sex workers were recruited into the study through snowball sampling.

The prolonged period spent by the researchers engaging with the women enabled sufficient time to build rapport and also to create trust-based working relationships. A focus group discussion guide with open-ended questions was designed by the researchers. The questions sought to explore the narratives and individual experiences of participants in the selected cities. The common experiences and pertinent issues raised by interviewees in the four study sites are presented in this chapter.

Our adoption of the narrative approach is in line with the African feminist theologians' emphasis on the need for academic researchers to provide a platform for African women to tell their own stories. Mercy Oduyoye and Musimbi Kanyoro aptly say that:

> African women theologians have come to realize that as long as men and foreign researchers remain the authorities on culture, rituals, and religion, African women will continue to be spoken of as if they were dead.[3]

Hence, the narrative approach was chosen because it gives room to the study participants to vocalize their lived experiences.

All of the women who participated in this study lived and worked in the low-income areas in Accra, Pietermaritzburg, Kampala and Harare. They were aged between 19 and 60 years old. Sixty-one percent had attended up to primary school, 27 percent had completed the first four years of secondary school, 7 percent had completed secondary school, 2 percent attained university education and 3 percent did not have any form of education. Over 56 percent of the study participants considered sex work to be their primary means of earning an income. Approximately 44 percent had other means of earning an income such as restaurant waitressing, bar attending, food vending on the streets and domestic work. Hence, for the latter, sex work was an additional source of income since they were earning very little from regular jobs.

Through the lens of agency theory, this chapter highlights the need for the contemporary Christian community to recognize and acknowledge the agency that is being exhibited by these women and offer unconditional support and respect. The term agency in this chapter is used to reiterate the fact that female sex workers are not victims per se who are acted upon. Rather, their agency is foregrounded in their intentional effort to take charge of their lives amidst economic vulnerability, dispossession and neglect in order to transform their status quo. The act of engaging in commercial sex work is therefore perceived as a tool utilized by women for their economic and social emancipation.

This chapter also draws insights from decolonial and postcolonial theories as lenses for critiquing the numerous injustices, discrimination and dehumanization endured by African sex workers. In light of this, the chapter further adopts the postcolonial African feminist conceptual framework, which places African women at the centre stage to proactively transform all sectors of life, not only for their benefit but for the benefit of all. The relevance of this framework lies in the fact that it provides the means for retrieving and reclaiming the holistic agency of African women, which was pertinent during the precolonial era.[4] Acknowledging that the adoption of sex work for many females in Ghana, South Africa, Uganda and Zimbabwe is a survival strategy not only for themselves but their dependents as well, this framework lays a foundation upon which the chapter proceeds to wrestle with the human rights abuses, violations and injustices that women in the sex industry are exposed to. Since decolonial theory is agency-oriented, a combination of principles from this framework with postcolonial theory bolsters our argument.[5]

The main standpoint is that female sex workers are agents who are transforming their lives even though the method they are using contradicts Christian moral teaching on sex and sexual relations. Hence, the Church and society at large must be intentional in capacitating them with resources and opportunities so as to equip them to use their agency in alternative ways besides sex work. More so, the Church needs to start asking pertinent questions such as "what do these women want from the Church and society at large?" Introspecting on these pertinent questions might lead the Church to the realization that instead of burdening women with sexual moral teachings that condemn their choices for survival, compelling them to leave the industry and find "respectable" work, rather, it is the Church that needs to change its understanding of sex.

Economic Constraints, Poverty and Unemployment

Poverty and unemployment were mentioned as the key factors pushing women into sex work. In its 2016 press release statement, the International Labour

Organization reported that unemployment and vulnerable employment in Africa is on the rise. A combination of these factors exacerbates the pervasive labor market distress especially among women and youth. It further notes that creating productive jobs remains a key challenge especially in Sub-Saharan Africa.[6] Such factors have driven many women into sex work as a means of survival. Many of the participants in the study are mothers, they also have partners who are not able to provide for the household alone due to the menial jobs they do. Therefore, the women have no option but to do everything in their power to fend for their families. A majority of the women said that they are involved in sex work because it is the easiest available option for them to earn a livelihood and support their loved ones.

Economic challenges are typified by subsistence poverty and a lack of employment opportunities in both the formal and informal sectors. As such, there is an inability for women to meet basic needs such as food, clothes, decent shelter, healthcare and school fees for children. With the increasing cost of childcare, coupled with the fact that many women lack education to provide them with good jobs, the women choose sex work as a way to meet their needs. Our findings are congruent to the study conducted by Wanyenze et al. on the experiences and perceptions of sex workers in accessing HIV services in Uganda. In this study, over 69 percent of sex workers revealed that they had no other formal employment/source of earning income and were totally dependent on sex work for survival.[7] A participant from Accra said that:

> I am in this trade because I have nothing else to do in order to survive. The standard of living is high and since there are no readily available jobs, I have to think of alternatives that will support me and my children.

Another 56-year-old woman from Harare averred:

> Life was not easy. I needed to provide for my children. I could not afford to see my children starve to death and yet there was something I could do to save the situation.

A participant in Pietermaritzburg recounted:

> I was forced to get married to reduce the economic burden at home. Upon reaching the man's home, he was also very poor and he could not afford to take care of me. I then decided to find an alternative means of survival. I would go to sell my body for money and buy all that we needed in the house. My husband was happy that he was relieved of the responsibility of taking care of the home. He has never asked me about what I do to get the money that I use to run the home.

From Kampala, a participant lamented:

> I was involved in sex work before and that is where I met the father of my child. When I conceived, he took very good care of me and dissuaded me from selling my body for money. After the birth of our child, the man continued to take care of us. There was absolutely no reason for me to go back to selling my body. Unfortunately, he died when our child was four years old. I started struggling again financially. I made a decision to go back to sex work. I had to do it in order for us to survive.

From the above responses, it can be deduced that sex work is a source of survival not only for the women but also their dependent kin. In the absence of support from family or elsewhere, there is a limited range of options especially if the women have children to take care of. With the increasing levels of unemployment and poverty in the study areas, these women are doing whatever is in their means to address their situation. Many of these women have resorted to sex work as a livelihood option, since, according to them they have nothing else to do.

Because sex work is criminalized in all the four countries, it is apparent that women who engage in it do so not because it is an easier option. Life in the industry is a hard life as evidenced through the narratives of torture and inhuman treatment they have had to endure at the hands of police officers. A majority of the sex workers we interviewed reiterated that they are living in "hell" through sex work but for lack of other livelihood options, they continue to trudge on.[8] Akomah et al. cited by Fawole Olufunmilayo and Dagunduro Abosede note that the "economic motive for commercial sex work is so strong that it engenders a state of helplessness amongst prostitutes with respect to when, where, and whom to have sex with and whether or not to use condoms in the act."[9] The challenges encountered by sex workers raise key issues regarding the need for addressing the human rights abuses perpetrated in this industry. This includes the decriminalization of the sex industry, confronting police and client violence, safe working conditions, setting up unions to build collective political power as well as providing support, making safe sex resources freely available and according to sex workers the much needed respect in society rather than stigmatizing them.

Positive Aspects of Sex Work

All participants said that although they despised the work they do, in addition to the economic benefit, it also gives them some degree of independence that not many other jobs could provide. This shows the women's complex agency; by naming poverty and stigma as the problem, they are revealing their own agency and confronting structural oppression. Van den Borne notes that "for them [women] sexual networking has become a strategy to escape poverty, get access to modern lifestyle and some of its gadgets and maximize their autonomy."[10] Similarly, Dori Possel affirms that:

> Prostitution serves both as a means of economic survival for women with few skills, and a more lucrative form of employment than that available to them in the formal labour market. Some women turn to prostitution as the only means to secure their (and their families') economic survival. They cannot find any other employment that offers enough to support themselves and possibly their children and for their (common -law) husbands.[11]

Van de Borne's and Dori Possel's assertions are clearly evident as all the women involved in the study echoed that the money they get from the trade allows them to live an independent life and they do not have to rely on support from elsewhere to pay their rent, keep children in school and provide food and other basic household needs. Most poor women see sex work as real work and have "sacrificed everything to ensure that their families survive."[12] This is in line with the comments from one of the participants from Kampala. She said:

> I get frustrated with the thinking of most people, this is the work that is sustaining my family. I don't mind doing it as long as my family is fed. As women, we have to sacrifice for our children, even those working in government departments also sacrifice a lot: after work, tired and exhausted they have to sacrifice their comfort and do house chores.

Another participant from Harare reiterated this by stating that:

> This is my choice and as long as it provides me with all I need, I don't mind. I cannot imagine working for someone. I am my own boss.

The above discussion makes it apparent that there are numerous positive stories in sex workers' accounts, despite the "hellish" conditions in their complex lives. As activist scholars, there is therefore need for us to interrogate the tension between the women's agency and the oppression they inadvertently endure.

Orphaned at an Early Age

Being orphaned at an early age, leading to a lack of support from caretakers and increased responsibility, was also mentioned as one of the factors that pushed women into sex work. One participant from Kampala had this to say:

> When our parents died, I was forced to drop out of school in primary five to take care of my siblings because I wanted them to continue with school. Where do you think I could find a job that pays well enough to take care of them? Of course, I had to use my body. I am glad two of my siblings have completed school and I am now left with only one.

Another participant from Harare echoed the same life experience:

> Upon the death of our parents, my siblings and I were left on our own. Relatives chased us out of our parents' house and we found refuge on the streets. Life on the streets is not the best. I remember the first night I went to sell my body, I was very scared but I managed to make 63 US dollars. I was so happy. From that time on, selling my body became the norm. Today I am able to sustain myself, my two children and siblings from the sale of my body. I don't care what people say or think. As long as I can provide for my loved ones, I am a better individual and I don't need anyone's approval on how to earn a living. I am content.

These stories narrated across the four countries illustrate the fact that the entry point for many sex workers is economic reasons and it would be unfair to judge them harshly as they make a living. In adopting sex work, they have become agents of change and transformation of not only their lives but their families' lives, utilizing the only means of survival at their disposal. They do not just sell sex for pleasure but they are forced by circumstances that bar them from having access to alternative means of survival. The harsh reality of life was also reiterated by Mbonye et al. who state that:

> Economic strains and unstable relationships put many women in Africa at a disadvantage as they seek to finance children's needs as well as their own. Many women confessed that they lack help from their partners and this has opened the route to sex work as a readily available option.[13]

Peer Pressure and Lifestyle Choices

In addition to economic challenges, peer pressure was also identified as an emerging factor contributing to the high rates of commercial sex workers in the study locations. Some women acknowledged that they engaged in this industry to gain access to "luxurious" goods they would not otherwise have, but for which there is social pressure among peers to acquire. Some of these goods include perfumes, clothes, flat-screen televisions and smartphones among others.

A participant from Kampala said that she got into commercial sex work through peer pressure.

> You look at your friends with beautiful clothes, and you also want to have something similar or even better. Then when you ask them how they got it and they tell you that you have to find a man to cater for such luxuries. Later I wanted to have another man to get more things and I ended up in the sex trade.

Another participant based in Harare concurred:

> As a young female student at a tertiary institution, there is immense pressure to have the essential three "Cs", (car, cash and an expensive cell

> phone). Seeing my colleagues with the bling of driving the latest car models around campus, with a wallet full of cash and trending with the latest smartphones led me to wonder how they did it. As I befriended them and learnt their source of bling, I followed in their footsteps. I am now hooked to commercial sex work.

A Pietermaritzburg based participant also shared similar sentiments:

> It all started during my matric year when we were preparing for the matric ball. I was under immense pressure since my family could not afford to pay the hefty amount required for the matric ball and the stylish attire to wear on the long-awaited day. I overheard some of my classmates excitedly discussing how they were planning to go on a shopping spree in preparation for the matric ball. When I shyly remarked that I could not even afford the bare minimum, they all laughed at me and introduced me to the concept of rich men called blessers.[14] I was then coerced to find my own blesser to bless me with all I needed for the matric dance. Since then, I have traversed from one blesser to the next.

These narrations and many others indicate that some women end up in sex work, not because they are materially needy but mainly because they want to have what their peers have. This also speaks to the broader social pressures of living in a globalized world that is heavily influenced by Western consumerism and raises a number of ethical issues such as, how do we challenge over-consumption without blaming individual women who want access to luxurious goods? Why shouldn't they have nice things?

Adverse Childhood Experiences

Difficult and abusive relationships characterized by violence and limited educational opportunities are some of the common factors that were identified by the participants as push factors which drove them into the industry. Several sex workers shared that they were raised in a cruel environment at the hands of caretakers and that such cruelty pushed them into sex work as an escape route from such brutality.

A participant from Kampala chronicled her ordeal:

> When our father died, my siblings and I were left under the care of our step mother who was so bitter and angry towards us because she had no biological children. She always tortured us and many times we were denied food. She even refused to pay for our education claiming that we weren't her responsibility. I ran away from home and found myself on the streets and since then, I have never looked back.

Another participant from Harare tearfully related her experience:

> Our parents died when we were still very young. I am the eldest of five siblings and our parents died when I was fourteen years old. Our maternal aunt took us in but this did not go down well with her husband and her in-laws. They considered us as an unwelcome financial burden. In order to punish us, our aunt's husband used to physically and sexually abuse me and my younger sister whenever our aunt had gone to work in the fields or to work in the vegetable garden. I finally gathered courage to escape from this abusive home at the age of 16 and I came to Harare to find work as a domestic worker. Unfortunately, my female employer was emotionally abusive and her husband started to sexually abuse me whenever the wife had travelled for cross-border trading in South Africa. I ended up quitting my job unwillingly and found myself living off commercial sex work. I am currently renting a place where I am raising my other four siblings through sex work.

A Pietermaritzburg-based participant also shared similar traumatic experiences:

> I was raised by a step mother who harshly mistreated me and my siblings. I then decided to get married at an early age to escape from the hostility at home. Unfortunately, immediately after giving birth to my first child, my husband turned abusive and married another woman. At first I persevered hoping that the more children I bore with him, the more he would respect me. Unfortunately, the abuse persisted until I had four children. I eventually decided to leave him and I took my four children for fear that their step mother would mistreat them in the same way I had been mistreated by my step mother. With no other source of livelihood, I resolved to engage in commercial sex work to fend for my children and myself.

From the foregoing narratives, it is evident that many of the women who engage in sex work have the interests of their loved ones at heart, hence their choice to adopt sex work comes from a good place rather than for selfish reasons. From the narratives of the women engaged in commercial sex work, it is not uncommon for many of them to engage in the trade in order to finance their basic needs and also augment their household income.

While many people hold the view that sex work is immoral and a result of the collapse of moral values, they do not look at the many social and economic inequalities related to this practice. They tend to judge those involved in the trade calling them names and subjecting them to abuse, torture, stigmatization and degrading treatment. They have also been accused of not fearing God. In an interview conducted by Sharon Thumboo on community perceptions about sex work in Chatsworth Durban, South Africa, one of the interviewees had this to say: "I think these women do not fear God; if they do, they will not sell their bodies to so many different men."[15] Based on our findings, our stance is that sex work should not only be understood through the moral and religious lens but also through the socio-economic context of unemployment, poverty, migration, seasonal work and social disruption due to reasons beyond the sex workers' control among others.

Negative Experiences They Face

From the study participants' narratives, there emerged a number of negative experiences that were shared in common across the four sites. Apart from having to endure stigmatization as mentioned above, the study participants mentioned incidents of violence and abuse often perpetrated by clients, particularly clients who do not want to pay after the service is offered. They also complained about some clients who take advantage of their vulnerability knowing that due to the nature of their trade, they are not able to report them to the police or even to seek medical support.

A participant from Pietermaritzburg who is a street sex worker narrated that:

> Some clients are very abusive and mean. After offering them the service, they will turn around and say that they were not impressed and they will refuse to pay. They know that we cannot go to the police, and because I for one I cannot fight them, they end up going away without paying.

Another participant from Harare reiterated that:

> One major challenge associated with our industry is violence and abuse. In this age of HIV, some clients still insist that they do not want to use condoms. They argue that using condoms is tantamount to eating a sweet without removing its cover. Even if you tell them that you do not want to fall pregnant, they still insist on not using condoms. You just have to agree because there is nothing you can do. Unless you are part of a network group, you have no protection.

Clearly, the above narratives are chockfull with evidence of violence and abuse, which is rampant in this industry. This raises major concerns surrounding sex workers' health and well-being. It also foregrounds the important need for them to understand the potential health risks and to be able to use the different forms of contraceptives that are available to protect themselves from unwanted pregnancies, HIV and STIs. This is where the role of the Christian community becomes important, particularly its ministry to all the marginalized and dehumanized as well as its prophetic voice on behalf of these women whose voices are not heard within the Christian circles. In this light, the next section proceeds to reflect on the ethical and theological implications of sex work.

The Ethical and Theological Implications of Sex Work

So far, the discussion has revealed two major areas that have remained in the private sphere within the Christian arena. The first is the issue of sexuality and the second is the status of women in the Church. These two issues have not been adequately addressed by Christianity and in particular the African church. For instance, Christian sexual ethics holds that sex is sacred and therefore should be enjoyed in the confines of marriage. Additionally, the Christian teaching on sexual morality perceives sex work as fornication or adultery. We are aware that the Bible does not answer all our ethical questions, however, there are still clues for people who are both sexual creatures and Christians at the same time.[16] Genesis 2:24 notes that upon marriage, man and woman "become one flesh". Thus, breaking this bond through adultery is a breach of faith with one's spouse and with God. Regarding fornication, Christians are encouraged to remain chaste until they marry/are married, only then can they engage in sex. As such, most "Christians and the Church tend to shy away from talking about sex, premarital sex and sex outside of marriage."[17]

The narratives presented in this chapter reveal the push factors as well as the positive and negative consequences of sex work. The fact that hundreds of young girls and women are flocking daily into this industry has forced these issues onto the public agenda. The Church has not been equipped to deal with the moral complexities of this industry. Clearly, the attempt by Christians to address issues of sex, sexuality and women have led to several inadequacies coming to the surface. According to the Christian tradition, the sacredness of sex suggests that it cannot be commodified, therefore perpetrators are often met with apathy or ambivalence. While many of the sex workers we interacted with are aware of these moral teachings, they revealed that due to the harsh economic conditions, they are left with no other livelihood options.

A participant from Accra mentioned that:

> The Church's teaching can make sense when you have all that you need but when there is no food on the table and your children are starving, you will have to do whatever you can, in fact you don't think about the teaching.

On this same issue, another participant asked a very pertinent question in the Pietermaritzburg interviews. She asked the interviewer:

> … tell me, what will you do if your child is very sick and you don't have money to take the child to the hospital and someone says let me sleep with you and give you money to take the child to the hospital, will you refuse and let the child die saying it is immoral? Which one is immoral, to let the child die or to exchange sex for money?

The above stories confirm that sex work is one of the ways for them to earn an easy and a quick source of livelihood, becoming agents of their own lives. Such a status quo foregrounds the paradoxical reality and the apparent clash between the values enshrined in Christian sexual ethics and the women's adoption of commercial sex work as a livelihood strategy. Anthony Giddens believes that agency suggests a situation where human action offers freedom in action. He adds that free will and rationality allow the agent to act and monitor their conduct.[18] This suggests that agents are able to shape the world or structures around them for their benefit. Relating this theory to the current study, we realise that instead of relying on structures in society to meet their need, the participants have chosen to become agents to change their own lives, which the Church can honour instead of condemning. They do not want to be a burden but rather use their creativity to be agents of their own circumstances.

Besides having to constantly grapple with the ethical dilemma whereby their trade is frowned upon and castigated within the Christian moral tradition, which provides the foundation for Christian sexual ethics, another major dilemma bedevilling female sex workers is the criminalization of their trade, which makes them susceptible to undue harassment and dehumanization. The precise number of commercial sex workers in the study areas remains unknown. This is because ascertaining the number of sex workers is challenging as the industry is usually conducted clandestinely and the population is ephemeral, with people moving in and out of the industry depending on the circumstances. Female sex workers often remain undocumented and since sex work is illegal in all the four countries, a number of sex workers prefer not to reveal their sex work activities at all for fear of being arrested and fined.[19] The combined effects of the criminalization of their trade and the intense stigma attached to sex work, as well as being ostracized by their family, fellow community members, and societal structures such as the police and social services, makes them adopt fluid identities so as to conceal their sex worker status.[20]

According to Section 274 of the Ghanaian Criminal Offences Act 1960 (Act 29), sex work is illegal in Ghana and this has resulted in negative cultural attitudes towards sex workers. Tenni, Carpenter and Thomson attest to the fact that women are criminalized for soliciting sex in Ghana.[21] They are mostly ostracized by the larger community as they work in order to meet their basic human needs.[22] In a study conducted in Epworth just outside Harare focusing on legislation surrounding child prostitution, Nyakurerwa affirmed the same views. She put it across as follows:

> In Zimbabwe, prostitution is illegal and legislation has been put in place to criminalise it. Prostitution is a criminal offence in terms of the criminal code. Division E of the code, section 81 to section 87 deals with crimes relating to prostitution or the facilitation of sexual crimes. In section 81 soliciting is defined as soliciting in a public place and the section also covers the means used to solicit such as print or electronic media.[23]

Solicitors are often charged and fined or given a prison term of six months in such circumstances. Sections 82 to 85 relate to "living off the earnings of a prostitute, coercion, detaining of persons in order to engage in unlawful sexual conduct."[24] Similarly, in Uganda's Penal Code Act, sex work is illegal. Chapter 139 of the Act notes that it is a criminal offense for women to live wholly or partly on sex work.[25] Resultantly, any person who practices or engages in the trade is liable for an imprisonment of seven years. In South Africa, sex work is criminalised by the 1957 Sexual Offences Act and subsequently the Sexual Offences Amendment Act of 2007. These laws ban brothels, making money through sex work and solicitation or enticing customers.

Although sex work is regarded as a criminal offence in all the four study sites, the recurring fact raised by the study participants is that it is an easy means to earn and save money. Consequently, a number of people join or have remained in this trade because it is profitable. In the study by Okyere-Manu among some sex workers in Pietermaritzburg, one of the participants, a 27-year-old, mentioned that sex work is profitable, because with a rate of "between R50–R80 per session" she is able to charge "between R500–700 per night" and on good days she gets up to about "10 clients per day."[26] The inference here is that if we go with the lower rate, it suggests that as far back as 2014–2015, the 27-year-old was earning at least R5000 per day. To the participants in the study, this was one of the most profitable jobs because they are able to pay their bills, pay their children's school fees, purchase daily essentials for themselves and their extended families. In fact, most of the participants reported that they are in this industry because it is flexible, they can decide to drink on duty, can decide to work at any time, they are their own bosses, etc. It also came out that some individuals choose sex work even though they have other equally profitable jobs. A number of them supplement their income with part-time or short-term sex work.[27]

Walking through particular spots in most of these cities, particularly the study areas, one observes many sex workers waiting for pickup from clients especially at night or in the early morning hours. The criminalization of sex work is believed to have increased sex workers' vulnerability to HIV and other related diseases, stigmatization as well as abuse and torture by police and the clients.[28]

Studies demonstrate that stigma continues to play a key role in shaping sex workers' lives.[29] Notably many of them "take on fluid and multiple identities that would give them space to manoeuvre" to avoid the stigmatization that comes along with engaging in sex work.[30] One of the participants mentioned that "No one in my family knows what I am actually doing to avoid stigmatization, all they know is that I am working in the hospitality industry."

It is against this backdrop that we tap into decolonial and the African-feminist postcolonial theories as pillars to propound for the Christian community to strive to become a redemptive community that embraces sex workers. Cognizant of the ethical dilemma confronting most sex workers in light of Christian sexual ethics, we are proposing that the Christian community deconstructs judgmental and stigmatizing attitudes and perceptions around sex and sex workers. If Christian communities profess to be inclusive and healing communities, this should beckon the Church not to exclude and judge female sex workers. Instead, they should lend their listening ears to enable them to understand where these women are coming from. As one participant commented:

> The problem with members in the Church is that they are quick to condemn without knowing one's story. I had a very bad experience when one

> church member saw me on the roadside and spread it in the women's fellowship group.

This suggests that it is only in lending a listening ear that the Church can be relevant to the daily struggles endured by women, especially the bulk of those who have chosen the sex work industry due to circumstances beyond their control and even those who are in the industry by choice. Hence, the starting point for anyone who wishes to journey along with the female sex workers is to begin by hearing their stories and their experiences.[31] Acknowledging them as agents of their own destinies will be an important step towards formulating strategies aimed at addressing the multifarious factors that are pushing them into this industry. Hence, we resonate with Maseko whose contention is that:

> The criminalization of sex work dehumanizes sex workers and makes them an invisible group, marginalized and excluded from society... but gradually, women are pushing back against oppressive forces that seek to dictate to them what they should do with their bodies. Women are gradually reclaiming their bodies through the language of rights and sex workers are leading the way.[32]

So practically what does it mean for the Church to be an inclusive and redemptive community to sex workers? The next section will highlight how Christianity's attitude to sex and sexual practices are to be redeemed to offer dignity to all.

Inviting the Church to Redeem the Humanity and Dignity of Sex Workers

True to its goal and mission, the Church ought to be welcoming to all God's people whether sex workers or not. On the basis of the narratives presented in this chapter, it is pertinent that the Church pays attention to the plight of women who find themselves trapped in sex work so that they can be empowered and equipped to do what they think is best with their lives, to have greater choices and not to be condemned if they decided to remain as sex workers. The same applies to those who are engaging in sex work out of their free will; the Church should minister to them as well. In fulfilment of its mandate as the light to the world and the salt of the earth, the Church should become the agent for change and transformation of the cultural and economic factors that expose women to sex work.

Additionally, the Church should create a safe space for women who have been forced into sex work, especially those trafficked and those who are forced into the industry against their will.[33] In such a space, sex workers should be free from any form of stigma in order to help them to rediscover who exactly they are in the face of their creator. Finally, the church ought not to be judgemental of those involved in sex work. Much of the stigma faced by sex workers stems from religion and culture. Being judgemental creates a divide between "us" and "them" where those involved in sex work are viewed as "sinners" while those who are not are viewed as the "holy ones." Consequently, the Church must lead the way in accepting sex workers within church spaces. The Church has a responsibility of finding a common ground for all believers to share in the grace of God and with the freedom that comes from accepting oneself and others. This may eventually help other Christians not to view sex workers with a negative attitude and mindset.

If the Church is sincerely committed towards holistic ministry, it should create a platform for a mutual discussion with the female sex workers in a bid to come up with practical solutions to the factors pushing women into sex work. Doing this would be the Church's acknowledgement that it is not enough to simply identify a moral problem and not offer solutions to the problem at hand.[34] The findings in this study resonate with other scholars who have researched on the same subject in Africa. It is befitting to conclude our discussion by citing Maseko at length, whose views echo the findings and arguments in this chapter:

> Sex work has been blamed for denigrating the morality of African societies. The common regional response has been the formulation of legal laws criminalizing sex work. This is because the laws are founded on a moral code, but they equally seek to impose a concept of morality on all citizens. The laws governing sex work are equally premised on a moral and religious code that purports to protect women's chastity and purity. Where morality and religion are used as arguments, those who are seen to be deviant are often subject to stigmatization. For instance, sex work is highly stigmatized in Africa and considered a 'moral issue', which results in social, religious and cultural ostracization and discrimination. Female sex workers are doubly discriminated against, because they are women and because they are sex workers.[35]

Adding to Maseko's terminology on African female sex workers being doubly discriminated on the basis of their gender and their social class, we are proposing the addition of a third component: race. Hence, in our view, African female sex workers suffer a triple oppression because of their race (color), gender (female) and social class (sex work). It is from the clutches of these three layers of oppression and dehumanization that our chapter is advocating that African female sex workers be released from.

Notes

1 Victor Lewis, and James Larson. "Sex work is one of the oldest professions in the world" *Journal of International Business and Cultural Studies* 9 (January 2015): 1–9. 1

2 Rhoda K. Wanyenze, Geoffrey Musinguzi. Juliet Kiguli, Fred Nuwaha, Geoffrey Mujisha, Joshua Musinguzi, Jim Arinaitwe, Joseph K. B. Matovu. "'When they

know that you are a sex worker, you will be the last person to be treated': Perceptions and experiences of female sex workers in accessing HIV services in Uganda." *BMC International Health and Human Rights* 17, No.11 (May 2017): 2–11 doi10.1186/s12914–017–0119–1. 3

3 Mercy Amba Oduyoye and Musimbi R. A. Kanyoro Eds. *The Will to Arise: Women, Tradition, and the Church in Africa.* Maryknoll, New York: Orbis Books, 1992:1.

4 See Mercy Amba Oduyoye. "Feminist theology in an African perspective." In *Paths of African Theology* edited by Gibellini Rosino, 166–181. London: SCM Press, 1994; Dube, Musa. "Postcoloniality, Feminist Spaces, and Religion." In *Postcolonialism, Feminism, and Religious Discourse*, edited by Donaldson, Laura E and Kwok Pui-lan, 100–20. New York: Routledge, 2002.

5 Gabriele, Dietze. "Decolonizing Gender – Gendering Decolonial Theory Cross-Currents and Archaeologies." In *Postcoloniality-Decoloniality-Black Critique: Joints and Fissures* edited by Broeck, Sabine and Junker Carsten, 253–276. Frankfurt/ New-York: Campus Verlag, 2014.

6 International Labour Organization. "Facing the growing unemployment challenges in Africa." World Employment Social Outlook Press Release January 20th, 2016 https://www.ilo.org/africa/media-centre/pr/WCMS_444474/lang–en/index.htm

7 Wanyenze et al., "When they know," 3.

8 Sex workers confessed to living in "hell" as they suffer many injustices from the police, the clients as well as stigma within the communities.

9 Falowe I. Olufunmilayo and Dagunduro T. Abosede. "Prevalence and correlates of violence against female sex workers in Abuja, Nigeria" *African Health Sciences* 14, No. 2(2014): 299–313 DOI: http://dx.doi.org/10.4314/ahs.v14i2.4. 10

10 Francine, Van de Borne. "'I am not a prostitute': Discords in targeted HIV/AIDS prevention interventions in urban and trading centers in Malawi." Series on HIV/AIDS in sub Saharan Africa. *Sex, Gender and Policy Working Paper Series* 13, No.8 (July 2003): 1–33. 13

11 Doris Posel. The sex market in the inner city of Durban. Economic research Unit. Durban: University of Natal. *Occasional paper* No. 28 (1993). 19

12 Beatrice Okyere-Manu. "The livelihood challenges posed by the commercial Sex Industry to Christian concern for poor women in Pietermaritzburg." Masters Thesis, University of KwaZulu- Natal, Pietermaritzburg, 2005. 79

13 Martin Mbonye, Winifred Nalukenge, Sarah Nakamanya Sarah, Teddy Nalusiba, Racheal King, Judith Vadepitte and Janet Seeley. "Gender inequity in the lives of women involved in sex work in Kampala, Uganda" *Journal of International Aids Society* 15, No.3 (June 2012):1–9 http://dx.doi.org/10.7448/IAS.15.3.17365. 2

14 The concept of blesser and blessee has become a subject of controversy on social media in South Africa and it has started receiving attention from academic authors. See Johannes Ntshilagane (2018) "Exploring the 'Blesser and Blessee' Phenomenon: Young Women, Transactional Sex, and HIV in Rural South Africa" SAGE Open October-December 2018: 1–9: DOI: 10.1177/2158244018806343 journals.sagepub.com/home/sgo

15 Sharen Thumboo. "Sex work: A community speaks" *Agenda* 17, No.56 (April 2011):107–110. 108.

16 Anet E. Dreyer and Andries van Aarde. "'n Krities-hermeneutiese perspektief op die huwelik in 'n postmoderne era", *HTS Teologiese Studies/Theological Studies* 63, No. 2 (May 2007): 653–681. http://dx.doi.org/10.4102/hts.v63i2.225. 483–491

17 Marilize E. Tukker. "Where sexuality and spirituality meet: An assessment of Christian teaching on sexuality and marriage in relation to the reality of 21st century moral norms." *HTS Teologiese Studies/ Theological Studies* 69, No.1 (September 2013):1–8 dx.doi.org/10.4102/hts.v69i1.1343. 1

18 Anthony Giddens. *Central Problems in Social Theory: Action, Structure, and Contradiction in Social Analysis.* Berkeley: University of California Press, 1979. 24.

19 Sian Maseko. "Sex on trial: The moralisation and criminalisation of sexuality in Zimbabwe" *A Journal on African Women's Experiences* (2012): 56–61. 57.
20 Joycelyn Elmes, Morten Skovdal, Kundai Nhongo, Hellen Ward, Catherine Campbell, Timothy B. Hallett, Contance Nyamukapa, Peter J. White, and Simon Gregson. "A reconfiguration of the sex trade: How social and structural changes in eastern Zimbabwe left women involved in sex work and transactional sex more vulnerable" *PLoS ONE* 12, No 2 (March 2017): 1–23. doi:10.1371/journal.pone.0171916
21 Brigitte Tenni, Jenae Carpenter and Nicholas Thomson. "Arresting HIV: Fostering partnerships between sex workers and police to reduce HIV risk and promote professionalization within policing institutions: A realist review." *PLoS One* 10, No.10 (October 2015): 1–12 doi:10.1371/journal.pone.0134900. 2
22 Jolien Van der Geugten, Berno van Meijel, Marion H. G den Uyl and Nanne K. de Vries. Virginity, sex, money and desire: Premarital sexual behaviour of youths in Bolgatanga municipality, Ghana. *African Journal of Reproductive Health* 17, No.4 (December 2013): 93–106.
23 Sekai Techkla Nyakurerwa. "An analysis of the law and the effectiveness of government and non-governmental organisations' interventions in curbing under age commercial sex work in Epworth and along the Mukuvisi river bank Harare, Zimbabwe." PhD Dissertation, University of Zimbabwe, 2016. 22.
24 Nyakurerwa "An analysis of the law" 22.
25 The Uganda Penal Code Act Uganda. Legal Information Institute (1950). http://www.ulii.org/ug/legislation/consolidated-act/120
26 Okyere-Manu, "The livelihood challenges posed by the commercial Sex Industry" 112
27 UNAIDS. Sex work and HIV/AIDS. Technical update June 2002. http://data.unaids.org/publications/irc-pub02/jc705-sexwork-tu_en.pdf
28 Many women in the study confessed that when they are arrested by the police, they are tortured, beaten and sometimes even raped by the police.
29 Ine, Vanwesenbeeck. "Another decade of social scientific work on sex work: a review of research 1990–2000". *Annual Review of Sex Research* 12, No.1 (2001): 242–289. Doi:10.1080/10532528.2001.10559799; Beatrice Okyere-Manu. "Sacrificing Physical Health for Wellbeing: A Theological Challenge". *Journal of Theology for Southern Africa* 124, (Mar 2006): 20–32. 124
30 Van de Borne, Francine. "I am not a prostitute," 271.
31 Sophia Chirongoma. "In Search of A Sanctuary: Zimbabwean Migrants in South Africa." In *Walking Together: Christian Thinking and Public Life in South Africa*, edited by Joel Carpenter, 150–175. Texas: ACU Press, 2012, 169.
32 Maseko, "Sex on trial" 57–58.
33 Chirongoma, Sophia. "Women's and Children's Rights in the time of HIV and AIDS in Zimbabwe: An Analysis of Gender Inequalities and its impact on people's health," *Journal of Theology for Southern Africa* 2, No.126 (November 2006): 48–65; also see Sonjelle, Shilton and Chitando, Sophia. 2016. YWCA Safe Spaces Training Guide (2016). http://www.worldywca.org/wp-content/uploads/2014/02/Safe-Spaces-long-web.pdf
34 Chirongoma, "Women's and Children's Rights," 60
35 Maseko, "Sex on trial" 60–61.

Bibliography

Chirongoma, Sophia. "Women's and Children's Rights in the time of HIV and AIDS in Zimbabwe: An Analysis of Gender Inequalities and its impact on people's health," *Journal of Theology for Southern Africa* 2, No.126 (November 2006): 48–65.

Chirongoma, Sophia. "In Search of A Sanctuary: Zimbabwean Migrants in South Africa." In *Walking Together: Christian Thinking and Public Life in South Africa*, edited by Joel Carpenter, 150–175. Abilene, TX: ACU Press, 2012.

Dube, Musa. "Postcoloniality, Feminist Spaces, and Religion." In *Postcolonialism, Feminism, and Religious Discourse*, edited by Donaldson, Laura E and Kwok Pui-lan, 100–120. New York: Routledge, 2002.

Dreyer, Anet E. and van Aarde, Andries G. "'n Krities-hermeneutiese perspektief op die huwelik in 'n postmoderne era", *HTS Teologiese Studies/Theological Studies* 63, No. 2 (May 2007): 653–681. http://dx.doi.org/10.4102/hts.v63i2.225.

Dietze, Gabriele. "Decolonizing Gender - Gendering Decolonial Theory Cross-Currents and Archaeologies." In *Postcoloniality-Decoloniality-Black Critique: Joints and Fissures* edited by Broeck, Sabine and Junker Carsten, 253–276. Frankfurt/New York: Campus Verlag, 2014.

Elmes, Jocelyn., Skovdal , Morten, Nhongo, Kundai, Ward, Hellen, Campbell, Catherine, Hallett, Timothy B., Nyamukapa, Constance, White, Peter J. and Gregson, Simon. "A reconfiguration of the sex trade: How social and structural changes in eastern Zimbabwe left women involved in sex work and transactional sex more vulnerable" *PLoS ONE* 12, No 2 (March 2017): 1–23. doi:10.1371/journal.pone.0171916.

Giddens, Anthony. *Central Problems in Social Theory: Action, Structure, and Contradiction in Social Analysis*. Berkeley, CA: University of California Press, 1979.

Lewis, Victor and Larson, James. "Sex work is one of the oldest professions in the world" *Journal of International Business and Cultural Studies* 9 (January 2015): 1–9.

Mampane, Johannes N. "Exploring the "Blesser and Blessee" Phenomenon: Young Women, Transactional Sex, and HIV in Rural South Africa" *SAGE Open* (October 2018): 1–9. doi:10.1177/2158244018806343.

Maseko Sian "Sex on trial: The moralisation and criminalisation of sexuality in Zimbabwe" *A Journal on African Women's Experiences* (2012): 56–61.

Mbonye, Martin, Nalukenge, Winifred, Nakamanya, Sarah, Nalusiba, Teddy, King, Racheal, Vadepitte, Judith and Seeley, Janet. "Gender inequity in the lives of women involved in sex work in Kampala, Uganda" *Journal of International Aids Society* 15, No.3 (June 2012): 1–9http://dx.doi.org/10.7448/IAS.15.3.17365.

Nyakurerwa, Teckla. Sekai. "An analysis of the law and the effectiveness of government and non-governmental organisations' interventions in curbing under age commercial sex work in Epworth and along the Mukuvisi river bank Harare, Zimbabwe." PhD Dissertation, University of Zimbabwe, 2016.

International Labour Organization. "Facing the growing unemployment challenges in Africa." *World Employment Social Outlook Press Release* January 20th, 2016https://www.ilo.org/africa/media-centre/pr/WCMS_444474/lang–en/index.htm.

Oduyoye, Mercy Amba and Kanyoro, Musimbi R.A., Eds. *The Will to Arise: Women, Tradition, and the Church in Africa*. Maryknoll, NY: Orbis Books, 1992.

Oduyoye, Mercy Amba. "Feminist theology in an African perspective." In *Paths of African theology* edited by Gibellini, Rosino, 166–181. London: SCM Press, 1994.

Olufunmilayo, I. Fawole and Abosede, Dagunduro T. "Prevalence and correlates of violence against female sex workers in Abuja, Nigeria" *African Health sciences* 14, No. 2 (2014): 299–313. http://dx.doi.org/10.4314/ahs.v14i2.4.

Okyere-Manu, Beatrice. "The livelihood challenges posed by the commercial Sex Industry to Christian concern for poor women in Pietermaritzburg." Masters Thesis, University of KwaZulu- Natal, Pietermaritzburg, 2005.

Posel, Doris. *The sex market in the inner city of Durban.* Durban: University of Natal, Economic Research Unit. Occasional paper No. 28 (1993).

Scorgie, Fiona, Vasey, Katie, Harper, Eric, Chersich , Matthew F., Richter, Marlise, Nare, Prince, Maseko, Sian. "Human rights abuses and collective resilience among sex workers in four African countries: a qualitative study". *Globalization and Health* 9, No. 33 (2013) doi:10.1186/1744-8603-9-33.

Sonjelle, Shilton and Chitando, Sophia. *YWCA Safe Spaces Training Guide (2016).* (2016) http://www.worldywca.org/wp-content/uploads/2014/02/Safe-Spaces-long-web.pdf.

Tenni, Brigitte, Carpenter, Jenae and Thomson, Nicholas. "Arresting HIV: Fostering partnerships between sex workers and police to reduce HIV risk and promote professionalization within policing institutions: A realist review." *PLoS One* 10, No.10 (October 2015): 1–12 doi:10.1371/journal.pone.0134900.

Legal Information Institute. The Uganda Penal Code Act Uganda, 1950. http://www.ulii.org/ug/legislation/consolidated-act/120.

Thumboo, Sharen. "Sex work: A community speaks." *Agenda* 17, No.56 (April 2011): 107–110.

Tukker, E. Marilize. "Where sexuality and spirituality meet: An assessment of Christian teaching on sexuality and marriage in relation to the reality of 21st century moral norms." *HTS Teologiese Studies/ Theological Studies* 69, No.1 (September 2013): 1–8. doi:10.4102/hts.v69i1.1343.

UNAIDS. Sex work and HIV/AIDS. Last modified June 2002. http://data.unaids.org/publications/irc-pub02/jc705-sexwork-tu_en.pdf.

Van de Borne, Francine. "'I am not a prostitute': Discords in targeted HIV/AIDS prevention interventions in urban and trading centers in Malawi." Series on HIV/AIDS in sub Saharan Africa. *Sex, Gender and Policy Working Paper Series* 13, No.8 (July 2003): 1–33.

Vanwesenbeeck, Ine. "Another decade of social scientific work on sex work: a review of research 1990–2000". *Annual Review of Sex Research* 12, No.1 (2001): 242–289. doi:10.1080/10532528.2001.10559799.

Vandepitte, Judith, Lyerla, Rob, Dallabetta, Gina, Crabbe , Francois, Alary , Michel and Buve , Anne. "Estimates of the number of female sex workers in different regions of the world". *Sexually Transmitted Infections Journal* 82, Supplement No. 3 (July 2006): 18–25. doi:10.1136/sti.2006.020081.

Van der Geugten, Jolien, van Meijel, Berno, den Uyl, Marion H.G. and de Vries, Nanne K. "Virginity, sex, money and desire: Premarital sexual behaviour of youths in Bolgatanga municipality, Ghana". *African Journal of Reproductive Health* 17, No.4 (December 2013): 93–106.

Wanyenze, K. Rhoda, Musinguzi, Geofrey, Kiguli, Juliet, Nuwaha, Fred, Mujisha, Geoffrey, Musinguzi, Joshua, Arinaitwe , Jim, Matovu, K.B and Joseph, K.B. "'When they know that you are a sex worker, you will be the last person to be treated': Perceptions and experiences of female sex workers in accessing HIV services in Uganda." *BMC International Health and Human Rights* 17, No.11 (May 2017): 2–11 doi:10.1186/s12914-017-0119-1.

Afterword

To Shape the Changes for Which We Long

Yvonne C. Zimmerman

The chapters in *Religious Responses to Sex Work and Sex Trafficking: An Outrage Against Any Decent People* leave me with two rather contradictory conclusions swirling in my mind. One is that the form of Christianity that dominates faith-based antitrafficking activism, advocacy, and service provision is terribly ill-equipped to deal with the contemporary realities of sex work and human trafficking. The other is that there are real possibilities for humanizing Christian antitrafficking work. Maybe Christians can learn to respond to commercial sex without reiterating worn moralisms about sexual morality. Maybe Christians can extricate themselves and their moral frameworks from seductive cycles of legitimating and perpetuating harm. Nothing is evitable, of course; yet these essays remind me that anything is possible. In the space of this Afterward, I want to probe both of these conclusions and describe some of the specific contributions this volume makes to postcolonial perspectives and practices of Christianity and justice.

There are some necessary qualifications to my assertion that Christianity is unprepared to deal with sex work and human trafficking constructively. First, I am speaking of a particular form of Christianity, not making a blanket statement about all Christians or all Christianities. Christianity is not, and never has been, singular. Second, I recognize that Christianity is a historical religion and as such, it is shaped by and through the social, political, and contextual environments of the times and places in which it is practiced. Therefore, I do not intend to make any claim concerning the essential nature of Christianity; only to make an observation about the form of Christianity *as practiced and existing as a set of social and cultural forces at the present moment in time.*

Third, I understand that the problem is not just Christianity. Here I want to highlight the necessity of using intersectional analyses that accounts for "how numerous systems of oppression interact to regulate…the lives of most people."[1] Coined by legal scholar and critical race theorist Kimberlé Crenshaw in 1989 to describe a complex analytical approach to conceptualizing power and oppression, intersectionality recognizes that systems of oppression are always multiple and mutually reinforcing rather than discrete and additive.[2] The lens of intersectionality suggests that Christianity's inability to deal constructively with sex work and human trafficking is not simply a religious problem, and

DOI: 10.4324/9780429328824-10

therefore cannot be fully understood without consideration of how Christianity intersects with colonialism, white supremacy, patriarchy, capitalism and more. Virtually every chapter in this collection wrestles with these intersections. Consequently, while it is crucial to recognize the ways that Christianity has contributed (and continues to contribute) to the systems of oppression that people in sex work and who experience human trafficking navigate, Christianity does not function as *a*, let alone *the*, singular force of oppression. No discrete line of power, whether religion (Christianity or other), race, class, gender, sexuality, nationality, ability, etc. ever functions alone.

With those qualifications in mind, I can now begin to unpack what I mean by characterizing Christianity as ill-equipped to deal with contemporary realities of sex work and human trafficking.

Ill-equipped

Evangelical Christianity dominates faith-based antitrafficking efforts around the world, exerting influence at the levels of activism and advocacy, as well in service provision. Further, as Carly Daniel-Hughes notes, and various chapters in this volume clearly exemplify, the impact that evangelical Christianity exerts over and in global antitrafficking extends well beyond the conservative, white, Protestant religious subculture of its origin.[3] Whether in mainline churches, secular Western governments, or in the faith-based humanitarian organizations that exist in virtually every country of the world, one of evangelical Christianity's defining features is the sexual ethic it espouses. This sexual ethics disapproves of all non-hetero-marital sexual activity. The only sexual activity and expression evangelical Christian sexual ethics recognize as fully moral, legitimate, and compatible with Christian faith and practice is that which takes place between married, monogamous, heterosexual couples. To be sure, this sexual ethic is not evangelical Christianity's only characteristic. Theologically, the experience of conversion, or being "born again" by accepting Jesus as personal savior, is central to evangelical faith. But "accepting Jesus" is understood to indicate a spiritual shift within an individual toward God that manifests externally in the cessation of all nonmarital, non-monogamous, non-hetero sexual activity. While engaging only in married, monogamous hetero sex is not itself *sufficient* for salvation in an evangelical theological worldview, this sexual ethic essentially functions as a principal mark of salvation.[4] Hence, accepting Jesus as personal savior is evangelical Christianity's defining theological characteristic and its defining moral characteristic is its ethic of sex. This sexual ethic is principally what I have in mind in saying that evangelical Christianity is ill-equipped to deal with contemporary realities of sex work and human trafficking.

Nkiruka Okafor and Lauren McGrow describe the Christian sexual ethic that teaches that sexual relations should be confined to monogamous, heterosexual marriage as "the sin perspective around the issue of sexuality" since this ethic holds that all nonmarital, non-monogamous, non-hetero sexual activity is sinful.[5] Sin is a theological category in evangelical Christianity that denotes immorality and transgression of divine law and purpose. Sin impedes an individual's capacity to be in full and flourishing relationship with God and, in this way, degrades individuals insofar as a relationship with God constitutes human beings' fundamental purpose. This Christian sexual ethic of monogamous heterosexual marriage gives rise to what Anna Kasafi Perkins and Dane C. Lewis call the "condemnatory perspective" of sex work.[6] What makes commercial sex morally wrong—i.e. sinful and degrading—according to the evangelical worldview is that it is not married monogamous hetero sex.

Of course, the condemnatory perspective is not just callously judgmental toward people who sell sex (although it can be) and can, as Mark A. Levand acknowledges, undergird "pastoral response[s] of support and charity."[7] Perkins and Lewis describe how this perspective generally entails the twin assumptions that people who sell sex are caught up in "a horrendous system" from which they need to be rescued, and that Christians are the ones to perform such rescue.[8] This "caughtness" is often described with the language of slavery, invoking a powerful set of familiar and intersecting socio-political and theological scripts. Socio-politically, the language of slavery calls to mind the institution of chattel slavery and the social movements that led to its abolition. Depicting human trafficking as modern-day slavery is a common trope, and suggests that trafficked people are enslaved and require free people to emancipate them. Theologically, the language of slavery invokes a familiar Christian theological binary that imagines unsaved people as in a state of bondage (i.e. enslaved) to sin and saved people as redeemed (i.e. rescued or emancipated) through faith in Jesus into freedom. Through the framework this theological binary provides, evangelical Christians understand themselves as quintessentially free people—politically, socially, and spiritually. In relation to human trafficking, this self-understanding authorizes them to take up helping roles as missionaries, pastoral caregivers, humanitarians, aid workers etc. who work to rescue trafficking victims from slavery. Okafor and McGrow's and Daniel-Hughes's chapters each explore how the freedom/slavery binary is an appealing conceptual framework for pastoral caregivers, and other antitrafficking actors because it legitimates their moral authority and social power in relation to those receiving help and support.[9]

Reliance on the freedom/slavery binary as the primary conceptual framework for understanding the moral situation of people who sell sex (i.e. as caught in "a horrendous system" from which they need to be rescued) has some powerful implications.[10] As this binary understanding intersects with, and is refracted through, the condemnatory perspective of sex work Perkins and Lewis describe and the sexual ethic of monogamous heterosexual marriage (or "sin perspective" per Okafor and McGrow) in which evangelical Christianity roots the condemnatory perspective, these implications are further amplified. Many of these implications are explored in this volume. The one I want to highlight is how this intersection contributes to the conflation of sex work with human trafficking, or the idea that there is no meaningful moral distinction between making the decision to sell sex and being forcibly compelled to do so.

By now, the conflation of sex work and human trafficking is an exhaustingly familiar one. But how does this conflation even make sense? The theological framework that undergirds this conflation holds that *all* nonmarital, non-monogamous, non-hetero sex is contrary to God's desire and therefore is immoral and wrong. The particular circumstances under which a person sells sex—that is, whether they freely choose to sell sex, are compelled to do so by outside forces (whether from another person or persons or life circumstances), or any other possible scenario on the continuum between these poles—are not morally determinative. Arguments about the presence, absence, or degree of choice essentially boil down to distinctions with no moral difference. In fact, they are actually morally irrelevant. Intersecting with and refracted through both the freedom/slavery binary and the saved/unsaved binary, any and all nonmarital, non-monogamous and/or non-hetero sex is indicative of slavery and sin; indeed, even, a state of slavery *to* sin. And in the evangelical lexicon, slavery to sin is a state from which all need to be rescued (i.e. "for all have sinned fall short of the glory of God" [Romans 3:23]). In this theological framework, moreover, slavery and sin (as well as slavery *to* sin) require spiritual interventions first and foremost. Sin is understood as responsive only to divine grace through faith in Jesus. Hence, in the terms of this theological framework, no matter how human agency is defined or redefined, it is completely impotent in relation to sin. The consequence of the intersections and refractions is that quite *regardless* of how or whether choice is present, absent, or operative in some intermediate degree, the sale of sex is always already read as unfreedom, or slavery, and, as Beatrice Dedaa Okyere-Manu, Margaret Ssebunya and Sophia Chirongoma's analysis astutely notes, indicative of moral collapse.[11]

In addition to the hetero-marital sex/non-hetero-marital sex, saved/unsaved, and freedom/slavery binaries, through which conservative evangelical Christianity understands and responds to sex work and human trafficking, the innocent/guilty binary also plays an important yet complicated—or, better, *complicating*—role in this larger moral formation. At a basic level, innocence implies *absence* of culpability and responsibility, while guilt implies their *presence*. As the innocence/guilt binary is inflected through evangelical conceptions of sin, things become complicated.

As discussed above, Christian theology understands sin as that which alienates people from God. In specifically evangelical understandings of sin, sin is an intractable part of the human condition that affects all equally by virtue of being human. In this sense, sin is not personal but a condition of the species. At the same time, and consistent with the theological emphasis evangelical Christianity places on the individual, evangelical theology holds that each *person* is responsible for choosing to live according to God's standards (i.e. morality) in the context of their individual lives and that each person bears responsibility for failure to do so. In this way, sin is mapped onto individuals and their discrete actions, thereby becoming more than just a condition of the human species, but intensely and immediately *personal*. At the heart evangelical theology is the claim that individuals are fundamentally unable be in the right relationship with

God and live according to God's moral standards on their own. The only way to restore the right relationship with God that is every human being's fundamental purpose is the grace that is freely and universally available through Jesus. "Conversion" is the name of the process through which individuals avail themselves of salvation by accepting Jesus as personal savior. The state of salvation, or being "saved", means that a person has been restored to right relationship with God.

Binary frameworks dictate that people can occupy one of the two categories offered, but not both simultaneously. There is no gray area; no third space or option. The question the innocent/guilty binary raises, as inflected through evangelical understandings of sin and salvation and applied to people who sell sex, is whether they are most truly *innocent* victims (of human trafficking, despite engaging in non-hetero-marital sex) or *guilty* sinners (for engaging in immoral sexual activity). The non-theological framing of this question is whether all commercial sex is sex-trafficking, or whether sex workers should be considered criminals (perpetrators of harm) or trafficking victims (those who suffer harm). Hannah Estabrook perceptively describes what is going on this process:

> "When we ask about the difference between sex trafficking and prostitution, it actually seems to me that we're attempting to create a line of demarcation about where we should view women as victims (and therefore care about them) and criminals (and therefore care *less* about them)."[12]

Okafor and McGrow point out that drawing such lines of demarcation are less helpful than they might seem since the reality is that people make choices less from one clearly distinguished category or the other, and more from *the continuum in-between* the two poles.[13] Similarly, Lauren McGrow emphasizes that the ideas of fully realized agents and completely destitute victims are both stereotypes that "fail to account for the human complexity of people in sex work, their life events and inner psycho-spiritual experiences."[14]

The conflation of sex work and human trafficking removes the need to define which women selling sex are victims and which are not, insisting that *both* sets of women are victims. As victims, they are not guilty and thus are recognized as worthy of care and concern. Positively, this has the effect of expanding the pool of who is recognized as legitimately needing and worthy of support, services, and help. Negatively, this conflation comes at price of refuting the sense of agency that some women who sell sex have and of disaffirming their experiences and interpretations of their own lives and choices. Further, in Christian contexts that deny the morality of all sexual activity except for monogamous hetero-marital sex, and that treat sexuality purity as crux of Christian morality, the conflation of sex work and human trafficking is easily leveraged to imply "a diminished human dignity" that "could lead others to treat sex workers with less respect," as Levand discusses.[15] The idea that the core human dignity of people in the sex industry is compromised or diminished reinforces the social stigmatization they face. The notion of stigma denotes the imposition of cruelties that are fundamentally unjustified.[16] Levand calls attention to how "discriminatory thinking and policies causing undue to harm to those in the sexual economy" both participate in and amplify this stigma. While the conflation of sex work and human trafficking is a move that can expand the scope of who is recognized as worthy of care and concern, this expansion is accomplished at the expense of recognizing the agency and dignity of people who sell sex, and in ways that systematically amplify the presumed moral superiority of those who are not in the industry over those who are. This conflation is therefore a deeply ambivalent move.

In summary, there are two dimensions to the reason conservative evangelical Christianity is ill-equipped to deal with contemporary realities of sex work and human trafficking. One dimension is how the ethic of monogamous heterosexual marriage is ensconced at the center of this theological system. Particularly for women, sexual behavior, and specifically sexual purity, or refraining from non-hetero-marital sexual activity, is the primary mark of Christian virtue. As feminist cultural critic Jessica Valenti argues in *The Purity Myth,* the consequence of making sex definitive of morality is that "nothing else matters—not what we accomplish, not what we think, not what we care about and work for."[17] This moral construction determines a person's moral worth, and often their entire worth as a human being, by their body—by what they do with and what is done to it. Regardless of any other attributes that a woman may have (like courage, determination, intelligence, resilience, tenacity, generosity, or kindness), the only one that registers as morally significant is sexual purity.

The second dimension is how the distinction between sexual purity (morality) and sexual impurity (immorality) that this sexual ethic establishes creates moral hierarchy that, as McGrow explains, positions white, heteronormative, married, Christian women (who are ostensibly sexually pure) as morally superior to people who are sex workers (who are ostensibly sexually impure).[18] Okafor and McGrow confirm the presence of this sexual moral hierarchy in their observation that "The work that nuns in Nigeria do with women prostitutes is mostly seen from the view of 'higher women' helping 'lower women.'"[19] Nuns (who ostensibly are sexually pure) are understood as morally superior to women who sell sex (who ostensibly are sexually impure).

Simply put, the equation of sexual purity with morality is a false equivalence that must be challenged. The center and substance of morality is justice, and particularly for marginalized groups; and the fundamental logic of justice is equality and freedom.[20] By contrast, the fundamental logic of sexual purity is hierarchy. Hierarchy does not move in the direction of equality in freedom and thus cannot lead to justice. For this reason, insofar as Christianity remains invested in logics, structures, and practices of hierarchy, its ability to join and participate in pursuits of the freedom and equality that justice requires cannot but be, at best, exercises in ambivalence. Perkins and Lewis write that the fundamental gospel call is "*to confront…whatever thwarts the ability of human beings to live fully, personally and communally, to defy all which denies personal and communal well-being in solidarity.*"[21] This means that the gospel confronts *Christianity*—conservative evangelical Christianity—and invites it to defy the moral and theological logic that has become ensconced at its center. A Christianity that is poised to deal constructively with the realities of sex work and human trafficking must divest itself from theological and moral hierarchies.

Humanizing Christian Antitrafficking Work

In observing that Christianity is theologically and morally unprepared to deal with contemporary realities of sex work and human trafficking, I do not intend to downplay or deny that there are significant resources within Christianity and the Christian tradition for dealing differently—even constructively—with sex work and human trafficking. Christianity and the Christian tradition have done great harm; yet that harm was not inevitable. It is always possible that Christianity could have been (and sometimes is) enacted differently. There are resources within Christianity that make it possible to enact Christian identity and mission in relation to sex work and human trafficking in ways that humanize, empower, and liberate. This collection treats readers to glimpses of Christian theological and moral reflection as well Christian praxis (practice) that are consistent with these values.

Notably, several of the authors specifically recommend postcolonial frameworks and approaches as a type of different enactment of Christianity consistent with values of humanization, empowerment, and liberation. Feminist theologian Kwok Pui-lan describes postcolonial approaches as "seek[ing] to unmask colonial epistemological frameworks, unravel Eurocentric logics, and interrogate stereotypical cultural representations."[22] The purpose of these unmasking, unraveling, and interrogating activities is to make as transparent and visible as possible the relationship between power and knowledge. Various regions of the world, including Sub-Saharan Africa, the Caribbean, and Australia, that have been shaped by colonialism and its aftermaths are the focus of chapters in volume.[23] The authors write with great insight about colonialism's ongoing and contemporary consequences: Prostitution generally, and the emergence of the contemporary commercial sex trade under the conditions of modernization and globalization, and tourist economies (and the way sex work is located within them), specifically. They clarify the links between colonialism, the African slave trade and the institution of chattel slavery, and the contemporary commercial sex industry. Kwok proposes a postcolonial imagination as "a desire, a determination, and a process of disengagement from the whole colonial syndrome" that aims at "creat[ing] a little more space to imagine that an alternative world and a different system of knowing are possible."[24] In drawing from voices variously situated around the world whose perspectives are formed by different varieties of Christianity, and who are committed to justice and freedom and to growing in their conceptions of and practices thereof, *Religious Responses to Sex Work and Sex Trafficking* contributes to the postcolonial imagination Kwok describes. I highlight several themes emerging from the chapters that I believe provide particularly promising routes of disengagement from colonial processes. These themes of colonial refusal are seeing, listening, and recognizing.

Seeing

Multiple authors extend the invitation to readers to see human trafficking, people in sex work, projects designed to intervene and help, and the people who staff them differently from how they are constituted through the colonial gaze. Framed around Jesus' words in Luke 7: 44: "Simon, Do you see this woman?", Estabrook articulates this invitation to see people in sex work—those who sell sex under a range of varying circumstances as well as those who buy sex and/or facilitate its sale—beyond simplistic categories and characterizations.[25] Broadly, the kind of seeing the authors encourage readers towards is what which perceives the limitations of the dominant "Reach, Rescue, and Restore" approach to sex work and human trafficking out of which most Christian organizations operate.[26] It means seeing that participation in the sex industry cannot be read simply as flawed or collapsed morality.[27] It means seeing that the presence of good intentions and wanting to help do not automatically translate into effective support for marginalized people.[28] In essence, the kind of seeing encouraged throughout these chapters is an invitation to see how the categories and categorizations provided by dominant frameworks and models of response to the sex industry and human trafficking obfuscate "complicated and fluid realities of exploitative labor conditions, migration, and sex work, and promote[s] a binary of agency or victimhood."[29] The theme of seeing is a summons for people who care toward greater self-reflexivity about how religious values about gender and sexual morality often work to intensify rather than alleviate the stigma that people in the sex industry must bear, and the threat of violence they must navigate as a result.[30] Finally, it gestures toward a different model of justice that is not focused on administering punishment and sanction, but on collective transformation; "a transformative justice that restores…the lot of us," as Estabrook puts it.[31] This type of inclusive, transformative justice requires a fundamentally different vision.

Listening

Stemming from the invitation to see differently, the second theme of colonial refusal is listening. Okafor grounds this invitation in the story of Jesus' encounter with the woman caught in adultery in John 8: 1–11, arguing that seeing differently begins with listening to the perspectives and experiences of marginalized people.[32] My chapter describes how one non-profit organization serving trafficked youth and young adults placed listening or, in her words, "the culture of relationship" at the very center of its service model. Certainly this listening included conversations about trafficking and experiences of harm and exploitation, but it also included a lot of conversation about regular life things like the weather and how one's day is going.[33] Listening requires the ability to pay attention to the range of life experiences, from the significant to the mundane.

Although coming from varying perspectives, the authors in this volume insist virtually unanimously that such a listening practice will readily reveal that frameworks and perspectives positing immorality as the primary driver of sex work and the sex industry are both too simplistic and inherently flawed. Perkins and Lewis, for example, argue powerfully that any and all frameworks positing immorality as a driver of sex work ought to be confronted and abandoned.[34] Pointing out that presumptions that sex work is sinful obstruct authentic and generous listening, Okyere-Manu et al. suggest as an alternative to moralizing frameworks understanding sex work through the socio-economic contexts of unemployment, poverty, migration, seasonal work, and social disruption due to reasons beyond the sex workers' control, among others.[35] Together, the authors insist that when those who (claim to) want to end human trafficking bring themselves to carefully and genuinely listen, they will find that there is more to sex workers' lives than the degradation, victimization, and alienation than the dominant "Reach, Rescue and Restore" antitrafficking paradigm portrays. As Okafor and McGrow argue in "Walking with Women in Sex Work," when pastoral care workers listen carefully, deeply, and without moral judgement to how women who sell sex talk about their lives and stories, it is possible to perceive more than alienation and degradation.[36]

Recognizing

Seeing and listening are not ends in themselves, but together form the foundation for recognition, the third theme of colonial refusal. For instance, Okafor and McGrow emphasize that when pastoral care workers listen carefully, deeply, and without moral judgement to how women who sell sex talk about their lives and stories, they may begin to recognize how their autonomy and bodily choice are expressed *in* sex work.[37] Such recognition enables the creation of new frameworks of support for sex-working women that proceed on different premises than that of moral and free Christians helping unsaved people who are immoral and subjugated. In essence, listening to sex workers and genuinely seeing them in the context of their lives and the choices available to them enables recognition of them as agents.

Complexity—the ability to recognize and work with it—is a theme threading throughout this volume. McGrow defines *complexity* as a feature of situations "in which it is difficult to state exactly what is going on or to predict what will happen next."[38] She explains that complexity acknowledges that there is no easy solution to the problems of gender bias, poverty, racism, ableism and social exclusion that people in the sex industry experience. In this way, the concept of complexity is less about problems to be solved than it is a way to characterize complex and intractable situations that must be dealt with. Life situations cannot always be dramatically transformed or changed; sometimes they simply must be navigated.

Recognizing complex circumstances means that those who provide pastoral and material care and support to people in the sex industry need to abandon clinical and pastoral models of care that focus on the achievement of specific pre-determined outcomes (like exiting the sex industry or giving up drugs) as the primary measures of success. When considered in the context of complex circumstances, exit and abstinence may not always be realistic, desired, or even desirable outcomes. Instead, recognition of complex circumstances elicits an emphasis on building connection, support, and resilience rather than "solving problems" or performing "rescue."[39]

Connected to this, recognition of complex circumstances calls for recognizing complex agency. Agency is often conceived as the ability to choose judiciously between options and is assumed to be an outcome of freedom; that is, agency is an ability exercised by free and empowered people. In contrast, the notion of complex agency does not assume freedom as a condition of agency. Okyere-Manu et al. describe complex agency as "intentional effort to take charge of their lives amidst economic vulnerability, dispossession and neglect in order to transform their status quo."[40] They highlight how complex agency emerges as individuals confront and navigate structural oppression, not just as an outcome of definitively escaping or transcending it. As an example of this concept, they point out how all the participants in their study reported that they either dislike selling sex altogether or dislike aspects of what selling sex entails, while simultaneously acknowledging the economic benefit they get from it and lifting up that selling sex "gives them some degree of independence that not many other jobs could provide." They continue, "This shows women's complex agency; by naming poverty and stigma as the problem, they are revealing their own agency and confronting structural oppression."[41] Complex agency is the survival skills that complex circumstances elicit. Complex agency does not necessarily transcend or transmute oppression, and thus is easily misunderstood, unrecognized, or discounted. It also does not depend on extrication from or transcendence of difficult circumstances. Instead, this concept highlights the ways individuals resist oppression and take action to sustain their lives materially in the midst of intractable difficulty. Through confronting and navigating oppression, complex agency offers the possibility of survival.

The notion of complex agency resonates with Katie Cannon's analysis of Black women's moral wisdom in her ground-breaking book *Black Womanist Ethics*. Cannon writes that the ethical code that guides the lives and choices of Black women in the U.S. is not one that turns on fixed rules and absolute moral principles, but "develops out of the various coping mechanisms related to the conditions of their own cultural circumstances."[42] Cannon points specifically to the effects of racism, sexism, and capitalism, arguing that, in response to these relentless systems of oppression, Black women have "fashioned values patterns and ethical procedures in their own terms, as well as mastering, transcending, radicalizing and sometimes destroying pervasive, negative orientations imposed by the mores of the larger society."[43] She acknowledges that this moral wisdom "does not rescue Black women from the bewildering pressures and perplexities of institutionalized social evils" but instead, "exposes those ethical assumptions which are inimical to the ongoing survival of Black womanhood."[44] In the same way that Cannon recognizes that "Black women's analysis and appraisal of what is right or wrong and good or bad develops out of the various coping mechanism related to the conditions of their own cultural circumstances," the notion of complex agency empowers recognition of how people in the sex industry are similarly navigating *their* contexts and options and, as we see throughout this book, in contextually specific ways.[45] Additionally, in the same way that Cannon argues that Black women have thus "justly regarded survival against tyrannical systems of triple oppression as a true sphere of moral life," the concept of complex agency accounts for survival as a significant moral accomplishment under oppressive historical, social, political, economic/material conditions.[46]

A further dimension of complex agency is the contribution it makes to restorative and transformative justice frameworks. Estabrook relates the transformation that she and her organization, Sanctuary Night, experienced in relation to men in and adjacent to the sex industry. She explains that when the Covid-19 pandemic forced their operations outdoors, they found themselves interacting more with the men who are in the lives of the women they serve. These interactions allowed them to begin to get to know the men personally. As they learned to know them, they began to recognize how the categories they usually applied to them, like "trafficker," "pimp" or "perpetrator of violence," reduced them simplistically to "monsters who deserve punishment." Getting to know them as people confronted them with "the utter humanity of these men."[47] Estabrook explains that as they began to hear their stories, they slowly began to see that the men were more complex than the categories the dominant trafficking narrative assigns to them. In this process, they began to recognize how a logic of othering had unwittingly been shaping the way they understood and approached (or didn't) these men. As "other," they considered the men as bad people who deserve to be punished—and only that. Estabrook's insight is that this sort of simplistic and totalizing reduction is "the first step to violence" *even when it is waged in the name of justice*.[48] She presses readers to consider a transformative, humanizing model of justice that interrupts the automatic dehumanization of those who perpetuate harm and, in so doing, refuses the logic of othering. A justice that transforms and genuinely restores must include *everyone* in its humanizing scope.

There is no doubt that making the shift from retributive models of justice that prioritize identifying who or what is legitimately deserving of punishment, to transformative models of justice that seek to respond to violence and harm in ways that prioritize healing, repair, and accountability can be difficult. It is certainly not a change that happens in a single moment. The concept of complex agency is a tool that facilitates certain moments in this shift. For instance, in Estabrook/Sanctuary Night's case, the process of expanding and complexifying their understanding of the co-existence of victimization and agency as relates to *women* on the street served as the basis for expanding and complexifying their understanding of the *men* in these women's lives. Recognition of complex agency expands space for *all* parties in processes of transformation and justice.

Complex agency also illuminates the ambivalences that social helpers—those who "fight trafficking"—navigate in their lives and social situations as well. Daniel-Hughes' analysis reveals the predominantly white evangelical Christian women who the antitrafficking movement mobilizes and organizes into various humanitarian, helping endeavours as morally complicated social actors who, not unlike the people they serve, are also intractably situated in large systems of oppression that complicate the exercise and experience of *their* moral agency. She interprets evangelical antitrafficking activism and advocacy as "a performance and assurance of religious power and authority," noting that the gender politics of their own communities makes public recognition of such power and authority unavailable to evangelical women in their own contexts.[49] Here it is possible to recognize antitrafficking activities that "save other women elsewhere" as a way that evangelical women are able to confirm their sense of themselves as free as they negotiate "tensive gender politics inside of their own communities."[50] In this way, antitrafficking activism and advocacy offers evangelical women some measure of "compensation for the stubborn, and painful, gender politics operative within...evangelical contexts."[51] Their sometimes considerable privilege notwithstanding, these (predominantly) women "anti-traffickers" also are not the pure moral agents they perceive themselves to be. They too are complex agents.

If transformative justice is a project of creating justice together by getting in "right relation," the concept of complex agency can be a crucial tool in producing and creating the conditions of justice. Complex agency illuminates how social agents negotiate and resist relations of power no matter where or how they are positioned in situations of social inequality. That is, complex agency helps reveal not only *sex workers'* formations of agency, but also *buyers'* and *social helpers'/anti-traffickers'*. This recognition contributes to the vision transformative justice casts insofar as it acknowledges the agency—fraught and complex—that *all* parties exercise as they seek to survive and thrive. In turn, this inclusive recognition helps expand space for *all* parties in processes of transformation and justice.

Conclusion: Working with the Nature of Change

Is there any hope that the dominant form Christianity in faith-based antitrafficking activism, advocacy, and service provision will become better equipped to deal constructively with sex work and human trafficking? Could evangelical Christians learn to engage commercial sex workers without relying on worn sexual moralisms? It seems to me that a theme these questions share is wondering if things will ever be different. On this point, I find social justice facilitator adrienne maree brown to be a valuable teacher. Brown helps me recognize that things will for sure be different—are already becoming different—because of the nature of change. Change is constant and inevitable. Things are already changing.[52] And, at the same time, brown insists on the necessity of *shaping* change toward justice and liberation.[53] Processes of change are always already under way; but the world (and ourselves) will only become more humane and just through persistent, collective work to make these iterations possible. Premised on these teachings about change, I offer the routes of disengagement from colonial mindsets and modes of action in responding to and engaging sex work and human trafficking as possibilities for shaping the kinds of transformative, justice-oriented changes that many activists, advocates, and care providers long for.

Finally, speaking of the inevitability of change and by way of acknowledging how change often contains an element of surprise, I would be remiss not to mention the Covid-19 pandemic that has reshaped life, collective and individual alike, since early 2020. Many changes—social, economic, political, personal, and even spiritual—have been both (and simultaneously) accelerated *and* delayed, and even altogether stalled, on account of the pandemic. The best way, if there is one, to characterize the overall impact of the pandemic and the changes it has engendered (is engendering) is yet unclear. However, what does seem clear is that so much oppression remains. The ways that poverty, illness, loneliness, and the focus on national/international borders have increased and intensified will likely lead to renewed interest in the issues on which practitioners in this field have considerable expertise. This suggests that possibilities for collectively shaping change in ways that enact a postcolonial imagination—that is, that hold open spaces for imagining and creating a more just, humane, and survivable world—not only remain in a post-Covid world, but are even newly available.

Notes

1 Cathy J. Cohen as quoted by Nikki Sullivan, *A Critical Introduction to Queer Theory* (New York: NYU Press, 2013), 49.
2 Melissa M. Wilcox, *Queer Religiosities: An Introduction to Queer and Transgender Studies in Religion* (New York: Rowman and Littlefield, 2021) viii; Nikki Sullivan, *A Critical Introduction to Queer Theory*, 49.
3 Carly Daniel-Hughes, "Abolition Mommas: Evangelical Women as Exceptional Citizens in the Fight to End "Global Sex Trafficking," in *Religious Responses to Sex Work and Sex Trafficking: An Outrage Against Any Decent People*, ed. Lauren McGrow (London: Routledge, 2023), 13.
4 Yvonne C. Zimmerman, *Other Dreams of Freedom: Religion, Sex, and Human Trafficking* (New York: Oxford University Press, 2013), 96.
5 Nkiruka Okafor and Lauren McGrow, "Walking with Women in Sex Work: An Appraisal of the Role of the Nigerian Conference of Women Religious," in *Religious Responses to Sex Work and Sex Trafficking: An Outrage Against Any Decent People*, ed. Lauren McGrow (London: Routledge, 2023), 56.
6 Anna Kasafi Perkins and Dane C. Lewis, "Jesus Ate With Pras: Christianity and Commercial Sex Work in the Caribbean," in *Religious Responses to Sex Work and Sex Trafficking: An Outrage Against Any Decent People*, ed. Lauren McGrow (London: Routledge, 2023), 140.
7 Mark A. Levand, "Human Dignity in Sex Work and the Catholic Tradition," in *Religious Responses to Sex Work and Sex Trafficking: An Outrage Against Any Decent People*, ed. Lauren McGrow (London: Routledge, 2023), 66.

8 Perkins and Lewis, "Jesus Ate With Pras," 140.
9 Okafor and McGrow, "Walking with Women in Sex Work," chap. 3; Daniel-Hughes, "Abolition Mommas," chap. 1.
10 Perkins and Lewis, "Jesus Ate With Pras," 141.
11 Beatrice Dedaa Okyere-Manu, Margaret Ssebunya and Sophia Chirongoma, "When Survival Precedes Faith: Decolonial perspectives on the ethical dilemma confronting female Christian sex workers in Africa," in *Religious Responses to Sex Work and Sex Trafficking: An Outrage Against Any Decent People*, ed. Lauren McGrow (London: Routledge, 2023), 163.
12 Hannah Estabrook, "Do You See This (Wo)man? Lessons Learned from Sex Workers," in *Religious Responses to Sex Work and Sex Trafficking: An Outrage Against Any Decent People*, ed. Lauren McGrow (London: Routledge, 2023), 33.
13 Okafor and McGrow, "Walking with Women in Sex Work," 45.
14 Lauren McGrow, "Towards an Ethical Framework for Practice: Three 'touchstones' for faith-based organizations at the margins." in *Religious Responses to Sex Work and Sex Trafficking: An Outrage Against Any Decent People*, ed. Lauren McGrow (London: Routledge, 2023), 114.
15 Levand, "Human Dignity in Sex Work," 68.
16 Sarah Schulman, *Conflict is not Abuse: Overstating Harm, Community Responsibility, and the Duty of Repair* (Vancouver, BC: Arsenal Pulp Press, 2016), 146.
17 Jessica Valenti, *The Purity Myth: How America's Obsession with Virginity is Hurting Young Women* (Berkeley, CA: Seal Press, 2010), 24.
18 McGrow, "Towards an Ethical Framework for Practice," 110.
19 Okafor and McGrow, "Walking with Women in Sex Work," 45.
20 Meredith Minister, *Rape Culture on Campus* (Lanham, MD: Lexington Books, 2018), 61.
21 Perkins and Lewis, "Jesus Ate With Pras," 132.
22 Kwok Pui-lan, *Postcolonial Imagination and Feminist Theology* (Louisville: Westminster John Knox Press, 2005), 2.
23 Colonialism can be defined in multiple ways. Kwok Pui-lan describes colonialism as a mindset that imposes one's own (narrow) cultural attitudes on other people who may not share them, and then interprets their lives according to one's own values and not the values of the people whose lives are subject to interpretation. Whether at the level of politics or interpersonal relations, the basis on which colonialism rationalizes itself is alleged inferiority of non-Western cultures and peoples. The site to which colonialist logics most readily point as manifesting this inferiority are these cultures' patriarchal customs and practices, which claim the necessity of rescuing indigenous women. In this way, colonial power and modes of relationship, then, self-rationalize as a force of freedom. Kwok Pui-lan, *Postcolonial Imagination and Feminist Theology* (Louisville: Westminster John Knox, 2005), 17; Saba Mahmood, *Politics of Piety: The Islamic Revival and the Feminist Subject* (Princeton, NJ: Princeton University Press, 2012), 189–190.
24 Kwok Pui-lan, *Postcolonial Imagination*, 2–3.
25 Estabrook, "Do You See this (Wo)man?" chap. 2.
26 Daniel-Hughes, "Abolition Mommas," 10.
27 Okyere-Manu, Ssebunya and Chirongoma, "When Survival Precedes Faith," 163; Perkins and Lewis, "Jesus Ate With Pras," 132.
28 Daniel-Hughes, "Abolition Mommas," 20.
29 Daniel-Hughes, "Abolition Mommas," 11.
30 McGrow, "Towards an Ethical Framework for Practice," 110.
31 Estabrook, "Do You See this (Wo)man?" 40.
32 Okafor and McGrow, "Walking with Women in Sex Work," 56.
33 Yvonne C. Zimmerman, "'A Catholic and an Agnostic Walk into a Homeless Camp…' Collaborating Across Religious Differences," in *Religious Responses to Sex*

Work and Sex Trafficking: An Outrage Against Any Decent People, ed. Lauren McGrow (London: Routledge, 2023), 89.
34 Perkins and Lewis, "Jesus Ate With Pras," 143.
35 Okyere-Manu, Ssebunya and Chirongoma, "When Survival Precedes Faith," 164.
36 Okafor and McGrow, "Walking with Women in Sex Work," 58.
37 Okafor and McGrow, "Walking with Women in Sex Work," 44.
38 McGrow, "Towards an Ethical Framework for Practice," 114.
39 McGrow, "Towards an Ethical Framework for Practice," 114.
40 Okyere-Manu, Ssebunya and Chirongoma, "When Survival Precedes Faith," 157.
41 Okyere-Manu, Ssebunya and Chirongoma, "When Survival Precedes Faith," 159.
42 Katie G. Cannon, *Black Womanist Ethics* (Atlanta, GA: Scholars Press, 1988), 4.
43 Cannon, *Black Womanist Ethics*, 76.
44 Cannon, *Black Womanist Ethics*, 4–5.
45 Cannon, *Black Womanist Ethics*, 4.
46 Cannon, *Black Womanist Ethics*, 4.
47 Estabrook, "Do You See this (Wo)man?" 37.
48 Estabrook, "Do You See this (Wo)man?" 37.
49 Daniel-Hughes, "Abolition Mommas," 9.
50 Daniel-Hughes, "Abolition Mommas," 9.
51 Daniel-Hughes, "Abolition Mommas," 17.
52 adrienne maree brown, *Emergent Strategy: Shaping Change, Changing Worlds* (Chico, CA: AK Press, 2017), 41.
53 brown, *Emergent Strategy*, 3.

Bibliography

Brown, Adrienne Maree. *Emergent Strategy: Shaping Change, Changing Worlds*. Chico, CA: AK Press, 2017.

Cannon, Katie G. *Black Womanist Ethics*. Atlanta, GA: Scholars Press, 1988.

Mahmood, Saba. *Politics of Piety: The Islamic Revival and the Feminist Subject*. Princeton, NJ: Princeton University Press, 2012.

McGrow, Lauren, ed. *Religious Responses to Sex Work and Sex Trafficking: An Outrage Against Any Decent People*. London: Routledge, 2023.

Minister, Meredith. *Rape Culture on Campus*. Lanham, MD: Lexington Books, 2018.

Pui-lan, Kwok. *Postcolonial Imagination and Feminist Theology*. Louisville: Westminster John Knox Press, 2005.

Schulman, Sarah. *Conflict is not Abuse: Overstating Harm, Community Responsibility, and the Duty of Repair*. Vancouver, BC: Arsenal Pulp Press, 2016.

Sullivan, Nikki. *A Critical Introduction to Queer Theory*. New York: NYU Press, 2013.

Valenti, Jessica. *The Purity Myth: How America's Obsession with Virginity is Hurting Young Women*. Berkeley, CA: Seal Press, 2010.

Wilcox, Melissa M. *Queer Religiosities: An Introduction to Queer and Transgender Studies in Religion*. New York: Rowman and Littlefield, 2021.

Zimmerman, Yvonne C. *Other Dreams of Freedom: Religion, Sex, and Human Trafficking*. New York: Oxford University Press, 2013.

Index

A21 Campaign 8, 10–11, 13, 16
abolition: of sex trafficking 8, 10–11, 14–20; of sex work 51
abuse, sexual 35–36
Acquired Immunodeficiency Syndrome (AIDS) 131, 136, 140
activism, moral 106–107
advocacy 90–91, 135–137, 140
Africa: poverty in 155, 157–159, 161; research in 156–157; stigma in 169; *see also* Ghana; South Africa; Uganda; Zimbabwe
agency: ambiguity about 21, 178; and choice 33–34, 47–48, 49, 53; complex 183–185; denial of 68; and language 101; theory of 157, 165–166
Agustin, Laura 107
AIDS *see* Acquired Immunodeficiency Syndrome (AIDS)
anti-trafficking campaigns: Christian 13–14; combined religious and secular 92–95; critique of 9, 10–12; effects of religion on 86–87; motivations for 20–21; and progressive Christians 87; and rescue narratives 13–14, 16; spread of 10; *see also* collaborative anti-trafficking campaigns
Aquinas, St. Thomas 46, 51, 71, 76
Augustine of Hippo, St. 46, 51, 71, 76
Australia 10, 106, 108–109, 112, 116, 121–122
authority 17–18
autonomy 159–160; *see also* agency

Bernstein, Elizabeth 12, 86
blame, self 35–36
blessers 162; *see also* sex work: consumers of
Bowler, Kate 17, 19
Brazil 50–52
brokenness 107
Butler, Josephine 15

Caine, Christine 8, 10, 17
Cambodia 10
Canada 10
Cannon, Katie 183
Caribbean region 133; sex work in 133–135; sex work laws in 137–139; sex worker liberation in 145–147; sex worker organizations in 135–137; *see also* Jamaica
CATCH Court 29, 31; historical limitations of 33; and restorative justice 32–33
categorization 45, 181; *see also* terminology: for sex work and sex workers
Catholic social teaching: and Catholic social thought 70; and prostitution 67; and sex work 66, 67
Catholic social thought: and Catholic social teaching 70; and sex work 69–78
change 185–186
charitable work 20–21
child sexual abuse 35–36
choice 34, 35, 48, 177
Christian Women's Temperance Union 15
Christianity 174–175; evangelical 175–180; progressive 87
Church (in general): listening and discussion by 167–169; and prostitution 50–52, 142, 157
clients, sex *see* sex work: consumers of
coercion 33, 34
collaborative anti-trafficking campaigns: boundaries in 98–9; conceptions of trafficking in 99–101; friendship in

95–96; mutual respect in 96, 104n16; relational intelligence in 97–98; trust in 96–97
colonialism 133, 180, 187n23; refusal of 181–185
colonization 54
Committee for the Support of the Dignity of Woman (COSUDOW), Nigeria 44–45, 55–56
commodification 139
common good 70–71, 75–76, 81n41
compassion 37–38, 56, 76
complexity 114–118, 182–185
consent 80n27
conservatism: Christian 12, 133, 175–180; religious 107
conversion 51–52, 178
corruption 139–140
COSUDOW *see* Committee for the Support of the Dignity of Woman (COSUDOW), Nigeria
Covid-19 pandemic 131, 186
criminal justice system 102
criminality 11, 41, 135, 138–139, 166–167, 178
criminalization 32, 71, 77–78, 87, 139

decency 1–2
decolonial theory 157
decriminalization 111, 112–113; and legalization 141–142
degradation of human persons 68
dehumanization 37
Denver Homeless Ministry 88–89, 92–95
dignity 68, 69–70, 75, 134, 168–169, 178–179
discernment 39–40, 77
diversity 113
dockets, specialized 31
drop-in centers 112

egalitarianism, gender 19
emancipation 60–61
empowerment 53, 60
"end demand" strategies 37
equality 53
Esther 53
ethics: Black women's 183–184; *see also* sexual ethics
evangelical Christianity 175–180; women adherents to 14–20, 184; *see also* Protestantism
exceptionalism 14, 19
exploitation 68, 69, 101–102

faith-based organizations 106–107; aims of 106; analysis of practice of 109, 122; criticisms of 107–108; faith of 121; leadership of 108; networking between 108–109; research into 108–109; in social hierarchy 110; structure of 106
family life, brutal 162–163
feminism 12, 35, 146, 157
forced labor *see* slavery
forgiveness of sin 39, 40
Francis, Pope 72
freedom 12, 33–34, 69, 176, 183
fulfilment 70
fundamentalism, religious 139

gender 137–138
gender non-conforming persons 87
gender politics 14, 17, 18–19
Germany 55
Ghana: law in 166; sex worker narratives from 158, 165
God, love of 41
Goffman, Erving 109
goods: luxury 161–162; moral 82n74
Gospel of Luke 38–40
Greece 10
Guider, Margaret 50
guilt 177

harassment 139
harm reduction 75–76, 82n68, 89, 91
healing 71
health risks 164
"helping imperative" 16, 20
Helping Individual Prostitutes Survive (HIPS) 52
heteronormativity 145
HIPS *see* Helping Individual Prostitutes Survive (HIPS)
HIV *see* Human Immunodeficiency Virus infection (HIV)
homecoming 111–113
homelessness 88–89
hookers 30, 132; *see also* sex workers
hospitality 39, 111–113
Human Immunodeficiency Virus infection (HIV) 131, 136–137, 140, 143, 164, 167
human persons: African notions of 57; degradation of 68; dignity of 68, 69–70; nature of 57; rights of 74–76, 159
human trafficking 33; conceptions of 99–101, 104n7; fighting against 35; perspectives on 1, 88, 99; as a prominent issue 86; and respectability

87; services for survivors of 91; and sexual violence 87; systemic dimensions of 102; *see also* anti-trafficking campaigns; sex trafficking

imago Dei 38, 56–57
independence 159–160; *see also* agency
India 48
individualism 12, 34, 177–178
innocence 11, 177
"International Justice Mission" 10
intersectionality 174–175
introspection 60
Italy 54, 55

Jakobsen, Janet 86
Jamaica 139–143; Church action in 140; sex work laws in 138; terminology for sex workers in 132; US Christian ideology in 139; *see also* Caribbean region
Jesus: and prostitutes 144–145; and woman caught in adultery 56; and woman who washed His feet 38–40, 145
John XXIII, Pope 73, 74
John Paul II, Pope 68, 71
johns 30, 36–38; *see also* sex work: consumers of
judgement 39–40
justice 179–180; and equity 36; models of 30; restorative 29–30, 31, 32–33, 40, 184; retributive 30, 36; transformative 40, 181, 184

kenosis 120–121

labor, forced *see* slavery
Latin America 49
law enforcement 139–140
leadership, pastoral 17–18
legalization 141–142; *see also* decriminalization
LGBTQ+ persons 87, 131
liberation theology 2, 50–52, 131–132
lifestyle choices 161–162
listening 56, 59–60, 167–168, 181–182
LIVE model of pastoral care 58–61
love 41, 52–53
Luke, Gospel of 38–40
Luther, Martin 47
luxury goods 161–162

Mac, Juno 69
Madonna/Whore model 46–47; *see also* terminology: for sex work and sex workers
marginalization 34, 107–108
marginalized persons 51–52, 72–73
market forces 49
migration 49, 54–55, 107, 138
missing persons 36
Moldova 49
moral activism 106–107
moral goods 82n74
moral probity 15
moral standards or teaching 1, 60, 155, 179; *see also* sexual ethics
morality 76–77, 82n74, 134–135, 175, 177, 179, 182

narratives, research through 156
NCWR *see* Nigerian Conference of Women Religious (NCWR)
Netherlands, the 55
Nigeria 44–45, 53–61
Nigerian Conference of Women Religious (NCWR) 44, 55
Nordic Model approach to prostitution 37
Nouwen, Henri 113
nuns 58, 59

objectification 44
oppression 38–39, 47, 174–175, 183; structural 3, 34–35
orphans 160–161
"othering" 37; *see also* objectification; oppression
outreach 143; street 88–90; *see also* drop-in centers

pandemics 131, 136, 186
participation, political 73–74
pastoral care for sex workers: LIVE model of 58–61; "trafficked model" of 44
peer pressure 161–162
play 114–118
police 139–140, 171n28
postcolonial theory 157, 180–181
poverty 33–34, 48, 72–73, 155, 157–159, 161
power: abuse of 119; biblical references to 120; imbalance in 70–71, 119; and language 101; loss of 40; sharing of 17–18, 118–121
pras 131, 132; *see also* sex workers
Prax(us) 88, 89–95
preferential option for the poor 72–73
prejudice 39–40, 45, 52–53, 76–77, 163
prohibition 51
promiscuity 110
"Propel Women" 17–18

proportionality 76–77
prostitutes 30, 33, 140–141; and Jesus 144–145; *see also* sex workers
prostitution: and Catholic social teaching 67; and Church (in general) 50–52, 142, 157; decriminalization of 37; disparagement of 66; entry into 34, 53; and human dignity 78n1; legal definitions of 137; and liberation theology 50–52; and oppression 38–39; renaming of 134; rescue from 15–16; and sex trafficking 67; and sin 68; as slavery 12, 67; stereotypes about 34; toleration of 130; and violence 34, 120; *see also* sex work; terminology: for sex work and sex workers
Protestantism 12; *see also* Christianity: evangelical

racism 87–88, 102
Rahab 51, 53
recognition 182–185
rehabilitation 12, 55–56
rescue 8, 10, 12, 55–56, 176
rescue narratives: and anti-trafficking campaigns 13–14, 16; biases underlying 14, 107; subversion of 45, 52
responsibility 71; *see also* solidarity
revenge 36
rights *see* human persons: rights of
risks 49–50

safe space 112, 113
salvation 16, 58, 175, 178; *see also* "helping imperative"; rescue narratives
Scholl, Lia Claire 52, 74, 75
self-blame 35–36
self-determination 48
self-examination 60
sex industry *see* sex work
sex slavery *see* sex trafficking
sex trafficking: and Catholic social teaching 67; conflated with sex work 3, 68, 76–77, 146, 176–180; differentiated from sex work 33, 67, 77; disgust at 1–2, 13; elimination of 77–78; ending demand for 37; extent of 11; and gender politics 14; as problem to be solved 2–3; as prominent cause 2; punishment for 11; as slavery 14, 176, 177; survivors of 30; victims of 11, 30, 33, 48–49, 178; *see also* anti-trafficking campaigns
sex work 130; abolitionists' view of 50; assumptions about 76–77, 143–144; and brokenness 107; and Catholic social teaching 66, 67; and Catholic social thought 69–78; and Church (in general) 50–52, 142, 157; and common good 70–71; conflated with sex trafficking 3, 68, 76–77, 146, 176–180; consumers' benefits from 70, 77; consumers of 68, 70, 75, 111, 137, 162; dangerous social conditions for 70–71; departure from 114, 143; differentiated from sex trafficking 33, 67, 77; and dignity 69–70, 134; as discouraged yet patronized 54, 167; entry into 48, 114, 137, 155, 157–164; and human rights 74–76; and independence 159–160; and migration 138; and morality 76–77, 134–135; and peer pressure 161–162; and political participation 73–74; and poverty 72–73; as slavery 3, 55, 67, 177; and social or structural sin 71–72; and solidarity 71; and stigma 49, 69, 163, 166, 169; and survival 157–161; terminology for 75, 134; and values 134; as violence against women 67; as work 69–70, 75, 134; workers' benefits from 35, 77; and workers' migration 49, 54–55, 107; *see also* prostitution; sex workers
sex workers: advocacy for 135–137, 140; characterizations of 30, 110–111, 112, 114, 137; dignity of 111; diversity among 67, 78n6, 114; empowerment of 33; legitimacy for 141–142; loving response to 52–53; in moral hierarchy 179; outreach to 143; and pandemics 131, 136; religious 58–59, 155; rights of 135–136, 159; self-identification of 35; in social hierarchy 110; street-based 107; suffering of 117, 135, 159, 164; terminology for 132; *see also* sex work
sexism 18–19
sexual abuse 35–36, 67
sexual economy 49
sexual ethics 165–168, 175–176; *see also* touchstones: ethical
sexual order 110
sexual politics 107
sexual purity 179
sexuality, and sin 56, 175–177
sexually transmitted infections (STIs) 131, 136–137, 140, 143, 164, 167
Showden, Carisa 47

sin: and forgiveness 39, 40; and prostitution 68, 71–72; and sexuality 56, 175–177; social or structural 60, 71–72, 76
slavery: abolition of 11; Christian responses to 87; condemnation of 68; prostitution as 12, 67; sex trafficking as 14, 176, 177; sex work as 3, 55, 67, 177
Smith, Molly 69
social exchange theory 49
social justice 12
solidarity 52, 58–61, 71, 76
South Africa 10; law in 167; sex worker narratives from 158, 162, 163, 164, 165
Spain 49
spirituality 114, 115
Stand Up for Kids 92
Star Light Ministries 52
stigma 52, 74, 141, 179; manifestations of 109; overcoming 109–113; persistence of 111; and secrecy 167; and sex work 49, 69, 163, 166, 169
STIs *see* sexually transmitted infections (STIs)
structural oppression 3, 34–35
survival 157–161, 184; *see also* poverty

Tamar 52
terminology: and access to services 100–101; in Catholic documents 66–69; of 'human trafficking' 99–101; and lived experience 30, 35, 68–69; pejorative vs. preferred 68; and provision of care 33; for sex work and sex workers 75, 132, 134
Thailand 3, 10, 13
Thomas Aquinas, St. 46, 51, 71, 76
toleration 51, 68, 76
touchstones, ethical 109, 122; about dealing with complexity 114–118; about overcoming stigma 109–113; about sharing power 118–121
trafficking, human *see* human trafficking
transgender women 135, 137

Uganda 155; law in 166–167; sex worker narratives from 158–159, 160, 161, 162
United Kingdom 10, 87
United States of America: 19th and 20th century campaigns in 15; 21st century campaigns in 10, 17–18; Black women's ethics in 183–184; effects of religious campaigns in 86–88; restorative justice in 29–30; solidarity with sex workers in 52

Valenti, Jessica 179
validation 60
values 134
victims 11, 30, 31, 33, 48–49, 178
vision 181; *see also* categorization
vulnerability 120–121
vulnerable persons 72–73

"Walk for Freedom" 10
Ward, Kate 75
welcome 111–113, 167–168
wellbeing 112
Western exceptionalism 14
"White Slave panic" 15, 16
women: advancement of 15–16; Church's regard for bodies of 46–47; empowerment of 17–18, 21; evangelical Christian 14–20, 184; and Jesus 38–40, 56, 145; marginalized 51; religious 44, 55, 58, 59; rights of 12; transgender 135, 137; violence against 67
Women Religious 58, 59
work 69–70, 75, 134

Zimbabwe: law in 166; sex worker narratives from 158, 160–161, 162, 163, 164
Zimmerman, Yvonne 12

Made in the USA
Las Vegas, NV
06 November 2024

e934e7f7-a287-4656-9c33-6e081906b6c1R01